MODERN GROUP BOOK III

Groups and Drugs

BOOKS BY DRS. KAPLAN AND SADOCK

Comprehensive Textbook of Psychiatry
Alfred M. Freedman and Harold I. Kaplan, Editors

Studies in Human Behavior
Alfred M. Freedman and Harold I. Kaplan, General Editors

Modern Synopsis of Comprehensive Textbook of Psychiatry
Harold I. Kaplan, Benjamin J. Sadock, and Alfred M. Freedman

Comprehensive Group Psychotherapy
Harold I. Kaplan and Benjamin J. Sadock, Editors

Modern Group Books
Harold I. Kaplan and Benjamin J. Sadock, Editors

HAROLD I. KAPLAN

Harold I. Kaplan received an undergraduate degree from Columbia University and an M.D. from the New York Medical College. He trained in psychiatry at the Kingsbridge Veterans Hospital and Mount Sinai Hospital in New York and became a Diplomate of the American Board of Psychiatry and Neurology in 1957; presently he is an Associate Examiner of the American Board. He began the practice and teaching of psychiatry and was certified in psychoanalytic medicine at the New York Medical College in 1954 where he became Professor of Psychiatry and Director of Psychiatric Training and Education in 1961. He is Attending Psychiatrist at Metropolitan Hospital Center, Flower and Fifth Avenue Hospitals and Bird S. Coler Hospital. He is the Principal Investigator of ten National Institute of Mental Health training programs, specializing in the areas of undergraduate and graduate psychiatric education as well as the training of women in medicine. He is the author of over seventy scientific papers and co-author and co-editor of the books listed on this page.

BENJAMIN J. SADOCK

Benjamin J. Sadock received his A.B. from Union College and his M.D. from New York Medical College. He trained at Bellevue Psychiatric Hospital. During his military service as an Air Force psychiatrist he was also on the faculty of Southwestern Medical School. Dr. Sadock became a Diplomate of the American Board of Psychiatry and Neurology in 1966 and is an Assistant Examiner for the American Board. Currently Associate Professor of Psychiatry and Director of the Division of Group Process at New York Medical College, Dr. Sadock directs the training program for group therapists and is Chief of Continuing Education in Psychiatry, Chief Psychiatric Consultant to the student health service and co-director of the Sexual Therapy Center. He is on staff of Flower and Fifth Avenue Hospitals, Metropolitan Hospital, and the New York State Psychiatric Institute. Dr. Sadock is active in numerous psychiatric organizations, an officer of the New York County District Branch of the American Psychiatric Association, a Fellow of the New York Academy of Medicine, and has written and lectured extensively in general psychiatry and group psychotherapy. He is co-editor with Dr. Harold I. Kaplan of *Comprehensive Group Psychotherapy* (1971) and co-author with Drs. Alfred M. Freedman and Harold I. Kaplan of *Modern Synopsis of Comprehensive Textbook of Psychiatry* (1972).

Groups and Drugs

Edited by

HAROLD I. KAPLAN, M.D.

Professor of Psychiatry and Director of Psychiatric Education,
New York Medical College, New York, New York

and

BENJAMIN J. SADOCK, M.D.

Associate Professor of Psychiatry and Director,
Division of Group Process, New York Medical College,
New York, New York

Jason Aronson, Inc.
New York, New York

Library of Congress Catalog Card Number: 72-96935
Standard Book Number: 0-87668-079-1

The editors express their appreciation to the following persons, publishers and publications for permission to reprint portions of the works cited.

Aldine-Atherton, Inc. for ''The Marathon Group,'' by G. R. Bach, reprinted from Hendrik M. Ruitenbeek, editor, *Group Therapy Today* (New York: Atherton Press, 1969); copyright © 1969 by Atherton Press. Reprinted by permission of the author and Aldine-Atherton, Inc.

Bruner/Mazel, Inc. for ''The Use of Videotape in the Integrated Treatment of Individuals, Couples, Families, and Groups in Private Practice,'' by Milton M. Berger, M.D., reprinted from *Videotape Techniques in Psychiatric Training and Treatment*, Milton M. Berger, M.D., editor. Bruner/Mazel, Inc., New York, 1970.

Dr. Herbert Holt for the unpublished essay, ''Existential Group Therapy: A Phenomenological Methodology for Psychiatry.''

International Journal of Group Psychotherapy for ''Sexual Acting Out in Groups,'' by the members of the Workshop in Group Psychoanalysis of New York: A. Wolf, R. Bross, S. Flowerman, J. Greene, A. Kadis, H. Leopold, N. Locke, I. Milburg, H. Mullan, S. Obers, and H. Rosenbaum. *International Journal of Group Psychotherapy*, Vol. 4, pp. 369-380, 1954.

for ''Accelerated Interaction: A Time Limited Approach on the Brief Intensive Approach,'' by Frederick H. Stoller. *International Journal of Group Psychotherapy*, Vol. 18, pp. 220-235, 1968.

for ''Group Therapy and the Small Group Field: An Encounter,'' by Morris Parloff. *International Journal of Group Psychotherapy*, Vol. 20, pp. 267-304, 1970.

International Universities Press for ''Group Therapy with Alcoholics,'' by A. Stein, M.D. and Eugene Friedman, Ph.D., Chapter III of *Fields of Group Psychotherapy*, S. R. Slavson, editor. International Universities Press, 1956.

American Psychiatric Association for ''Phoenix House: Therapeutic Communities for Drug Addicts,'' by M. S. Rosenthal and D. V. Biase, *Hospital and Community Psychiatry*, Vol. 20, p. 27, 1969.

W. W. Norton & Co., Inc., and the Hogarth Press Ltd. for an excerpt from *An Outline of Psycho-Analysis*, Volume XXIII of Standard Edition of Sigmund Freud, revised and edited by James Strachey. Copyright 1949 by W. W. Norton & Co., Inc., and copyright © 1969 by the Institute of Psychoanalysis and Alix Strachey.

The Williams & Wilkins Co. for an excerpt from ''Group Therapy in Married Couples,'' by Helen Papanek, M.D., reprinted from *Comprehensive Group Psychotherapy*, Harold I. Kaplan and Benjamin J. Sadock, editors. Copyright © 1971 by The Williams & Wilkins Co.

for an excerpt from ''Videotape Feedback in Group Setting,'' by F. Stoller. *Journal of Nervous and Mental Disorders*, Vol. 148, No. 4, pp. 457-466.

Seymour Lawrence/Delacorte Press for an excerpt from *Cat's Cradle* by Kurt Vonnegut, Jr. Copyright © 1963 by Kurt Vonnegut, Jr. A Seymour Lawrence Book/Delacorte Press. Reprinted by permission of the publisher.

Contents

Preface

The emergence of group psychotherapy within the past two decades constitutes one of the most significant and extraordinary developments in the field of psychiatry. Gradually during this period, but particularly within the past five years, group therapy has come to be chosen for the treatment of a widening range of patients with highly diverse problems. Concurrently, professionals and laymen alike see a growing interest in the relationship of group therapy to sociocultural and educational concepts, processes, and systems. Predictably, these theoretical developments are accompanied by the development of myriad therapeutic approaches which vary with respect not only to their underlying philosophy but also to the planning and conduct of treatment.

Psychotherapy is an art as well as a science. What is taught via the lecture hall or seminar room constitutes just one aspect of the teaching curriculum. Training in psychotherapy must also include clinical exercises performed under the supervision of an experienced clinician who acts as a model for the student. The editors' commitment to this project, and its concomitant goals, evolved from their extensive experience as both educators and clinicians. The editors' special interest in group psychotherapy as a treatment technique, and an awareness of the need for more intensive training in this discipline to ensure its continued growth and development, led to the establishment, at the New York Medical College, of the first medical-school-affiliated postgraduate certification program

in group psychotherapy. In addition, they have participated in the organization of training programs in group therapy for workers in other mental health disciplines —psychology, psychiatric social work, and psychiatric nursing.

The stated goal of this series—to provide a survey of current theoretical and therapeutic trends in this field—carries with it the obligation to pursue an eclectic orientation and to present as comprehensive an account of events at every level of its development as is possible. The organization and orientation of this series attempts to provide a comprehensive survey of the theories, hypotheses, and therapeutic techniques which dominate contemporary group practice. There are no final answers, as yet, to the problems and issues which currently face group psychotherapy. But we may help to identify these problems and issues and place them in proper perspective.

This book is one of a series of paperback volumes based on *Comprehensive Group Psychotherapy,* which we previously edited. New articles have been written for each of these volumes and certain subjects have been updated or eliminated in an effort to reach a wider audience. Invitations to participate were extended to those workers who have made major and original contributions to the field of group psychotherapy and who are acknowledged experts in a particular area of theory and/or practice. Thus the preparation of this series afforded the editors a unique opportunity to engage in a stimulating interchange of ideas and to form many rewarding personal relationships. As a result, what would appear to have been an ardous undertaking has in fact been a most gratifying experience.

The editors have received dedicated and valuable help from many people to whom they wish to express their appreciation. For their secretarial and editorial help, we would like to thank Robert Gelfand, Sylvia Houzell, Mercedes Paul, Paulene Demarco, Louise Marshall, and in particular Lois Baken, who coordinated these efforts. Spe-cial thanks are extended to our publishers, E. P. Dutton, and to our outstanding editor, Robert Zenowich.

Finally, the editors wish to express their appreciation to Virginia Sadock, M.D., who acted in the capacity of assistant to the editors and assumed the multitudinous tasks of that office with grace and charm.

HAROLD I. KAPLAN, M.D.

BENJAMIN J. SADOCK, M.D.

Introduction

The World Health Organization has defined drug addiction as a condition requiring repeated consumption of a natural or synthetic drug. Its manifestations include an overwhelming need to take the substance into the body with an equally overpowering desire to obtain the drug by any means. Doses increase as time goes by and there ultimately develops a psychological and/or physiological dependence on the drug's effects.

According to this definition, any drug can be abused by developing a dependency upon it. Indeed, medical literature abounds with descriptions of an almost endless variety of substances upon which man has become pathologically dependent. Of these, two stand out throughout history in bold relief: alcohol and narcotics.

Etiology

The causes of addiction to these substances are myriad and complex, and there is evidence to support both a genetic and a psychological predisposition toward alcoholism or narcotics addiction. There is also evidence that supports the theory of social and cultural predispositions to the disease. Most workers in the field accept as etiologic factors all of these, with the major emphasis placed on psychological causes. Both classes of drugs are known to alleviate anxiety and certain individuals will turn to alcohol or narcotics to assuage overwhelming frustration, conflict, and resentment, whatever the source, while searching for the state of euphoria which these drugs temporarily provide.

Many alcoholics and addicts share certain personality characteristics in common, notably an extreme and pervasive passivity, a very low frustration tolerance, and an inability to delay gratification. Often the family histories give evidence of a parental figure who overprotected the patient from frustration and poorly prepared him, if at all, for the demands of living. A large number of these patients come from homes that are broken, and the absence of a stable family environment has caused chronic anger, hostility, low self-esteem, and other psychological damage. Other addicts display excessive needs for love as a result of this denial in childhood. In psychoanalytic terms these individuals are fixated at the oral level and seek nurturance by "taking-in." In these situations, the addicting substance symbolizes the wished-for nurturing mother.

Scope

Alcoholism and narcotics addiction are to be found in all strata of society in most parts of the world. In the United States the problem is immense. Present estimates are: over 6 million people diagnosed as suffering from some form of alcoholism; almost 500,000 people addicted to narcotics.

Treatment

The treatment for dependence on these substances is multifaceted and involves the use of a variety of methods. Psychological treatment (individual or group therapy), medical treatment (the use of disulfiram

[Antabuse] in alcoholism and methadone treatment for narcotic addicts), and hospital or community approaches are all used, usually in combination. Depending on the needs of the particular individual, one or more of these methods may be primary at any time.

Narcotics

In the two chapters that deal with the treatment of narcotics addiction, two approaches are discussed which have come to the fore in the last decade: methadone maintenance and the therapeutic community. In the former method, devised by Drs. Vincent Dole and Marie Nyswander of Rockefeller University, the narcotics addict is placed on daily doses of methadone, which block his craving for narcotics. This eliminates his need to go to any length (usually criminal) to obtain the illegal drug to which he is addicted. Simultaneously, he is able and urged to engage in vocational and psychological rehabilitation. The chapter by Lowinson and Zwerling describes this treatment program in detail.

In the latter method, the therapeutic community, the use of methadone on a long-term basis is avoided. Rather, the addict is confined in a drug-free environment in which the rules of the community—abstinence from any kind of drug—are rigidly enforced. In the chapter by Rosenthal and Blase, the programs of Phoenix House, one of the most successful therapeutic communities in New York City, are described.

Of particular significance is the section on follow-up studies, also by Lowinson and Zwerling, in which different approaches to curing drug addiction are compared. A reasoned and accurate overview of the results of various programs, it also includes statistics never available before in a single source. Such an overview is particularly important, because in this field proponents of one method are often unwilling or unable to see the benefits of the others. What is common to all programs, however, is the extensive use of groups in a variety of forms, from traditional group therapy, led by a psychiatrist or other mental health professional, to the use of specialized group approaches, such as the encounter or confrontation group conducted, in most instances, by ex-addicts themselves.

Alcohol

A group approach to the treatment of alcohol addiction won adherents many years ago, when organizations such as Alcoholics Anonymous proved successful in rehabilitating the victims of this disease. Organized as a self-help group, AA adopts an accepting attitude toward the alcoholic who often presents in dire personal circumstances. Within an accepting environment the benefits derived from abstinence from alcohol are vividly demonstrated by ex-alcoholics who successfully achieved this goal. Through this process, whereby the sick member identifies with the healthy member, and through the use of group pressure to maintain abstinence, the process of cure begins.

Traditional group therapy, outlined in the chapter by Stein, has also been of benefit to the alcoholic. In the group, attempts are made to explore the psychological antecedents to the patient's alcoholism, and he is encouraged to gain heightened awareness of how these processes led to and maintained his illness. The group goal and expectation are that, as insight develops, the need to rely on alcohol as an anxiety-reducing drug will diminish and eventually cease altogether.

Clinical Diagnosis

The editors' decision to include a chapter on clinical diagnosis was based on their belief in the importance of diagnosis in group treatment. We hold the firm conviction that careful evaluation and diagnosis of each patient is essential to the efficacy of group therapy. Moreover, it has become evident, in the light of recent therapeutic developments, that diagnosis is essential if casualties resulting from group experience are to be averted. Regardless of the group therapist's orientation—whether he emphasizes the here-and-now or the historical antecedents of behavior, whatever his goals—careful evaluation and diagnosis help him determine whether the patient is suited to group treatment and, if so, what type. In addition, the psychiatric interview, the major tool of diagnosis, may in itself serve an important function; it underscores the nature of the therapist's attitude toward and perception of the patient, which plays a crucial role in treatment. This chapter, therefore, presents a detailed discussion of the diagnostic process and the classification of psychiatric disorders set forth in the second edition of the American Psychiatric Association's *Diagnostic and Statistical Manual of Mental Disorders*. Such a diagnosis is important in determining the best therapeutic approach to the patient's disorder, in evaluating his motivation for treatment, his capacity for change, and the strengths and weaknesses of his personality structure. Thus, diagnosis is more than nosological pigeonholing. Those workers who suggest that diagnosis is unimportant in group therapy take too simplistic a view of the diagnostic process, which routinely should include an extensive examination of the patient's chief complaint and a detailed evaluation of his past developmental history. Such an evaluation examines functioning in a variety of areas—vocational, familial, social, marital, and sexual. The mental status examination provides clues about psychopathological processes at work, currently and in the past, and indicates the patient's future response to stress. Diagnosis also includes postulates about the psychodynamic and defense mechanisms involved, the causes of the patient's emotional disorder, and the desired goals to be achieved; from it the clinician should be able to make certain inferences about the patient.

However, the diagnostic examination is incomplete if data about the patient's physical health is not available. No patient should be placed in psychotherapy for an emotional disorder without a physical examination which rules out the presence of an organic disease that might account for some if not all of his symptoms. In short, the diagnostic interview is very important to effective treatment outcome.

Psychopharmacology and Chemotherapeutics

The chapter on the use of psychopharmacologic and chemotherapeutic agents in conjunction with group psychotherapy, written by Kline and Davis, presents a most important finding: In the treatment of schizophrenia, the most common mental disorder treated in mental hospitals, a combination of drug administration and group psychotherapy is superior to either form of treatment alone. In view of this, neither should be withheld from the hospitalized patient if he is to receive the most effective care. In such a situation, if the psychotherapy group is conducted by a nonmedical person, it is essential that a physician able to prescribe appropriate medication be available to work closely with the group leader. The effectiveness of such collaboration was borne out by results of a four-year study of group therapy patients at New York Medical College-Metropolitan Hospital Community Mental Health Center. Over 80 per cent of the patients receiving outpatient group psychotherapy also received some form of psychopharmacologic agent during their course of treatment.

Drug Treatment

The final chapter, on drug treatment, by Kline and Davis, offers an updated and comprehensive survey of the numerous chemical agents available for the alleviation of many kinds of mental disorders. Dosages, indications, contraindications, and side-effects, both desirable and undesirable, are outlined. For the nonmedical mental health professional such a review provides a ready source of useful information about the medication his patients may or perhaps should be using.

Groups and Drugs

1
Clinical Diagnosis in Group Psychotherapy

Harold I. Kaplan, M.D. and Benjamin J. Sadock, M.D.

INTRODUCTION

To be of help, the group therapist must have detailed knowledge of each individual patient's intrapsychic and interpersonal disturbances, and he must be aware of the patient's psychological strengths and assets. In addition, the therapist must understand how and why the patient's problems developed—which means that he must study the patient's developmental history. Finally, the therapist must try to identify the various causes of the patient's illness—the stresses, adverse social and cultural influences, and somatic factors. With all this information in hand, the therapist can then proceed with his formal diagnosis and begin treatment.

In one-to-one therapy, diagnostic evaluation and the first steps in treatment may sometimes be conducted at the same time. But not in group therapy. For one thing, the therapist is not able to concentrate on any one patient long enough to collect the extensive data he needs for accurate diagnosis. For another thing, the therapist may jeopardize the treatment of the group as a whole and the treatment of the individual if he is not aware of the patient's diagnostic classification beforehand. The presence of just one unsuitable patient in the group may reinforce the pathology of his co-patients and create intolerable tension.

Clearly, then, the therapist must see each prospective candidate for group psychotherapy individually before he is admitted to the group. One or more psychiatric interviews will give the therapist an opportunity to make his diagnostic evaluation. Of course, the therapist may later modify his initial assessment of the patient. Indeed, he must be alert to changes in intrapsychic and interpersonal functioning and in somatic structure and function. But he cannot start group treatment with any degree of confidence until he establishes the patient's diagnostic classification.

Diagnostic competence begins with an understanding of the psychodynamics of behavior—both how the patient acts and how his conscious and unconscious mind works.

PSYCHOANALYTIC THEORY OF BEHAVIOR

The Theory of the Instincts

The term instinct refers to the influence of body needs on mental activity and behavior. Mediated through the central nervous system, such influences are experienced psychologically in the form of various sensations and various perceptions of the environment associated with the satisfaction or frustration of body needs. In the course of a person's development, psychological representations of these experiences become established in his mind and are referred to as drives or instinctual drives.

Certain behavior and psychic activity aim at contact, union, or closeness with objects in the environment. Other behavior and psychic activity aim at the destruction of objects. This difference suggests the presence of two instincts—sexual instincts and aggressive instincts.

Libido. As defined by Freud, libido is that force by which the sexual instinct is represented in the mind. Sexual instinct undergoes a complex process of development and has many manifestations other than genital union. And sexuality is not limited to those sensations and activities typically considered sexual or to those parts of the body usually associated with erogenous zones.

Phases of Psychosexual Development. The earliest manifestations of sexuality involve bodily functions that are basically nonsexual. In the oral phase, which extends into the second year of life, erotic activity centers on the infant's mouth and lips and is manifested by sucking and biting. Between the ages of two and four, the child is increasingly preoccupied with bowel function and control, and his dominant erotic activity shifts from his mouth to his anal region. Usually by the fourth year, the child is increasingly aware of pleasurable feeling from his genitals. The penis and clitoris become the new erotic zones, and masturbatory activity is manifested.

Development of Object Relationships. In earliest infancy, the child depends on certain elements or objects in the environment and is driven to behave in ways that will assure the supply of these objects. Such behavior occurs without the infant's being aware of the external world or of the objects he seeks. In fact, he becomes aware of the objects partly because of some degree of frustration. Awareness of food evolves out of repetitive experiences of being hungry and then being fed. Awareness of his mother evolves out of separation and reunion with her.

At this point the mother starts to be recognized as the source of nourishment and as the source of the pleasure the infant derives from sucking. She becomes the first love object. Later sexual development and psychosocial development reflect the child's attachment to the crucial people in his environment and his feelings of love or hate or both toward them.

During the oral phase, the infant is essentially passive. His mother must gratify or frustrate his demands. But during the anal period his mother demands that he use the toilet, thereby giving up some of his freedom. And so the battle is joined as he attempts to continue enjoying the pleasurable sensation of excretion. Later on, he may derive even more pleasure by retaining the fecal mass, stimulating his anal mucosa. During this period, the child wields power over his mother by giving up or refusing to give up his feces. Expelling and retaining feces are endowed with erotic and aggressive meanings, symbolizing submission and defiance, love and hate, conflict and ambivalence.

During the oral and anal phases of development, the child makes some progress toward finding a love object, but most of his libidinal activity is autoerotic: He directs his sexual impulses toward his own body and discharges them by masturbating. The task of finding a love object belongs to the phallic phase of development. At that time the child discovers the anatomical differences between the sexes, and the pattern is set for later object choices—and for later psychoneuroses. The Oedipus complex—the intense love relationships, rivalries, hostilities, and identifications formed during this period—represents the climax of infantile sexuality. These oedipal strivings must be replaced by adult sexuality if the person is to develop normally. If he clings to oedipal tendencies, he will develop neuroses.

Aggression. At first, Freud equated aggression with sadism. Later, he thought of aggression as self-preservative impulse. But when he saw self-destructive tendencies in depressed patients, self-inflicted injuries among masochistic patients, and wanton destructiveness by small children, he concluded that aggression was often not self-preservative. So Freud gave aggression a separate status as an instinct, noting that the source of the instinct is largely in the skeletal muscles and that its aim is destruction.

The Psychic Apparatus

The Mind. Mental activity takes place on three levels: the unconscious, the preconscious, and the conscious. In the unconscious, personality forces strive for discharge, but strong counterforces block them from conscious awareness.

The preconscious, which develops in childhood, is accessible to both the unconscious and the conscious. Elements in the unconscious reach the conscious only by first reaching the preconscious. One of the functions of the preconscious is to repress or censor certain wishes and desires.

The conscious is the sense organ of the mind. Words, thoughts, impulses, and feelings may be brought to consciousness only with effort and attention, or they may intrude into consciousness unbidden. Keeping some things from becoming conscious and letting other things become conscious involves ego functions. Except for feelings, the things that come into consciousness are associated with symbols or words. The capacity to organize conscious experience in a logical, coherent, reality-oriented way marks the difference between primitive and mature mental functioning.

Structure of the Psychic Apparatus. The psychic apparatus is divided into three provinces: id, ego, and superego. The id, the locus of the instinctual drives, operates in accordance with the pleasure principle, with no regard for reality. The ego, on the other hand, is a coherent organization that controls contact with reality and avoids pain by inhibiting or regulating the discharge of instinctual drives to conform with the demands of the external world. The ego makes use of such defense mechanisms as repression, displacement, reaction formation, isolation, undoing, rationalization, intellectualization, denial, projection, regression, counterphobic mechanisms, withdrawal, and sublimation to oppose the id impulses. The superego, which contains the internalized moral values of parental images also regulates the discharge of id impulses. The aim of the human being is satisfaction of the basic biological influences and adequate adjustment within the environment.

DIAGNOSTIC PROCEDURES

The Psychiatric Interview

The clinical interview, as described by Ripley, whose work forms much of the basis for the discussion that follows, is the psychiatrist's principal diagnostic tool—one that may be supplemented by medical and neurological examinations and by psychological tests. During the interview, the psychiatrist tries to evaluate the patient's developmental history, his present life situation, and his current emotional status and mental capacity.

The psychiatrist begins with signs and symptoms. He listens to the patient's story, subjects him to various types of examinations, and then tries to diagnose his illness. Within this broad framework, the organization of the interview and the techniques employed vary from patient to patient and from one interview to another with the same patient. The therapist's personality, response to the patient, and clinical experience also modify the structure of the interview. Whatever his technique, however, the psychiatrist must focus his attention on the patient, not simply on the manifestations of disease. The psychiatrist must try to understand the disease in terms of the patient's life.

Goals. Before the therapist can make a diagnosis, he must get a description of the patient's symptoms. His symptoms are the focus of the patient's immediate concern, and the therapist must be tolerant of the patient's preoccupation with his symptoms and receptive to his efforts to describe them even if they are not evidence of psychiatric disease. Moreover, the therapist should become aware not only of the symptoms the patient describes but also of those symptoms he minimizes or conceals. The therapist must also understand what the patient says, have some insight into what he is trying to say but is reluctant to put into words, and realize when he is denying the presence of symptoms.

The psychiatrist's second task is to get information about every aspect of the patient's biological, psychological, and social history past and present. With this information, the therapist should be able to identify those factors that helped cause the illness. In addition, he will have a preliminary picture of the patient's personality—his attitudes, character traits, and intrapsychic conflicts and the psychological devices he uses to deal with these conflicts. And the therapist may have some insight into the causes of the patient's symptoms.

At the end of the interview, the therapist may try to make a tentative diagnosis and prognosis. He should also make a preliminary decision about the disposition of the patient. But if the therapist needs more information before he can make even a tentative conclusion about the patient's illness, he may schedule additional diagnostic interviews or recommend other diagnostic procedures—psychological tests and medical or neurological examinations. Once the diagnosis has been made, the therapist may accept the patient for treatment, refer him to another therapist, or recommend some other form of treatment.

The therapist must help the patient understand his illness. The patient who is symptom-free must be made aware of his illness. And the patient with subjective symptoms must learn to accept the fact that he has to change his underlying emotional attitudes.

The interview may be therapeutic as well as diagnostic.

The therapist must try to relieve the patient's immediate suffering by offering reassurance, understanding, and sympathy. Above all, he must empathize with the patient.

The Psychiatrist-Patient Relationship. Whether the psychiatrist achieves his goals depends on how he conducts the diagnostic interview and on the quality of his relationship with the patient.

A satisfactory psychiatrist-patient relationship depends on the psychiatrist's ability to achieve rapport with the patient—to create a feeling of harmonious responsiveness, to make the patient feel that the psychiatrist understands him, accepts him despite his liabilities, and recognizes his assets and that the psychiatrist is someone he can talk to.

Achieving rapport in a clinical setting is contingent on the psychiatrist's ability to understand the patient's symptoms, personality, and behavior on an intellectual level. More important, it is contingent on the therapist's capacity for empathy—his ability to put himself in the patient's place—and for self-examination—his constant awareness of his responses and attitudes toward the patient, and of the psychodynamic factors underlying those responses and attitudes.

The Patient's Attitude toward the Psychiatrist. The patient's reactions to his illness and to the interview as well as his usual ways of dealing with other people will influence the attitude toward the psychiatrist.

The patient's reactions to his illness depend on personal, social, and cultural factors. His personal experiences affect the manifestations of his illness and his affective responses to pathological changes in his personality and behavior. The defenses he mobilizes to deal with these unpleasant feelings reflect his usual way of dealing with such feelings. Social and cultural factors may determine what symptoms he describes to the therapist and what symptoms he conceals, since different cultures have different standards of what is acceptable and what is shameful. Social and cultural factors may also determine when, how, and where the patient goes for help.

Almost all patients approach the first psychiatric interview with some anxiety. The perception of psychiatric symptoms invariably gives rise to fears, realistic and unrealistic, that are as diverse and complex as the forms of psychiatric illness. The patient may express his fears and anxieties verbally or only in his nonverbal behavior. He may deliberately withhold information, give evasive answers, or, in extreme cases, simply refuse to communicate. He may try to charm or endear himself to the psychiatrist, or even behave seductively in an effort to divert him from the real issues. Or, he may use such defense mechanisms as denial and projection.

Some patients place the psychiatrist on a pedestal and endow him with magical powers. The inevitable disillusionment may strengthen their resistance to treatment. They may at times feel that, once they have consulted a psychiatrist, they don't have to do anything else. At other times they may see the seeking of psychiatric help as an act of surrender, an admission of weakness.

The patient often sees the psychiatrist as an authority figure who has the power to control every aspect of his life. This reaction grows out of anxieties and guilt feelings surrounding his illness and also out of his unresolved dependency needs, which may be reactivated during periods of psychological or physical stress and redirected toward an idealized parental figure, such as the psychiatrist.

Finally, the patient's attitude toward the psychiatrist reflects his usual way of relating to other people—aggressive and domineering or dependent and submissive, detached and disinterested or manipulative and seductive.

The Psychiatrist's Attitude toward the Patient. At some time, the patient is negative or ambivalent toward the psychiatrist. The effect of these attitudes on the psychiatrist-patient relationship is minimal if the psychiatrist understands their origins and deals with them appropriately. But if the psychiatrist's attitudes toward the patient are inappropriate, the effects on the psychiatrist-patient relationship, the diagnostic process, and the course and outcome of treatment can be disastrous. So the psychiatrist must be aware of his feelings toward the patient, understand the origins of his countertransference, and work through his inappropriate attitudes. Self-understanding is the key, which is why a personal analysis is considered an essential part of psychiatric training.

The psychiatrist's initial reactions to the patient are based on his first impressions. He may like the patient immediately and feel attracted, or he may automatically dislike him and be repelled by his appearance or behavior. These initial reactions often form part of the basis for a tentative diagnosis.

If the patient is hostile or aggressive, the psychiatrist may perceive such behavior as a personal attack and try to fight back, calling forth more hostility from the patient. Their relationship quickly reaches a stalemate in such a situation. Ideally, of course, the psychiatrist does not overreact. Instead, he evaluates and deals with the patient's attitudes objectively. To do so, he must understand the psychodynamics of the patient's behavior and the psychogenesis of his own response to such behavior.

If the patient's symptoms evoke anxiety, the psychiatrist may ignore them or sidestep the patient's efforts to discuss them. Or if the patient's behavior is unorthodox and unexplained by current theories of personality, the psychiatrist may condemn him out of hand. When he reacts with shock or fear, the psychiatrist may try to defend against his feelings. He may adopt a grave, magisterial facial expression that gives the patient the impression that he is being judged or that his condition is worse that it actually is. Or the psychiatrist may put on a cold, expressionless facade that freezes the patient or a pedantic expression that makes him feel like a small child. Whatever form they take, these defensive patterns convey a message of rejection.

A positive reaction that exceeds the proper limits of the therapist-patient relationship can be just as destructive as a negative reaction. If the psychiatrist overempathizes with the patient, he may want to solve his problems and make his decisions for him. Efforts to protect the patient from life can sabotage the psychiatrist's diagnostic and treatment efforts.

The psychiatrist's positive reactions to the patient may also be based on envy, awe of the patient's social or economic status, or admiration of his intellect. If the psychiatrist feels inferior to the patient, he needs to examine the roots of his own feelings. And, he must be alert to any effort by the patient to intimidate or manipulate him.

A written record of the psychiatrist's impressions of attitudes toward, and emotional responses to, the patient can facilitate systematic self-evaluation. A check-list of the variables that may shape the psychiatrist's reactions to the patient is particularly useful.

Number and Duration of Diagnostic Sessions. If, at the end of the initial psychiatric interview, the psychiatrist needs more diagnostic data, he will schedule at least one more diagnostic session. The need for more interviews depends on the skill with which the therapist conducts the initial interview and on factors he cannot control— the nature and severity of the patient's symptoms, the setting in which he is seen, and the time available. How the therapist conducts the initial interview and the quality of the patient-therapist relationship affect the patient's willingness to follow through and cooperate.

As a general rule, the psychiatric interview should last no more than an hour, but it may be extended to an hour and a half, if the patient is particularly alert and receptive. Whatever the length of the interview, the patient should not have the feeling that he is being rushed to produce the kind of information he thinks the therapist wants. Some patients need time to warm up and relax before they can discuss their symptoms. If the patient's anxiety is too great to continue the interview he should be allowed to leave if he wants. Trying to persuade him to stay serves no useful purpose. But the therapist should assure the patient that he is interested and concerned, and that his services are available whenever the patient is ready to discuss his problems.

The Physical Setting. The therapist's office is ideal for the interview, providing privacy, quiet, and seclusion. Such interruptions as telephone calls and the transmission of messages should be kept to a minimum. Sometimes an interruption serves a useful purpose—the patient has a chance to pull himself together and gather the courage to confide some shameful detail—but more often he uses the interval to mobilize his defenses and resistance. Moreover, the therapist has no assurance that the interruption will not occur at a strategic point. And the patient may interpret interruptions as a sign that the therapist is not interested or is hostile toward him.

When the therapist greets the patient he should introduce himself, invite the patient to be seated in a comfortable chair, and try to make him feel at ease. Explaining the purpose of the diagnostic interview is helpful. The therapist might tell a naive patient that he needs to know more about his difficulties if he is to help him. A more sophisticated patient may require a more elaborate explanation and a brief description of the treatment process. Questions about the therapist's professional qualifications should be answered frankly to reassure the patient.

Note-Taking. Notes should be made as unobtrusively as possible so that the patient will not be inhibited. If the patient objects, the therapist may reassure him that the notes are confidential and help to ensure diagnostic accuracy—and proper treatment. If the patient persists in his objections, the therapist should stop taking notes. By contrast, some patients object when the psychiatrist does not take notes. They look on note-taking as a sign of the therapist's interest and recognition of the importance of what the patient is saying.

If the therapist does not take notes during the interview, he can record the relevant data immediately after the patient leaves. But his own reactions may contaminate the patient's record. Sound recordings are a better alternative to note-taking. They are more complete than notes and do not interfere with spontaneous communication.

Observations of the Patient. Observation of specific details of the patient's appearance and behavior begins when the therapist hears the patient's voice on the telephone for the first time or sees him in his waiting room, and it continues throughout the interview. Agitated movements, disturbances in speech, changes in the patient's appearance, or changes in his respiration may give the therapist important clues about the patient's unconscious feelings and attitudes. Such observations may indicate inconsistencies between the emotional reactions the patient reports and those that exist on an unconscious level. In addition, the patient's attire, posture, behavior, and voice may indicate the nature and severity of his illness. Indeed, the therapist's observation of these nonverbal phenomena may be his only diagnostic tool when the patient talks too little, too much about irrelevant matters, or not at all because of his need to avoid discussion of his emotional conflicts.

The therapist should record his observations systematically, under such headings as patient's preinterview behavior, initial response to therapist, attire, body characteristics, facial expression and features, voice and speech, gait and posture, patterns of motor activity.

The patient's behavior in the waiting room, before he is summoned into the private office, gives the therapist his first clues about his mental and emotional status. The patient's behavior when he meets the therapist is an index of his response to his illness and his attitude toward the therapist and may provide insights into the quality of his object relationships.

Excessive fastidiousness in dress may suggest an obsessive-compulsive disorder. Extreme slovenliness may be an early sign of depression or schizophrenia. Seductive dress may indicate a hysterical neurosis. Exhibitionistic attire is worn by certain male homosexuals. Somber, drab clothing may indicate depression, or an effort to discourage sexual interest. Childish patterns of dress may express a regressive clinging to childhood. But the therapist should be aware of dress standards in different cultures—including the teen-age culture. Attire that looks eccentric to the therapist may be acceptable to or even required by the patient's peers.

The patient's physical characteristics may indicate distortions in his body image. He may be excessively preoccupied with particular body parts, feel inferior or proud because of his appearance, or be troubled by problems of sexual identity.

The patient's voice and speech, gait and posture, and pattern of motor activity are clues to his affective state. Increased motor activity—loud speech, chronic restlessness, excessive smoking, irritability—may be part of the anxiety and depression syndrome. Decreased motor activity, abnormal posture and gait, halting speech may express the underlying affects of helplessness and hopelessness found in simple depression.

Some aspects of the patient's behavior and appearance may be only transient phenomena. His increased or decreased motor activity, somber attire, angry or sad facial expression may not be components of his illness but simply his response to his illness and the interview situation.

Interviewing Techniques. The success of the initial interview depends on the therapist's knowledge of what he must find out from the patient and of how he can find it out. The good interviewer, like the good conversationalist, has verbal facility, intuitive tact, and, above all, the ability to listen. In addition, the therapist must have empathy, genuine interest in other people, and tolerance of human frailties.

Opening the Interview. The physical setting and the therapist's observance of the basic social amenities are particularly important at this point. He can use superficial techniques to convey his interest in and acceptance of the patient and his illness and to set the tone for the interview. Then the therapist proceeds to focus on the patient's chief complaint by asking a general question, such as, "What brings you here?" or "What seems to be your trouble?" This approach defines the purpose of the interview and shapes its direction.

Guiding the Interview. Listening is one of the therapist's major tools. By keeping his directive role to a minimum, he can encourage the patient to expand on his thoughts, bring up relevant topics, and lower his resistance.

The therapist's quiet attentiveness can generally lessen the patient's anxiety, blocking, and silences. But at times, he may have to play a more active, directive role. Traumatic, emotionally charged, or painful subjects may cause the patient to fall silent or become angry, tearful, or fidgety; or he may try to change the subject or terminate the interview. These reactions—forms of resistance or blocking—can be attributed to the emergence of a painful emotion, such as anxiety, conflict, shame, embarrassment, or guilt. The therapist can help the patient to overcome or lessen the intensity of these reactions.

If the patient suddenly falls silent, the therapist may ask him one or two direct questions or simply look at him questioningly and nod his head encouragingly. The patient often interprets such activity as a sign of the therapist's interest, which is a potent weapon against resistance.

If the patient remains silent, the therapist may return to the source of the patient's resistance ("You were saying. . ."). If the patient's pain is clearly apparent, the therapist may find it helpful to put into words what the patient is feeling as a sign that he understands him ("You seem to be feeling depressed [or angry, resentful, anxious, ashamed]"). Or the therapist may interpret the patient's reaction ("You suddenly became upset when you were talking about . . ."). Often the therapist tries to allay the patient's anxiety by expressing empathy and sympathy ("That must have been an upsetting experience.").

If the patient summarily drops a subject, the therapist may defer to his wishes and hope that he will resume the discussion at a later date. Or he may openly confront the patient about his reluctance to discuss the subject.

Blocking and emotional reactions are brought on not only by sensitive subjects but also by the patient's reactions to his illness and to the diagnostic situation. If the illness evokes feelings of guilt or shame, the therapist should try to bolster the patient's self-esteem by emphasizing his achievements and positive qualities and the facts that psychiatric illness is not a sign of weakness and that others also have the illness. And if the patient has fears and doubts about the diagnostic situation, the therapist's professional competence, confidentiality, and the treatment process, the therapist can best deal with them by bringing them out into the open.

The therapist must allow the patient to tell the story of his illness in his own words. Only if he is permitted to talk about himself frankly and to express his thoughts and feelings freely, without interruption, can the patient find out about himself. Early in the interview is no time to elicit all the details and the complete factual history. Gaps in the patient's account can be filled in later. Nor should the therapist at this time challenge the patient's statements or correct his misrepresentation or misperception of the facts. These areas can be explored later, when rapport is established.

Questions, however, can be helpful if injected at strategic points in the patient's monologue. When the patient provides appropriate leads, perceptive questions can help the patient develop an understanding of himself. Tactful questioning is indicated when the therapist is not sure what some piece of information means to the patient. And, by discreet questioning, the therapist can get information about intimate topics that the patient may be reluctant to discuss. Topics such as sex can be introduced by asking the patient questions about physical development, for example.

The questions should be open-ended,

somewhat ambiguous, leaving room for explanations and elaborations by the patient. Restrictive questions answered by a "yes" or "no" cannot help the therapist understand the patient or help the patient develop an understanding of himself.

The therapist should avoid leading questions. For example, in asking the patient about his current emotional status, the therapist should not ask him whether he has a bad temper. "How is your temper?" is a more appropriate question.

Excessive questioning should also be avoided. It may overwhelm the patient, interrupt his train of thought, or block his effort to express an emotional reaction. The therapist must overcome any tendency to use precipitate questioning as a way to cope with his own anxiety.

The therapist's questions should be relevant to what the patient is talking about. Questions from out of left field may confuse or inhibit the patient. If the therapist feels that he is belaboring a topic—a sign of resistance—he can change the subject by saying, "There are other important things to cover." As the patient gives his account of his problens, the therapist may ask him whether he had similar problems in the past. This question will bring forth information about the patient's past history, which will give the therapist an insight into the origins of the patient's illness.

Finally, the therapist's vocabulary and the content of his questions and comments should be influenced by the patient's intelligence, level of sophistication, and symptoms. Whenever possible, the therapist should use the patient's own words and phraseology. Doing so assures the patient that the therapist understands him. And the therapist, in turn, minimizes the possibility that the patient will distort what he says.

Concluding the Interview. At this point, the therapist must play a more active and directive role. He must make decisions about the patient's future management, and try to make sure these decisions are carried out.

No matter how little he feels he has accomplished, no matter how frustrated or discouraged he feels, the therapist must give the patient a feeling of optimism and convince him that the diagnostic interview has been useful. But the therapist cannot guarantee a cure or even a favorable response to treatment. Nor can he estimate how much treatment the patient will require.

If no further diagnostic interviews are needed, the therapist may recommend a plan of treatment. If additional interviews are needed, he may tell the patient that there is a need for further discussion, express his continued interest, and suggest that he think about the material covered so far and about the topics he would like to discuss in the next interview. The success of later interviews depends largely on how much the patient cooperates with the therapist.

If the patient cannot face the prospect of treatment or additional interviews, he may convince himself that such procedures are unnecessary, that he only needs to change some aspect of his current life situation—get a new job, earn more money, get divorced or married, take a vacation. The therapist must persuade him that such solutions are rarely effective—and only when the patient's illness is a transient situational disturbance.

During the final phase of the interview, the therapist must tell the patient what he needs to know about his illness. Giving the patient too much information or presenting it improperly may exacerbate the patient's symptoms or create new ones. But obviously withholding information may increase his anxiety by convincing him that the therapist is keeping something from him and that his illness is more serious than he had been led to believe. As a result, the patient's confidence and trust in the therapist are undermined. Generally, it is wise to give the patient whatever information is necessary to enlist his cooperation.

As a rule, the therapist's appraisal is reassuring to the patient. For one thing, it indicates the therapist's recognition and understanding of the patient's illness. Second, when the illness is brought out into the open, it no longer lurks in the realm of the mysterious and frightening unknown.

Later Interviews. The techniques used in subsequent interviews are much the same as those used in the initial interview. The patient is encouraged to continue telling his story and to express his thoughts and feelings freely. And the therapist asks appropriate questions, expresses empathy and understanding, and occasionally interprets the patient's remarks in an effort to help him overcome his reluctance to discuss the emotional conflicts evidenced by blocking and prolonged silences.

One difference is that the therapist usually plays a more directive role in later interviews. Since he scheduled further meetings with the patient to get additional information, the therapist may ask the patient to expand on topics introduced during the first interview, or he may ask about areas that were not discussed at all.

Whatever new information is disclosed, the therapist must maintain his nonjudgmental, understanding attitude, neither condoning nor condemning the patient's behavior and values. His questions may evoke emotional reaction, anxiety, shame, guilt, withdrawal. The therapist must counteract these responses or at least lessen their intensity by reassuring and supporting the patient and by indicating his awareness of the patient's strengths as well as his weaknesses.

Specialized Interviewing Techniques. Interviewing techniques vary according to the patient's personality reactions. The therapist's usual nondirective approach may at times make the patient feel abandoned and anxious. At such times, the therapist must modify, or temporarily abandon, his basic diagnostic technique in favor of guidance and more explicit reassurance.

At other times, the therapist must try to stimulate anxiety so that an apathetic patient experiences enough discomfort to talk about his conflicts. Or the therapist may probe, challenge, and confront the indifferent patient to arouse feelings that will make him participate actively in the diagnostic process.

Interviewing techniques may also vary according to the patient's illness. A depressed patient, for example, generally has a short attention span and should have a relatively brief interview. Moreover, the therapist may have to interrupt because the patient tends to reiterate in a destructive, self-deprecatory way. Often, such a patient does not mention his depression. Instead, he may complain of insomnia, loss of appetite, diurnal changes their patients verbally without making it a flesh-and-blood reality involving all the senses. This objectification, however, is apparently necessary to Moreno's way of doing things; he has to be shown in addition to being told.

The patient, depending on his personality, may derive a certain satisfaction from acting out rather than simply verbalizing his conflicts. For Moreno, acting out represents a great therapeutic maneuver; for the analyst, it is resistance.

The patient is said to gain insight from doing, but catharsis has a tendency to interfere with the acquisition of insight, and the outpouring of emotion may be the patient's only benefit. By training the patient through behavior therapy, the therapist attempts to alter fixed patterns of behavior.

The dramatic enactment of problems may be carried out through psychodrama, in which the patient relives an actual situation or acts out a situation posed by the director, who knows the patient's special problem; through sociodrama, in which the patient is confronted with some concrete social problem that characterizes the society to which he belongs; and through role-playing, in which the patient assumes the role of another person, thus allowing him to try out new types of behavior and new forms of communication in a relatively nonthreatening situation.

The theatre of spontaneous man is a brilliant idea, and it certainly deserves a place in the history and practice of group psychotherapy. But whether all the complex resistances that make up modern civilized man can be dissolved by means of a simple dramatic device is open to question. Is it indeed acting, or is it really acting out in the psychoanalytic sense?

The dramatic approach has spawned a large number of dramatic games that are used to warm up a patient in the initial phase of therapy. These exercises have been incorporated into training groups and other modern departures from classical therapy. In fact, Moreno has claimed with some truth to have pioneered the development of encounter groups, Gestalt therapy, transactional analysis, behavior therapy, and joy workshops. He feels that, together with

Buber, he has been responsible for the existential encounter—the real, concrete, complete experience involving both physical and psychic contact with a convergence of emotional, social, and cosmic factors. He feels that psychodrama is the essence of encounter, since it entails the experience of identity and total reciprocity.

Moreno is a creative, dramatic, spontaneous, and charismatic man whose quasi-religious, dithyrambic style of writing makes him sound at times like a latter-day Nietzsche. His sociometry is a genuine contribution to group psychology and has been widely used by the scientifically oriented who spurn the other side of Moreno, his psychodrama. To many group psychotherapists, he represents a detrimental influence that has split the group world in two, seducing many a group therapist from the careful and patient practice of classical group psychotherapy and leading him into wildly exciting, highly controversial, short-cut methods of treatment.

GROUP PSYCHOTHERAPY

Pioneer Efforts

In 1907, Pratt described what he called a class method of treating tuberculosis in the homes of the poor, and a year later he discussed his results. It was known then, as it is known now, that tuberculous patients are prone to be difficult people and to have emotional problems. Since tuberculous patients, like psychotics, are often herded together and are treated with fear and rejection by the general populace, it seemed appropriate to use group techniques. After Pratt's original efforts, other psychologically oriented physicians have tried to do the same thing.

The psychiatrists in mental hospitals were stimulated by the possibilities of this new technique. Lazell in 1921 and Marsh in 1931 instituted the group method with psychotics.

All these early practices were psychologically naive, and they made little or no use of group dynamics. The instructor lectured to a group of patients on their illness, and sometimes these lectures were broadcast through

Identification. This section should include the patient's name, age, sex, ethnic and cultural background, marital status, occupation, source of referral, housing situation, and hospitalizations. Identify informants.

Therapist's Personal Impressions. The therapist should give a brief, nontechnical description of the patient's appearance and behavior.

Chief Complaint. If possible, the patient's own words should be used to describe the complaint. He should be encouraged to explain its duration and occurrence, possible causes, intensity, and effects on him.

History of Present Illness. This section should include a chronological account, in the patient's own words, of how his symptoms and signs developed, including a description of his premorbid personality, his life circumstances when his symptoms began, the precipitating stresses or events, and the effects on his behavior, health, attitudes, and personal relationships.

Previous Illnesses. These illnesses may be categorized as emotional or mental disturbances, physiological disorders that may be psychogenic, medical conditions, and neurological disorders.

Personal History. This section should include a separate description of each period in the patient's life—infancy, childhood, adolescence, and adulthood. Gaps may be filled in later, when additional facts emerge during treatment, or information may be gathered from other sources. Also, such gaps may indicate that the patient is repressing particularly stressful or conflictual developmental events.

The personal history gives the psychiatrist an understanding of the patient's development, the environment in which it occurred, the significance of certain people, and the patient's adaptive techniques. The history is also a current commentary. It includes a description of the patient's present environment, of its stresses and sources of pleasure, and of the persons who are significant and influential. For each period of the patient's life, the report should include information about his social, sexual, and vocational functioning, the inhibitions imposed by excessive or inappropriate fear or guilt, and his sources of pleasure.

Family History. This section should include a description of the patient's parents and siblings and anyone else who lived with the family, including their names, ages, occupations, economic and social status, marital records, and major physical and emotional illnesses. Of particular importance are depression, psychiatric hospitalization, suicide, alcoholism, drug addiction, mental retardation, convulsive disorders, and syphilis. This section should also indicate how the patient felt about each relative, what their relationship was like, and what it is like now. Finally, the therapist should include a description of the family's ethnic and religious traditions and the psychological atmosphere in the home.

Mental Status Examination. The mental status examination gives the psychiatrist a precise picture of the patient's emotional status and mental capacity and functioning at the time of the psychiatric interview. The report should be organized in a certain order and according to certain categories, but the examination itself need not be conducted in that order. The psychiatrist may decide to emphasize certain areas of the mental examination, depending on the patient's problem and history, cooperation, and sensorium.

The report's categories might include a general description of the patient's appearance, behavior, and attitude; his speech; his alertness and orientation; his affective state; his level of anxiety; his stream of thought—including verbatim quotations—and content of thought; his memory; his information and intelligence; his ability to count, calculate, and do abstract thinking; his judgment and insight; and his dreams, fantasies, and value systems.

Summary of Positive Findings. The psychiatric report should include the findings derived from medical and neurological examinations and from psychological tests. The report should also list any drugs the patient has been taking, including dosage and duration of intake, since most sedative and hypnotic agents reduce perceptual acuity and motor skills when taken in small amounts and produce somnolence and stupor when taken in large amounts.

Diagnosis. Any diagnosis made after the psychiatric interview must be tentative. Some crucially important information may not have emerged, the patient may have withheld data deliberately, or he may have a severe disorder that is in a state of temporary remission. However, even the psychiatrist's tentative diagnosis should adhere to the standard nomenclature of the American Psychiatric Association.

Prognosis. The report should include the psychiatrist's assessment of the future course and outcome of the patient's illness, taking into account such factors as the particular illness and its natural history; self-limited treatment goals; the patient's assets and liabilities, such as his age, duration of the illness, and his early traumatic experiences; motivations for treatment; accessibility for treatment; and current life situation.

Recommendations for Treatment. After his systematic study of the patient, the psychiatrist should recommend an appropriate course of therapy—or no psychiatric treatment—on the basis of his understanding of the patient's development and the vicissitudes of his life experiences.

Ancillary Diagnostic Procedures

The psychiatrist may need findings derived from medical and neurological examinations and psychological tests to determine whether the patients' symptoms are psychiatric, physiological, or neurological in origin or whether he is suffering from a severe psychoneurosis or a borderline psychosis.

Medical Examination. The central nervous system can react to emotional stress or to physical stress by producing similar symptoms, and these symptoms can be physiological or psychological or both. Diagnostic difficulties arise when a systemic disease produces emotional symptoms. Anxiety, depression, fatigue, headaches, irritability, dizziness, poor or excessive appetite, drowsiness, and insomnia are usually due to psychogenic factors, but they may also be produced by infectious, toxic, metabolic, degenerative, neoplastic, and nutritional disorders. Depression may be an early sign of hepatitis, cirrhosis of the liver, or carcinoma of the pancreas. And fatigue, frequently associated with depression or anxiety, may be caused by a chronic infectious disease.

Neurological Examination. Disorders of perception and apperception, such as depersonalization phenomena or hallucinations, are sometimes caused by lesions or electrical stimulation of the temporal lobe or by certain chemical agents. Similarly, disorders of intellectual function—such as defects in memory, retention, and recall—may be caused by metabolic deficiency or damage to certain brain structures.

Behavioral assessment is a necessary part of neurological evaluation. Psychological tests and clinical observation sample the same aspects of behavior—speed of response, level of comprehension, use of language—but the tests are more reliable and precise. Psychological tests currently used to assess brain damage are summarized in Table 1 (Freedman and Kaplan).

Psychological Tests. Psychological tests are generally used to facilitate assessment of particular aspects of personality function, the nature and extent of psychopathology, the patient's intellectual potential, and possible brain damage. Some commonly used tests—measuring devices, which provide scores and normative standards; behavior samples, which allow qualitative observations within given areas of psychological functioning; and projective techniques—are described in Table 2, which was prepared for Freedman and Kaplan's *Comprehensive Textbook of Psychiatry.*

Psychological tests of personality function are particularly helpful when the psychiatrist needs more information about sensitive areas and he does not want to question the patient directly, lest his probing arouse excessive anxiety. And psychological tests of intellectual function can help the psychiatrist determine whether the patient's impaired functioning is due to cerebral disease, a basic intellectual deficiency, sociocultural factors, or a psychiatric disorder.

Nomenclature

Psychiatric clinical syndromes are currently classified according to the official nosological system of the American Psychiatric Association as published in the *Diag-*

Table 1. *Tests for Assessing Brain Damage**

Category	Subcategories	Remarks
General scales	Wechsler Adult Intelligence Scale (WAIS) Stanford-Binet Wechsler Intelligence Scale for Children (WISC)	Given the availability of adequate normative standards in relation to the patient's educational and cultural background, a performance significantly below expectations should raise the question of cerebral damage. This generalization applies to both adults and children.
Reasoning and problem solving	Abstractions (Shipley) Progressive matrices (Raven) Proverbs (Gorham) Perceptual mazes (Elithorn) Object and color-sorting tests (Goldstein and Scheerer)	Performance level is closely related to educational background and premorbid intellectual level. In general, the clinical application of these tests is more useful in the case of educated patients. If specific language and perceptual defect can be ruled out as determinants of defective performance, failure suggests frontal lobe involvement or diffuse cerebral disease.
Memory and orientation	Immediate auditory memory—repetition of digits Immediate auditory memory—reversal of digits Immediate visual memory (Benton, Graham-Kendall) Recent auditory memory—words or stories Recent visual memory—words or pictures Temporal orientation (Benton, Van Allen, and Fogel)	For complete assessment, a number of memory tasks (auditory vs. visual, verbal vs. nonverbal, immediate vs. recent) should be given. Minor defects in temporal orientation may be elicited and suggest weakness in recent memory.
Visuoperceptive and visuoconstructive	Identification of hidden figures (Teuber-Weinstein-Rudel) Identification of fragmented figures (Street-Gestalt) Block design construction (Kohs, Goldstein-Scheerer, Wechsler) Stick arranging (Goldstein-Scheerer) Copying designs (L. Bender, Benton visual retention) Three-dimensional block construction (Benton-Fogel) Inkblot interpretation (Rorschach, Holtzman) Perceptual mazes (Elithorn) Responsiveness to double visual stimulation (M. B. Bender)	These types of task are relatively sensitive indicators of the presence of cerebral disease. Analysis of qualitative features of performance and comparison of performance level with the status of language and reasoning abilities often provide indications with regard to locus of the lesion.
Somatoperceptual	Tactile recognition (Parker, Ross) Finger recognition (Benton) Right-left orientation (Benton) Responsiveness to double tactile stimulation (M. B. Bender)	Frequently useful indicators of the presence and locus of cerebral disease.
Language	Token test (De Renzi-Vignolo) Abstractions (Shipley) Proverbs (Gorham) Word fluency (Benton-Spreen-Fogel) Illinois test of psycholinguistic abilities (Kirk-McCarthy)	Test performance is dependent on educational background, and it is essential that clinical interpretation allow for this and other possibly significant factors. In adult patients, defective performance (particularly in relation to other abilities) suggests dysfunction of the cerebral hemisphere that is dominant for language. In children, defective performance does not have this localizing significance but does raise the question of the presence of cerebral damage.
Attention, concentration, and motor abilities	Continuous performance test (Rosvold) Visual vigilance (McDonald-Burns) Reaction time (Blackburn-Benton-Joynt) Motor impersistence (Garfield) Imitations of actions (Bergès-Lézine)	Valuable behavioral indicators of the presence (and sometimes locus) of cerebral disease that deserve more extensive clinical application.

* Adapted from *Comprehensive Textbook of Psychiatry*, edited by A. M. Freedman and H. I. Kaplan, Williams & Wilkins, Baltimore, 1967. Chart by Arthur Benton, Ph.D.

Table 2.   *Some Instruments Commonly Used by Clinical Psychologists**

Instrument	Description	Comments
Measuring Devices Benton Visual Retention Test	An individually administered test designed to measure visual memory, used for subjects 8 years of age and older.	This is one of a class of instruments used to investigate memory functions. It is most useful in differential diagnosis and in the evaluation of brain damage.
Cattell Infant Intelligence Scale	A downward extension of the Stanford-Binet test to cover ages 3 to 30 months.	This test has little predictive value for future intellectual level, particularly in the early ages. However, it does yield a good description of current functioning and is useful for the early diagnosis of mental retardation and brain damage.
Gesell Developmental Schedule	A scale based on behavioral observations, to measure development in different areas from the age of 4 weeks to 6 years.	Although the scale yields poor predictions for later developmental quotients, particularly during the early ages, it does yield a satisfactory picture of current functions. Clinically, it is most useful as a supplement to other data or when successive measurements are taken over a period of time.
Minnesota Multiphasic Personality Inventory	A questionnaire type of personality test for ages 16 years and over. May be administered individually or in groups. Yields 14 scores in scales representing diagnostic categories (such as hysteria, schizophrenia) and test-taking behavior (such as lying).	Besides the scales noted in the test manual, other scales, such as ego strength, have been reported in the literature. Although the administration and scoring of this test are quite simple, the interpretation of the score profiles may become rather complex and requires considerable experience.
Stanford-Binet Intelligence Scale, Form L-M, 1960	An individually administered age scale intelligence test designed to range from 2 years up. This is a revision based on the 1937 Forms L and M. It yields a mental age and a deviation I.Q.	This scale presents a wide variety of items and item difficulty. It is organized by item difficulty (i.e., age level). The choice between this scale and the WISC is often a matter of the preference of the individual clinician, with the Stanford-Binet usually being the most helpful at the lower age levels and at the extremes of intelligence.
Wechsler Adult Intelligence Scale (WAIS)	An individually administered intelligence test for ages 16 years and over. It yields scores for 11 subtests as well as verbal, performance, and full-scale I.Q.'s.	The items of this scale are organized according to the task presented, with a separate score for each type of task. Besides yielding information concerning the intellectual and cognitive functions, analysis of the pattern of subtest scores and qualitative examination of the protocol may yield information concerning the impact of psychopathology in these areas.
Wechsler Intelligence Scale for Children (WISC)	A downward extension of an earlier form of the WAIS to cover the ages below 16 years. Yields scores similar to the WAIS (one additional optional test) but with subtest scores based on chronological age; covers ages to 16 years.	As with the WAIS, the scale is often used for more than the determination of level of intelligence. The grouping of items by type of task involved makes it easier for the clinician in actual practice to use it as an instrument to investigate the impact of pathology in the intellectual and cognitive areas.

Table 2—Continued

Instrument	Description	Comments
Vineland Social Maturity Scale	An individual interview schedule aimed at determining rate of development. An age scale, it covers from birth to maturity. It yields a development quotient (D.Q.), which is the ratio of developmental age to chronological age.	This scale is simpler to administer and to score than is the Gesell scale, but it is based on reports rather than on direct observation. It does furnish a helpful picture of current developmental status, and it is strongest when used to supplement other data or to provide successive measures over time.
Behavior Samples Bender-Gestalt Test	An elicitation of visual-motor behavior by having the patient copy a set of geometric designs. Various modifications of administration may be introduced, such as having the designs redrawn from memory.	Although several scoring systems have been developed for this test, it is usually used qualitatively. Deficits in this area are often associated with brain damage, and the test is most used for differential diagnosis of brain damage. It may also be used to investigate developmental and intellectual levels in children and the characteristics of ego functions in adults. A number of clinicians use the instrument as a projective technique.
Examining for aphasia (Eisenson)	A systematic survey of the ability to receive and to express meaning through different modalities. It includes the aphasias, agnosias, and apraxias.	This instrument provides for behavior samples in various areas of language and symbolic function and at several levels within each area. As a quick survey, it is extremely useful where brain damage is suspected. However, further examination is usually necessary for treatment planning.
Goldstein-Scheerer Tests of Abstract and Concrete Thinking	A battery of five tests (cube test, color sorting, object sorting, color form sorting, stick test) to examine the ability to attain and to maintain the abstract attitude.	These tests afford opportunities to observe the patient attempting to solve problems that require abstraction and shifts in abstractions. Although other thought disorders, such as schizophrenic thinking, may be elicited, concrete thinking tends to be highlighted. The tests are most used for the diagnosis and the evaluation of brain damage.
Concept Formation Test (Kasanin and Hanfman)	A complex problem of grouping the Vigotsky Blocks is presented. Clues given and explanations of groupings are questioned.	The attempts to solve the complex problem provides opportunity to observe the patient's modes of thinking. The test is particularly useful in revealing patterns of schizophrenic thinking.
Projective Techniques Blacky Pictures	A series of 11 cartoons about a dog (Blacky) and his/her family. The patient makes up stories, answers more structured questions, and indicates like-dislike for the pictures.	The stimulus pictures depict different stages of psychosexual development. Its major use is with children, but it can be used with adults. Some writers suggest the following sequence: Blacky with younger children, CAT with older children and adolescents; TAT with adults. This, however, is very much at the discretion of the individual clinician.

Table 2—Continued

Instrument	Description	Comments
Draw a Person	The basic instruction is simply to draw a person, then to draw a person of the opposite sex. Many elaborations exist, including interviews about figures drawn.	This is one of a number of drawing projective techniques, including the drawing of a house, tree, person; of the family; of animals. The figure drawings, in general, may be interpreted as yielding data concerning self-concept, perception of significant figures, problem and conflict areas, mood, affect, and anxiety.
Rorschach	A series of 10 symmetrical inkblots. The patient tells what he sees in each. This is followed by an inquiry concerning the responses. Different sets of stimulus cards are available, but the original Rorschach plates are by far the most frequently used.	This is the most useful single instrument of the clinical psychologist. Through analysis of perception, cognition, and content, information concerning almost every aspect of psychological organization may be revealed.
Sentence Completion Test	Incomplete sentences are completed by patient (e.g., "My mother . . . ."). Sentences may be aimed at specific potential conflict areas. Standard forms, such as the one by Rotter, are available.	This technique may be used at different levels from the prediction of overt behavior to the uncovering of deep personality dynamics. It yields data concerning conflict areas and emotional attitudes. This technique has the advantage of flexibility, for the skilled clinician may devise incomplete sentences tailored for a specific patient.
Thematic Apperception Test (TAT)	Patient makes up stories about stimulus pictures. Some pictures are specially designed for girls, boys, women, or men. Other sets of stimulus cards for special groups are available, such as the Children's Apperception Test (CAT), which uses pictures of animals.	This test helps to furnish the content of the patient's inner life. It may be said with some truth that the Rorschach furnishes the skeleton on which to hang the flesh and blood of the TAT. It yields data concerning, among other things, needs, pressures, self-concept, motives, fantasies, attitudes, and feelings.

* Adapted from *Comprehensive Textbook of Psychiatry*, edited by A. M. Freedman and H. I. Kaplan, Williams & Wilkins, Baltimore, 1967. Chart by Herbert Fensterheim, Ph.D.

nostic and Statistical Manual of Mental Disorders (*DSM-II*) and as outlined in Table 3. This system of nosology is not entirely satisfactory, chiefly because the causes of many psychiatric disorders are not yet fully understood. The system is, therefore, based on superficial characteristics and must be considered artificial. But an artificial system is far better than none at all, and so it is generally used.

More than one category of disturbance may be seen in a patient, and so the first edition of the manual (*DSM-I*), published in 1952, supported the concept of multiple diagnoses, but certain combinations of diagnoses were not permitted. For example, Alcoholism could not be listed as a separate diagnosis when it was associated with an underlying disorder. In contrast *DSM-II* encourages clinicians to diagnose every disorder present, even if one is the symptomatic expression of another. Also, *DSM-II* makes greater use of qualifying phrases—acute and chronic, not psychotic, in remission, mild, moderate, and severe.

Table 3.   *Classifications of Mental Disorders According to DSM-II**

I. Mental Retardation—subnormal intellectual functioning. Retardation begins during the developmental period and is associated with impairment in maturation or in learning and social adjustment or both.

Borderline: I.Q. of 68 to 85
Mild: I.Q. of 52 to 67
Moderate: I.Q. of 36 to 51
Severe: I.Q. of 20 to 35
Profound: I.Q. under 20

Clinical Subcategories of Mental Retardation:

After Infection and Intoxication (congenital cytomegalic inclusion body disease, rubella, syphilis, toxoplasmosis; encephalopathy associated with other prenatal infections, due to postnatal cerebral infection, associated with maternal toxemia of pregnancy, bilirubin, and postimmunization).

After Trauma or Physical Agent (encephalopathy due to prenatal injury, mechanical injury at birth, asphyxia at birth, and postnatal injury).

Associated with Disorders of Metabolism, Growth, or Nutrition (cerebral lipoidosis, lipid histiocytosis, phenylketonuria, hepatolenticular degeneration, porphyria, galactosemia, glucogenosis, and hypoglycemosis).

Associated with Gross Brain Disease, postnatal (neurofibromatosis, trigeminal cerebral angiomatosis, tuberous sclerosis, encephalopathy associated with diffuse sclerosis of the brain).

Associated with Diseases and Conditions Due to Unknown Prenatal Influence (anencephaly, malformations of the gyri, congenital porencephaly, multiple congenital anomalies of the brain, craniostenosis, congenital hydrocephalus, hypertelorism, macrocephaly, primary microcephaly, and Laurence-Moon-Biedl syndrome).

Associated with Chromosomal Abnormality.

Associated with Prematurity.

After Major Psychiatric Disorder.

Associated with Psychosocial Factors (environmental deprivation).

II. Organic Brain Syndromes—disorders characterized by impairment of brain tissue function and resulting in impairment of orientation, memory, intellectual functions, and judgment and in shallow affects (the acute form is reversible; the chronic form is permanent).

A. Psychoses Associated with Organic Brain Syndromes:

Senile Dementia—occurs with senile brain disease in old people; manifested by self-centeredness, childish emotionality, difficulty in assimilating new experiences, and deterioration—sometimes to the point of vegetative existence.

Presenile Dementia—covers cortical brain diseases similar to senile dementia but occurring in younger people; examples include Alzheimer's and Pick's diseases.

Delirium Tremens—acute brain syndrome caused by alcohol poisoning and characterized by delirium, visual hallucinations, and coarse tremors.

Korsakov's Psychosis—(alcoholic) chronic brain syndrome caused by long-time alcohol poisoning and characterized by confabulation, memory impairment, disorientation, and peripheral neuropathy.

Other Alcoholic Hallucinosis—hallucinosis caused by alcohol but not categorized as delirium tremens, alcoholic deterioration, or Korsakov's psychosis. The patient may have threatening auditory hallucinations, while his sensorium is relatively clear.

Alcohol Paranoid State—paranoid state in chronic alcoholics characterized by excessive jealousy and delusions of the spouse's infidelity.

Acute Alcohol Intoxication—covers acute brain syndromes caused by alcohol and of psychotic proportion but not categorized as delirium tremens, acute hallucinosis, or pathological intoxication.

Alcoholic Deterioration—covers chronic brain syndromes caused by alcohol and of psychotic proportion but not categorized as Korsakov's psychosis.

Pathological Intoxication—acute brain syndrome of psychotic proportion after a small intake of alcohol.

Psychosis Associated with Intracranial Infection, General Paralysis—psychosis characterized by signs and symptoms of parenchymatous syphilis of the nervous system and usually by positive serology.

Table 3—Continued

Psychosis with Other Syphilis of Central Nervous System—covers all other psychoses caused by intracranial infection by *Spirochaeta pallida.*

Psychosis with Epidemic Encephalitis (von Economo's Encephalitis)—disorder caused by post-World War I viral epidemic encephalitis.

Psychosis with Other and Unspecified Encephalitis—includes disorders caused by encephalitic infections other than epidemic encephalitis and encephalitis not otherwise specified.

Psychosis with Other and Unspecified Intracranial Infection—covers acute and chronic conditions caused by nonsyphilitis and nonencephalitic infections, including meningitis and brain abscess.

Psychosis with Cerebral Arteriosclerosis—chronic disorder caused by cerebral arteriosclerosis; it may coexist with senile dementia or presenile dementia.

Psychosis with Other Cerebrovascular Circulatory Disturbance—disturbances such as cerebral thrombosis, cerebral embolism, arterial hypertension, cardiac disease, and cardiorenal disease.

Psychosis with Epilepsy—condition associated with idiopathic epilepsy; the patient's consciousness may be clouded or he may be dazed, confused, bewildered, and anxious; on occasion he may have an episode of excitement, hallucinations, fears, and violent outbreaks.

Psychosis with Intracranial Neoplasm—includes primary and metastatic neoplasms.

Psychosis with Degenerative Disease of the Central Nervous System.

Psychosis with Brain Trauma—covers posttraumatic chronic brain disorders and disorders that develop immediately after a severe head injury or brain surgery and that produce significant changes in sensorium and affect.

Psychosis with Endocrine Disorder—covers disorders caused by complications of diabetes and by disorders of the endocrine glands.

Psychosis with Metabolic or Nutritional Disorder—covers disorders caused by pellagra, avitaminosis, and metabolic disorders.

Psychosis with Systemic Infection—covers disorders caused by such severe general systemic infections as pneumonia, acute rheumatic fever, typhoid fever, and malaria.

Psychosis with Drug or Poison Intoxication (other than alcohol)—covers disorders caused by drugs such as psychedelic drugs and by hormones, gases, heavy metals, and other intoxicants except alcohol.

Psychosis with Childbirth—not used unless all other possible diagnoses have been eliminated.

Psychosis with Other and Undiagnosed Physical Condition—covers psychoses caused by physical conditions not already listed and brain syndromes caused by physical conditions not yet diagnosed.

B. Nonpsychotic Organic Brain Syndromes—children with mild brain damage often show hyperactivity, short attention span, easy distractibility, and impulsiveness; they are sometimes withdrawn, listless, perseverative, and unresponsive; a few have difficulty in initiating action. Subcategories include nonpsychotic organic brain syndromes with intracranial infection; with drug, poison, or systemic intoxication; with brain trauma; with circulatory disturbance; with epilepsy; with disturbance of metabolism, growth, or nutrition; with senile or presenile brain disease; with intracranial neoplasm; and with degenerative disease of central nervous system.

III. Psychoses Not Attributed to Physical Conditions Listed Previously:

A. Schizophrenia—covers disorders manifested by disturbances of thinking (alterations of concept formation that may lead to misinterpretation of reality and sometimes to delusions and hallucinations), mood (ambivalent, constricted, and inappropriate responsiveness and loss of empathy with others), and behavior (withdrawn, regressive, and bizarre).

Simple Type—schizophrenia characterized by slow reduction of external attachment and interests, by apathy and indifference, by impoverishment of interpersonal relations, by mental deterioration, and by a low level of functioning.

Hebephrenic Type—schizophrenia characterized by disorganized thinking, unpredictable giggling, shallow and inappropriate affect, silly and regressive behavior and mannerisms, frequent hypochrondriacal complaints, and, occasionally, transient and unorganized delusions and hallucinations.

Catatonic Type—the excited subtype is characterized by excessive and sometimes violent motor activity; the withdrawn subtype is characterized by generalized inhibition—stupor, mutism, negativism, waxy flexibility, or, in some cases, a vegetative state.

Paranoid Type—schizophrenia characterized by persecutory or grandiose delusions and sometimes by hallucinations or excessive religiosity; the patient is often hostile and aggressive.

Table 3—Continued

Acute Schizophrenic Episode—condition characterized by acute onset of schizophrenic symptoms and confusion, emotional turmoil, perplexity, ideas of reference, dreamlike dissociation, excitement, depression, or fear.

Latent Type—schizophrenia characterized by clear symptoms but no history of a psychotic schizophrenic episode; sometimes called incipient, prepsychotic, pseudoneurotic, pseudopsychopathic, or borderline schizophrenia.

Residual Type—covers patients with signs of schizophrenia after a psychotic schizophrenic episode but who are no longer psychotic.

Schizo-affective Type—covers patients with a mixture of schizophrenic symptoms and pronounced elation (excited subtype) or depression (depression subtypes).

Childhood Type—schizophrenia that appears before puberty. It is characterized by autistic, atypical, and withdrawn behavior; failure to develop identity separate from the mother's; and general unevenness, gross immaturity, and inadequacy in development.

Chronic Undifferentiated Type—schizophrenia with mixed symptoms or with definite schizophrenic thought, affect, and behavior not categorized elsewhere.

Other and Unspecified Types—schizophrenia not previously described.

B. Major Affective Disorders—psychoses characterized by a single disorder of mood—extreme depression or elation—that dominates the patient's mental life and is responsible for loss of contact with his environment but that is not precipitated by any life experience.

Involutional Melancholia—psychosis occurring during the involutional period and characterized by anxiety, agitation, worry, and severe insomnia and frequently by somatic preoccupations and feelings of guilt.

Manic-Depressive Illnesses—psychoses marked by severe mood swings and by remission and recurrence.

Manic Type—manic-depressive illness that consists of manic episodes only—excessive elation, talkativeness, irritability, flights of ideas, and accelerated motor activity and speech.

Depressive Type—manic-depressive illness that consists of depressive episodes only—severely depressed mood, mental and motor retardation, and sometimes apprehension, uneasiness, perplexity, agitation, illusions, hallucinations, and delusions of guilt.

Circular Type—manic-depressive illness characterized by at least one attack of a depressive episode and of a manic episode.

Other Major Affective Disorder—psychosis with no more specific diagnosis or mixed manic-depressive illness, in which manic and depressive symptoms appear almost simultaneously.

C. Paranoid States—psychotic disorders in which a persecutory or grandiose delusion is the essential abnormality.

Paranoia—a rare condition characterized by gradual development of an elaborate paranoid system based on an actual event; the patient often considers himself unique and superior; the chronic condition rarely interferes with his thinking and personality.

Involutional Paranoid State—paranoid psychosis characterized by delusional formation in the involutional period.

Other Paranoid State—covers paranoid psychotic reactions not previously classified.

D. Psychotic Depressive Reaction—psychosis characterized by a depressive mood caused by a real experience but with no history of repeated depressions or mood swings.

IV. Neuroses—disorders characterized by anxiety but not by gross personality disorganization or gross distortion or misinterpretation of external reality.

Anxiety Neurosis—neurosis characterized by anxious overconcern to the point of panic; often associated with somatic symptoms.

Hysterical Neurosis—neurosis characterized by involuntary psychogenic loss or functional disorder; symptoms begin and end suddenly in emotionally charged situations symbolic of underlying conflict.

Conversion Type—hysterical neurosis in which the special senses or voluntary nervous system is affected, causing blindness, deafness, anosmia, anesthesias, paresthesias, paralyses, ataxias, akinesias, or dyskinesias; the patient often shows inappropriate lack of concern and may derive some benefits from his symptoms.

Dissociative Type—hysterical neuroses in which alterations in the patient's state of consciousness or his identity produce amnesia, somnambulism, fugue, or multiple personality.

Table 3—Continued

Phobic Neurosis—neurosis characterized by intense fear of an object or situation that the patient knows is no real danger to him but that causes faintness, palpitations, perspiration, nausea, fatigue, tremor, and panic.

Obsessive-Compulsive Neurosis—neurosis characterized by the involuntary and persistent intrusion of thought, urges, or actions and often accompanied by anxiety and distress.

Depressive Neurosis—neurosis marked by excessive depression caused by an internal conflict or an identifiable event or loss.

Neurasthenic Neurosis—neurosis characterized by complaints of chronic weakness, easy fatigability, and exhaustion, which distress the patient.

Depersonalization Neurosis—syndrome characterized by a feeling of unreality and estrangement from the body, self, or surroundings.

Hypochondriacal Neurosis—condition marked by preoccupation with the body and persistent fears of presumed disease.

Other Neurosis—covers psychoneurotic disorders not classified previously.

V. Personality Disorders and Certain Other Nonpsychotic Mental Disorders:

A. Personality Disorders—disorders characterized by deeply ingrained, generally life-long maladaptive patterns of behavior that are usually recognizable by adolescence or earlier.

Paranoid Personality—behavioral pattern characterized by unwarranted suspicion, hypersensitivity, jealousy, envy, rigidity, excessive self-importance, and a tendency to blame and ascribe evil motives to others—symptoms that often interfere with ability to maintain satisfactory interpersonal relations.

Cyclothymic Personality—behavior pattern characterized by recurring and alternating periods of elation (marked by optimism, ambition, high energy, warmth, and enthusiasm) and depression (marked by pessimism, low energy, worry, and a sense of futility)—moods that are not attributable to external circumstances.

Schizoid Personality—behavior pattern characterized by shyness, oversensitivity, seclusiveness, avoidance of close or competitive relationships, and eccentricity and sometimes by autistic thinking without loss of capacity to recognize reality, by daydreaming, and by inability to express hostility and aggression.

Explosive Personality—behavior pattern characterized by sudden, gross outbursts of aggressiveness or rage that differ strikingly from the patient's usual behavior.

Obsessive-Compulsive Personality—behavior pattern characterized by excessive concern with conformity and standards of conscience; patient may be rigid, overconscientious, overdutiful, overinhibited, and unable to relax.

Hysterical Personality—behavior pattern characterized by emotional instability, excitability, overreactivity, vanity, immaturity, dependence, and self-dramatization that is attention-seeking and seductive.

Asthenic Personality—behavior pattern characterized by low energy, easy fatigability, lack of enthusiasm, inability to enjoy life, and oversensitivity to stress.

Antisocial Personality—covers unsocialized persons in conflict with society—persons who are incapable of loyalty, selfish, callous, irresponsible, impulsive, unable to feel guilt or learn from experience, with a low level of frustration tolerance and a tendency to blame others.

Passive-Aggressive Personality—behavior pattern characterized by both passivity and aggressiveness, which is often expressed passively in obstructionism, pouting, procrastination, inefficiency, and stubbornness.

Inadequate Personality—behavior pattern characterized by ineffectual responses to demands—by ineptness, poor judgment, social instability, inadapatbility, and lack of stamina.

Other Personality Disorders of Specified Types.

B. Sexual Deviations—covers persons whose sexual interests are primarily directed toward objects other than people of the opposite sex, toward sexual acts not usually associated with coitus, or toward coitus performed under bizarre circumstances. Included are such deviations as homosexuality, fetishism, pedophilia, transvestitism, exhibitionism, voyeurism, sadism, and masochism.

C. Alcoholism—covers patients whose alcohol intake damages their physical health or personal or social functioning and those to whom alcohol is essential.

Table 3—Continued

Episodic Excessive Drinking—condition when alcoholism is present and person becomes intoxicated at least four times a year.

Habitual Excessive Drinking—condition when alcoholic becomes intoxicated (impaired speech, coordination, or behavior) more than 12 times a year or is recognizably under the influence of alcohol more than once a week, though not intoxicated.

Alcohol Addiction—condition when patient is dependent on alcohol—suffers withdrawal symptoms.

D. Drug Dependence—covers patients addicted to or dependent on drugs other than alcohol, tobacco, and caffeine beverages. Patient may be dependent on opium, opium alkaloids, and their derivatives; synthetic analgesics with morphinelike effects; barbiturates; other hypnotics, sedatives, or tranquilizers; cocaine; *Cannabis sativa* (hashish and marijuana); other psychostimulants such as amphetamines; and hallucinogens.

VI. Psychophysiological Disorders—disorders characterized by physical symptoms caused by emotional factors and involving a single organ system, usually under autonomic nervous system control.

Psychophysiological Skin Disorder—covers reactions like neurodermatosis, pruritis, atopic dermatitis, and hyperhydrosis, caused by emotional factors.

Psychophysiological Musculoskeletal Disorder—covers disorders like backache, muscle cramps, myalgias, and tension headaches caused by emotional factors.

Psychophysiological Respiratory Disorder—covers disorders like bronchial asthma, hyperventilation syndromes, sighing, and hiccoughs, caused by emotional factors.

Psychophysiological Cardiovascular Disorder—covers disorders like hypertension, vascular spasms, paroxysmal tachycardia, and migraine caused by emotional factors.

Psychophysiological Hemic and Lymphatic Disorder—covers any hemic and lymphatic disturbances caused by emotional factors.

Psychophysiological Gastrointestinal Disorder—covers such disorders as peptic ulcer, constipation, chronic gastritis, ulcerative and mucous colitis, hyperacidity, pylorospasm, heartburn, and irritable colon caused by emotional factors.

Psychophysiological Genitourinary Disorder—covers such disorders as dyspareunia, impotence, and disturbances in menstruation and micturition that are caused by emotional factors.

Psychophysiological Endocrine Disorder—covers endocrine disorders caused by emotional factors.

Psychophysiological Disorder of Organ of Special Sense—covers any disturbance, except conversion reactions, in the organs of special sense that are caused by emotional factors.

VII. Special Symptoms Not Elsewhere Classified—covers psychopathologies manifested by a single specific symptom that is not the result of an organic or other mental disorder. Included are speech disturbance, specific learning disturbance, tic, other psychomotor disorder, sleep disorder, feeding disturbance, enuresis, encopresis, and cephalalgia.

VIII. Transient Situational Disturbances—temporary disorders of any severity that occur without any apparent underlying disorder and that are acute reactions to environmental stress. Disorders are classified as adjustment reaction of infancy, childhood, adolescence, adult life, or late life.

IX. Behavior Disorders of Childhood and Adolescence—disorders that are more stable, internalized, and resistant to treatment than transient situational disturbances but less so than psychoses, neuroses, and personality disorders. Characteristic symptoms include overactivity, inattentiveness, overaggressiveness, delinquency, shyness, feeling of rejection, and timidity.

Hyperkinetic Reaction of Childhood or Adolescence—disorder characterized by overactivity, restlessness, distractibility, and short attention span, especially in young children.

Withdrawing Reaction of Childhood or Adolescence—disorder characterized by shyness, timidity, seclusiveness, detachment, sensitivity, and inability to form close interpersonal relationships.

Overanxious Reaction of Childhood or Adolescence—disorder characterized by chronic anxiety, sleeplessness, nightmares, excessive and unrealistic fears, and exaggerated autonomic responses. The patient is usually immature, self-conscious, conforming, inhibited, dutiful, lacking in self-confidence, approval seeking, and apprehensive in new situations and places.

Runaway Reaction of Childhood or Adolescence—covers patients who characteristically run away from home for a day or more to escape threatening situations, who steal furtively, who are immature and timid, and who feel rejected at home, friendless, and inadequate.

Table 3—Continued

Unsocialized Aggressive Reaction of Childhood or Adolescence—disorder characterized by hostile disobedience, aggressiveness, quarrelsomeness, vengefulness, destructiveness, temper tantrums, solitary stealing, lying, and hostile teasing of other children. The patients usually have no consistent parental discipline or acceptance.

Group Delinquent Reaction of Childhood or Adolescence—covers patients, usually boys, who accept the values, behavior, and skills of their gang, with whom they steal, skip school, and stay out late at night.

Other Reaction of Childhood or Adolescence—covers children and adolescents with disorders not previously categorized.

X. Conditions without Manifest Psychiatric Disorder and Nonspecific Conditions:

A. Social Maladjustments without Manifest Psychiatric Disorder—covers persons who are psychiatrically normal but who have severe problems.

Marital Maladjustment—covers normal persons with significant conflicts in marriage.

Social Maladjustment—covers culture shocks and conflicts caused by loyalties to two cultures.

Occupational Maladjustment—covers normal persons who are grossly maladjusted in their work.

Dyssocial Behavior—covers persons who follow criminal pursuits but are not categorized as antisocial personalities.

B. Nonspecific Conditions—covers conditions not classified under any other category.

* This table is based on the American Psychiatric Association's *Diagnostic and Statistical Manual of Mental Disorders*, second edition (DSM-II).

REFERENCES

American Psychiatric Association. *Diagnostic and Statistical Manual of Mental Disorders*, ed. 2 (DSM-II). American Psychiatric Association, Washington, 1968.

Blum, R. H. *The Management of the Doctor-Patient Relationship.* McGraw-Hill, New York, 1960.

Deutsch, F., and Murphy, W. F. *The Clinical Interview*, vol. 1. International Universities Press, New York, 1955.

Finesinger, J. E. Psychiatric interviewing: principles and procedure in insight therapy. Amer. J. Psychiat., *105:* 187, 1948.

Freedman, A. M., and Kaplan, H. I., editors. *Comprehensive Textbook of Psychiatry.* Williams & Wilkins, Baltimore, 1967.

Freud, S. The dynamics of the transference. In *Collected Papers*, vol. 2, p. 312. Hogarth Press, London, 1946.

Freud, S. Fragment of an analysis of a case of hysteria. In *Collected Papers*, vol. 3, p. 13. Hogarth Press, London, 1946.

Gill, M., Newman, R., and Redlich, F. C. *The Initial Interview in Psychiatric Practice.* International Universities Press, New York, 1954.

Lewin, B. D. Counter-transference in the technique of medical practice. Psychosom. Med., *8:* 195, 1946.

Lewis, N. D. C. *Outlines for Psychiatric Examination*, ed. 3. State Hospitals Press, Utica, N. Y., 1943.

Menninger, K. *A Manual for Psychiatric Case Study.* Grune & Stratton, New York, 1952.

Ripley, H. Psychiatric interview. In *Comprehensive Textbook of Psychiatry*, p. 491, A. M. Freedman and H. I. Kaplan, editors. Williams & Wilkins, Baltimore, 1967.

Rogers, C. R. *Client-Centered Therapy.* Houghton Mifflin, Boston, 1951.

Sullivan, H. S. *The Psychiatric Interview.* W. W. Norton, New York, 1954.

Whitehorn, J. C. Guide to interviewing and clinical personality study. Arch. Neurol. Psychiat., *52:* 197, 1944.

2

Group Therapy with Narcotic Addicts

Joyce Lowinson, M.D. and Israel Zwerling, M.D., Ph.D.

INTRODUCTION

Classical approaches to the treatment of hard-core heroin addicts have proved to be unsuccessful in controlling opiate abuse. Therapists such as Nyswander have described very limited successes in the treatment of addiction by using psychoanalytic techniques but these techniques have failed to help the vast majority of patients alleviate their persistent narcotic craving. Because of the over-all failure of individual therapy, other approaches to the control of drug addiction have been sought and group therapy has been widely employed as a treatment modality, especially in hospital settings, by Blachly et al., Brett and Villeneuve, Einstein and Jones, and Johnston. It is the present purpose to describe the range of group approaches which have been used and to assess their effectiveness in altering addictive behavior.

Definition

The philosophical orientation of programs using group therapy techniques may range from classical analytically oriented therapy, where the therapist, psychiatrist, or other trained professional plays a central role, to encounters directed by trained ex-addicts who reject the central role of professionals. Group therapy may take place in an intramural setting, such as a hospital, rehabilitation center, therapeutic community, or prison, or in a community setting, such as a doctor's office, counseling clinic, induction center for a therapeutic community, probation or parole center or hospital aftercare center.

Circumstances

The reasons for an addict's involvement in group therapy and the degree of his volition vary. Some addicts enter treatment because the cumulative effect of social, legal, and financial pressures makes drug use egodystonic. Other addicts feel that their drug addiction stems from a psychological disorder for which they need treatment. Still others participate in group therapy because it is one of the conditions for being accepted into or remaining in a voluntary treatment program such as Synanon, Daytop Village, Odyssey House, or Phoenix House. And some patients in hospital situations attend group therapy because of boredom or the desire to ventilate complaints about the treatment facility or both.

In certain states, drug addicts must enter treatment before they can receive welfare assistance. And in civil commitment programs, such as those run by the California Rehabilitation Center and New York's Narcotic Addiction Control Commission, all patients are required to attend group therapy sessions.

Readiness for release to aftercare is based to a large degree on the extent of participation in therapy and on the insight and growth that the patient has derived from this experience.

The authors wish to thank Herman Joseph and John Langrod, who collaborated on the preparation of this chapter.

ABSTINENCE-ORIENTED TREATMENT PROGRAMS

Most abstinence-oriented treatment programs view heroin addiction as a manifestation of underlying character disorder. One of their principal goals is to effect the cessation or, at the very least, diminution of heroin use. However, this is not the case with all group therapy programs. A problem, related but separate, faced by practitioners of group therapy concerns the extent to which demands can be made of participants in groups. If the abstinence requirements for group participants are too lax, the unmotivated patient may thwart the therapeutic goal by using such defense mechanisms as superficial discussions or complaints about the agency's regulations and conversations revolving around drugs. If, on the other hand, the requirements are too stringent, a smaller number of addicts will remain in therapy.

The practitioners of classical group therapy hold that the addict seeks immediate gratification and demonstrates a low threshold of pain, frustration, depression, and anxiety. In 1961, Zucker noted that, in a group setting, peers may be more effective than the professional therapist in making the addict aware of his self-defeating, regressive behavior. This finding influenced the development of groups directed by ex-addicts. These groups are more concerned with the modification of present behavior and attitudes than with analysis of the patients' past histories and the unconscious factors in their addiction.

Therapeutic Communities

The ex-addict-operated programs had their origin in 1958 when Synanon was founded. Numerous programs based on the Synanon model have been developed in recent years. All these programs postulate that the addict is an immature person, a baby, who tends to blame others for his problems. Therefore, when the patient begins treatment, he starts at the lowest level, washing floors and dishes, because that is all the responsibility a child is capable of handling.

He is constantly confronted about his behavior and he takes instructions from a senior resident, who acts as a role model and as living proof that the new resident can succeed. In encounter therapy sessions, the patient's defenses are stripped away by heavy attack and ridicule to force him to be honest and more aware of his actions.

Because the residents do most of the work in a therapeutic community, the job structure takes the form of a sharply differentiated hierarchy in which each resident can theoretically work his way to the top. The structure is divided into separate departments ranging from the kitchen and maintenance staff at the lowest level to the policy-making administrative position at the top. Each resident begins his career at the bottom and his job performance is rated periodically. If a resident wants a different job, he is expected to assert himself and make his wishes known to the community leaders. Being shifted from job to job and having to wait for promotions are viewed as training designed to increase the patient's acceptance of change and frustration, which is considered as a sign of maturity and growth.

In addition to job promotions, rewards are given in the form of passes to leave the facility for short periods of time. In some programs the possibility of becoming sexually involved with another resident or with a nonresident spouse is also construed as a reward.

Punishment may take the form of verbal reprimand, loss of pass privilege, job demotion, and such ridicule as having to wear diapers and a sign stating "I am a baby." The ultimate punishment, short of expulsion from the community, is shaving of a resident's hair. This punishment is usually reserved for residents who steal or who leave the program and then return. Punishment must be accepted in good grace, as its acceptance by the resident is taken as a sign of maturity. Sometimes residents who are unfairly or severely punished leave the program.

Synanon. Synanon was founded in 1958 by Charles Dederich, a reformed alcoholic. By 1969 more than 1,100 persons were in residence in Synanon houses on the West Coast.

Synanon is viewed as a social movement whose goal is to teach people a better way of life. The treatment and cure of drug addicts and alcoholics is only one facet of the program. Synanon is not basically geared to returning persons to the community as is indicated by the organization's ownership of businesses, schools, and housing facilities. Rather, the program's goal is to provide and create a better society for its members. Persons who leave Synanon to assume positions in other addict treatment programs are considered splitters.

Increasingly, Synanon is attracting nonaddicts with a wide diversity of problems. Schizophrenic patients in particular and others who need a sheltered environment seem to find peace in this setting. The residents tend to be middle-class whites.

Synanon is wholly self-sufficient and applicants for admission are expected to contribute at least $500 as evidence of their motivation. The theory is that, if the addict can get money to buy drugs, he can do so to save his life. Synanon does not accept public funds because it opposes extramural evaluation.

Synanon also feels that research may interfere with treatment. Urine-testing for detection of drugs is resisted on the grounds that it conflicts with the principle of absolute honesty. Opposition to Nalline-testing is based on the premise that it involves the administration of a drug.

Although impartial statistics are not available, Dederich has estimated that 50 per cent of the residents leave during the first three months of treatment. Of those who stay in Synanon, 90 per cent remain drug-free. These figures, reported by Casriel in 1964, represent a possible but not impartially validated retention rate of 45 per cent.

Daytop Village. Daytop was founded in 1963, financed by a National Institute of Mental Health grant given to the Brooklyn Supreme Court Probation Department. Originally called Daytop Lodge, it was first directed by Daniel Casriel, a psychiatrist who had extensive experience at Synanon. In 1964, David Deitch, a former director at Synanon, was hired as Daytop's director. Later, the name of the program was changed from Daytop Lodge to Daytop Village and

addicts who were not on probation but who wished to enter were accepted after screening.

Daytop, like other therapeutic communities, accepts only the highly motivated addict who has demonstrated his desire for treatment. To get an appointment the applicant must repeatedly telephone the intake or induction center. Once granted an appointment, he may be made to wait for hours before being granted an interview. The addict must convince the intake worker, himself a former heroin addict, of his sincere desire to give up drugs. Treatment for the purpose of avoiding a jail sentence is not considered sufficient reason to enter the program. Bassin reports that, as the ultimate test of motivation, the heroin addict has to undergo "cold turkey"—withdrawal from heroin without the aid of methadone or tranquilizers. At the present time, the number of applicants eliminated in the screening process is unknown.

Daytop, as well as some other therapeutic communities, receives public funds, and so it is committed, at least in theory, to returning the patient to the community. In actual fact, most therapeutic community programs like to retain successful graduates as staff members to serve as role models and therapists for the new patients.

Phoenix House. Phoenix House was started in 1967 under the direction of Efrem Ramirez, a psychiatrist who had begun a similar program in Puerto Rico. Phoenix House is essentially a variation of the Synanon model and numerous former residents of Synanon were and are employed as directors and supervisors. The present director of Phoenix House, Mitchell S. Rosenthal, is a psychiatrist who had extensive experience at Synanon.

Phoenix House has a higher percentage of black and Puerto Rican patients than do other therapeutic communities. Screening criteria are similar to those of other therapeutic communities with the added requirement that applicants must participate in encounters prior to admission.

Although the director of the program is a psychiatrist, professionals are concerned principally with research; therapy and administration are under the direction of ex-addict staff members and senior residents.

A recent decision was made to terminate regular urine-testing because it interferes with treatment goals. And greater emphasis is now being placed on securing jobs for residents in the community and outside the addiction field.

Odyssey House. Odyssey House was started as part of a pilot research project at Metropolitan Hospital in 1960. A group of addicts had been receiving cyclazocine, a narcotic antagonist. They and their psychiatrist, Judianne Densen-Gerber, felt that they would be able to function normally if they were totally drug-free. The project was designed to test this theory.

Professionals including psychiatrists, internists, psychologists, and social workers participate in all phases of treatment. Therapy is conducted by a staff of professionals and ex-addicts. According to Densen-Gerber, Odyssey House has borrowed techniques from the Synanon and Daytop programs as well as Doctors Ramirez, Maslow, and Berne. Urine-testing is an important part of the program; the professional staff as well as the patients are subjected to testing. Patients who wish to complete the program must obtain a high school equivalency diploma and get a job outside the field addiction treatment.

Densen-Gerber has found that in about 30 per cent of Odyssey House residents, problems of a neurotic nature are unmasked once the encounter therapy lifts the sociopathic behavior patterns. These patients may then enter individual therapy. A significant difference between Odyssey House and other therapeutic communities is the fact that psychiatrists evaluate all patients and do a careful mental-status examination to determine whether encounters would harm them.

Civil Commitment. Both the California Rehabilitation Center and the New York State Narcotic Addiction Control Commission (NACC) employ group therapy as a treatment technique for the civilly committed patient. The specifics of group therapy as employed in commitment facilities may vary from institution to institution.

Generally, it is done by counselors who are college graduates with backgrounds in psychology and by narcotic rehabilitation officers who are trained by the agency. The narcotic rehabilitation officer functions as an attendant, guard, and co-therapist; he is usually a high school graduate from a socioeconomic background similar to that of the patient. Occasionally, a psychologist or psychiatrist may participate in the group. Patients are expected to attend groups two to three days per week for periods of one to two hours. A recent innovation of the New York State NACC program has been the use of ex-addicts who are in a state of narcotic abstinence and who have completed the state program or graduated from therapeutic communities.

Therapeutic techniques are basically of the classical type with adaptations and modifications of techniques employed in reality therapy and therapeutic communities. Emphasis is placed on the patient's behavior and the possibility of changing his life style.

The sessions are less intense than the prolonged encounter-type therapy found in therapeutic communities. However, the California Rehabilitation Center has employed marathon-type sessions which may last for two days. Also, family therapy has been introduced in the NACC program. Notwithstanding genuine attempts at group therapy while patients are institutionalized, reports from California and the New York State aftercare programs concede a high addiction relapse rate once the addict is returned to the community. Because of the relapse rate, NACC is currently expanding methadone maintenance programs within its aftercare service.

Use of Therapy

Drug addiction is viewed by practitioners of encounter therapy as symptomatic of an underlying character disorder. Drugs, in their view, are used by the addict as an encapsulating mechanism that blocks out stress or anxiety.

Notwithstanding the proliferation of encounter-type therapeutic communities, their basic philosophies and treatment methods do not vary extensively. In our view, this proliferation may be due to the closing off of upward mobility and the consequent clashes between charismatic leaders for positions of power.

Encounter Therapy. The universal therapeutic tool in these programs is the group encounter, which has been described by Densen-Gerber and Murphy, Rosenthal and Blase, Ramirez, and Casriel and Deitch. Although some programs vary their approach in small details, a basic format for encounters remains standard. A typical encounter group consists of eight to 15 residents who may or may not be representative of the make-up of the program. Some groups are composed of residents who are within the same age range or at the same level of job responsibility or who have been in the program for about the same length of time. Other encounter groups are designed to deal with specific grievances between residents. If a resident has complained about another resident by placing a grievance slip in a special box, the person in charge of setting up the encounter groups will schedule the complaint and the accused for the same group. Participants in encounter groups may also be selected at random by picking out names from a shuffled card deck. Still other groups represent a cross section of the population of the community.

The composition of an encounter group may vary from session to session, subjecting a resident to different experiences, attitudes, and viewpoints at each session. Or the population of a group may remain constant over a period of time. The needs of the participants determine the method used. Residents usually attend three encounter groups a week and the length of a session generally ranges from two to four hours.

Unlike groups led by a psychiatrist or some other qualified professional who observes, guides, and interprets the behavior of the patient group, the therapeutic community encounter group does not have a fixed, formal leader. Usually, the group is loosely directed by a more experienced resident who is himself in treatment and who participates both as an equal in treatment

and as a group leader. Often, encounter leaders emerge during the course of a session and leadership may shift from person to person, depending on the nature of the problems discussed.

Physical violence is not tolerated. However, extreme verbal hostility involving screaming and cursing is permitted and may even be encouraged as a form of catharsis, since such behavior is prohibited outside of the encounter sessions. Screaming, crying, and cursing are also viewed as indicators of the degree to which feelings are being aroused, feelings that had previously been encapsulated by the use of drugs.

All group members are expected to participate during an encounter session. Those who do not participate voluntarily are challenged. The session leader or facilitator seeks maximal participation and tries to focus on problems that the group is not dealing with adequately. Each participant is confronted individually for at least some part of a session and he is, in turn, expected to confront others.

Members of an encounter group are confronted about their negative attitudes toward others and themselves, poor job performance, sloppiness, pro-drug attitudes, irresponsible behavior, immature sexual acting out, and general appearance. The group does not encourage rationalizing of negative behavior and probing of a psychoanalytic nature. The emphasis is on each member's responsibility for his daily behavior, which in the beginning is usually described as stupid, self-destructive, and immature—but never as sick.

The group helps the resident view himself and the consequence of his behavior with greater objectivity. The focus of the group is on day-to-day problems and interactions within the group. Secondary importance is assigned to past experiences, because they were, themselves, consequences of attitudes still currently held that need to be attacked and changed.

The participant is presented with a standard of behavior and is expected to act as if he were a mature adult. The fact that he may not feel mature is immaterial; he must act as if he were responsible, and he must obey without question the more experienced residents and staff members. At the start of treatment, it is not important for the resident to understand the rationale of the rules, since, like a young child, he would be unable to comprehend the rationale.

During encounter sessions, all participants are expected to make a commitment to change their behavior. This commitment must be carried over from the encounter group to everyday life within the community.

Techniques used to elicit responses during an encounter session may range from a simple questioning about what is bothering a participant to abrasive accusations and ridicule. The participant who is being confronted is expected to be completely honest in his responses about himself and his behavior. An effort is made to strip the patient of his defenses. Discussion of repressed or denied material may be particularly traumatic. As a result, the patients are frequently reduced to tears during the confrontation.

At the end of the encounter a conscious effort is made to build up the participants. Affection may be shown to an individual member as a sign of responsible concern, love, and acceptance. And friendly interaction is sought by serving coffee and snacks to the group.

One complaint often heard about professionals is that they are easily conned and made to feel sorry for their addict patients. It is assumed that ex-addicts, having been through the experience, are not fooled by the actions of their peers. Admission about one's faults and negative attitudes are usually not held against a person; instead, they are mainly regarded as indications of growth and maturity. Tacit agreements known as "contracts" between participants to rationalize each other's behavior or attitudes in order to avoid the full impact of confrontation or assumption of responsibility for one's behavior are severely chastised. To grow, the participant must cope honestly with his behavior and attitudes.

Techniques to Build Verbal Skills. Participation in encounter groups requires the possession of verbal skills as does membership in therapeutic communities in general; those lacking such skills are at a disadvantage. The following are among the techniques used to assist the resident in acquiring these skills:

Morning Meetings—Because the encounter sessions tend to be critical, the morning meeting is intended to start the day off in a friendly fashion. The residents give talks, sing, and recite poetry. A resident presents a thought for the day derived from literature, the classics, or religous texts. The group then analyzes the phrase or poem, searching out its meaning and application to life.

Word for the Day—Each day a new word goes up on the bulletin board and residents are required to learn its meaning and its message.

Speaking Engagements—Residents go out into the community to explain the program and to solicit funds.

Grab-Bag Seminars—The residents pick topics out of a hat and give ad lib speeches on the topics selected.

Debates—Residents are arbitrarily assigned opposite sides in debates about controversial subjects. At the end of the debate, the participants are forced to switch sides and argue the other point of view.

Open House—Once a week the residents hold open house, when they are expected to communicate and interact socially with nonaddicted visitors.

Extended Encounter Techniques. Another type of group technique is the probe. This extended encounter session may last from 12 to 18 hours. At Daytop Village the probe is designed to deal with deep-rooted fears and anxieties that may not be resolved in shorter encounter sessions. An example would be anxiety resulting from repressed homosexual impulses. Probes are often more emotional than regular encounter sessions and the participating group is smaller, with two staff members in charge.

At Odyssey House probes are used for the purpose of judging whether an applicant can be fully accepted as a member of the community. The applicant has to assure the residents and the staff that he is fully committed to the philosophy of the program.

The probes take place after the applicant has been in the therapeutic community for about six weeks.

Group meetings called "cop-outs" at Daytop Village and/or "House Encounters" at Phoenix House are group sessions that involve all residents and staff members. Problems affecting the entire community are dealt with. Examples are failure to keep the community clean, extensive sexual acting out, secretive use of drugs within the community, and general misbehavior of cliques within the house. These problems are exposed and dealt with by the entire group. If these sessions fail, smaller motivation groups for those persons presenting serious problems may be established.

The most extended encounter group technique is the marathon, which can last for 30 or more continuous hours. The marathon is designed to enhance group solidarity and break down defenses that do not yield in regular encounters. Sears found that marathons have indeed enhanced lagging group solidarity and improved participation in groups. But marathons have recently been eliminated at Daytop Village because the results obtained were minimal in relation to the time spent. Furthermore, since 15 or more people may participate in a marathon, the group can become unmanageable in a prolonged session.

Classical Group Therapy. Groups used in the treatment of addicts have varied in size and composition. Therapy groups at Central Islip State Hospital in New York have been composed exclusively of male patients, as Brett and Villeneuve report. At New York's Baird House, a voluntary residential facility for female addicts, groups are made up exclusively of women. Einstein and Jones describe groups at New York's Riverside Hospital (now closed) composed of adolescents of both sexes. The Riverside patients were mixed with non-drug using college students to determine whether the nonaddicts would accept the addicts during the course of therapy. Although a majority of the addicts relapsed into drug use after

leaving therapy, they did form friendships with nonaddicts as a result of contact within the groups. Laskowitz et al. describe a group composed of both male and female addicts at New York's Greenwich House, a community-based counseling center. Most of the group members were using drugs while in therapy and the attrition rate of the group during a six-month period was about 50 per cent due to re-arrests and hospitalizations.

The Greenwich House group was directed by a team of male and female co-therapists, with a view toward the enhancement of transference relationships. In a variation of co-therapy developed at New York's Lincoln Hospital, each co-therapy team is composed of a professional and a nonprofessional.

Results

As shown in Table 1, abstinence-oriented treatment programs do not appear to be effective in retaining the majority of patients in treatment. Preliminary studies conducted by John Langrod at the Bronx State Hospital Methadone Program have shown that a number of participants in abstention-oriented group therapy programs and therapeutic communities relapsed to drugs once they left the sheltered environment.

Relapses to drug use occurred regardless of philosophy or therapeutic techniques. On the basis of current information, it would appear that the group therapy and abstention-oriented therapeutic communities are unable to halt persistent heroin craving for a substantial number of addicts. Except for the information received from the aftercare division of the California Civil Commitment program, none of the discharges in Table 1 were followed up by the respective agencies. Until thorough research and impartial evaluations are completed, the effectiveness of therapeutic communities and group therapy *per se* remains in doubt as to successful treatment for the majority of hard-core heroin addicts.

Table 1. *Results of Abstinence-Oriented Treatment Programs*

Name of Program	Type of Program	Addicts Admitted (No.)	Addicts Discharged prior to Completion of Treatment (No. and %)	Addicts Retained in Treatment after Admission (No. and %)	Addicts Who Successfully Completed Treatment (No. and %)	Observation Period for Patients	Source of Information
Synanon	Therapeutic community using encounter-type therapy	1,100 (minimum)	35–45%	Not given	25% (minimum)	2 years	Markoff (1969)
Addiction Research Center, Rio Pedras, Puerto Rico	Therapeutic community using encounter-type therapy	1,672	Not given	Not given	112 (7%)	54 months (1957–1961)	Ramirez (1961)
Greenwich House	Community-based counseling service using individual and group therapy	792	372 (47%)	418 (53%)	2 (¼%)	12 months (July 1, 1967–June 30, 1968)	Calof (1969)
Baird House for Women (Quaker Committee on Social Rehabilitation)	Residential center using group and individual therapy in combination	46	Not given	Not given	13 (27%)	12 months (July 1, 1967–June 30, 1968)	Calof (1969)
California Rehabilitation Center—Aftercare Outpatient Parole Division	Civil commitment program using group therapy	454	380* (84%)	74 (16%)	None	36 months (1964–1967)	Kramer et al. (1968)
Daytop Village	Therapeutic community using encounter-type therapy	694	382 (55%)	312 (45%)	38† (?)	12 months (1969–1970)	Collier (1970)
Phoenix House	Therapeutic community using encounter-type therapy	2,110	1,113 (53%)	918 (43%)	79 (4%)	33 months (1967–1970)	Levin (1970)
Exodus House	Community-based program using group therapy	1,041	1,000 (90%)	42 (4%)	59 (6%)	108 months (1958–1967)	Calof (1967)

* Of the 380 who are no longer on aftercare, 366 absconded, were recommitted, relapsed, or were re-arrested and 14 were removed from the program while in good standing by death or by court order (writ of habeas corpus).

† The 38 residents who graduated in 1969–1970 entered the program prior to 1969. As we do not know the exact number of people who entered Daytop, we cannot give an accurate percentage. However, for the years 1966–1970, 113 persons graduated from Daytop; 13 are known to have relapsed and about 70 are employed either by Daytop or by other drug programs. It is estimated that perhaps 1,000 addicts entered Daytop during the period 1966–1970. If this is so, then the successful graduates are approximately 10 per cent of the total admissions.

METHADONE MAINTENANCE TREATMENT PROGRAMS

Metabolic Factors

The limited success of individual and group psychotherapeutic approaches in the treatment of the heroin addict may be due to the fact that these approaches fail to deal with the physiological aspects of addiction. The addict's first contact with drugs depends on availability, social interaction, and undefined personality factors. His physical response to the drug depends in great measure upon biochemical factors that may result in either a positive (pleasure) or a negative (malaise, nausea) reaction. Intertwined with the physiological reaction are psychological and social components which may also influence the person's response to the drug. If the experimenter's reactions are consistently negative and if social pressures are brought to bear against continued experimentation, he may stop using drugs before he becomes addicted. In most instances, during the initial stages of experimentation, the drug-user is able to control usage. However, once addiction develops, control of drug use becomes much more difficult, if not impossible, even with the application of such external pressures as legal constraint and social censure. According to Dole and Nyswander, an ever-present narcotic craving or hunger is generated as the result of repeated exposure to heroin. This craving has a strong physiological component that appears to be symptomatic of an altered response to opiates resulting possibly from a metabolic change within the nervous system. Evidence for this metabolic change has been found in studies of both animal and human subjects.

Wikler has demonstrated that addicted laboratory rats exhibit persistent opiate-seeking behavior. The addicted rats drank from a bitter-tasting opiate solution that nonaddicted rats avoided. Cochin and Kornetsky have shown that tolerance to morphine is maintained in laboratory animals over long periods of time, and persistent metabolic effects of morphine, which is pharmacologically similar to heroin, have been isolated by Himmelsbach.

Martin et al. identified what is considered a prolonged secondary abstinence syndrome after detoxification. Unfortunately, the patients signed themselves out of the hospital and measurements had to be discontinued at the end of a six-month period. During the first seven weeks of this study, after detoxification, hypersensitivity of the respiratory center to CO_2 was recorded. However, after the seventh week, the respiratory center became hyposensitive to CO_2; this condition persisted unabated until the end of the six-month research period. Martin et al. have also reported persistent changes in blood pressure, pulse rate, body temperature, pupillary diameter, body weight, and synthesis of the neurotransmitter epinephrine during the six-month period following detoxification. These changes constitute adequate evidence of the prolonged effect of opiates, even after detoxification.

Also symptomatic of a prolonged metabolic alteration due to drugs is the immediate appearance of euphoria, without accompanying malaise, in response to a shot of morphine or heroin after a period of detoxification or abstention from drugs. Available evidence has shown that tolerance to the discomforting effects of heroin may persist for the duration of an addict's life.

Dole and Nyswander, recognizing the implication of these metabolic changes, set out to develop a treatment approach that would take into account the medical control of narcotic craving. The result was the methadone maintenance treatment program.

History of the Methadone Maintenance Program

The methadone maintenance treatment program was started in 1964 as a pilot project at Rockefeller University under the direction of Vincent P. Dole, a specialist in metabolic research, and Marie E. Nyswander, a psychiatrist with extensive experience in the treatment of opiate addiction.

They sought a medication that would end the addict's antisocial activity, stemming from his need for drugs, and restore him to a normal productive life within the community. On the basis of previous pharmacological, laboratory, and clinical studies, they hypothesized that opiate abuse can generate a prolonged narcotic hunger or craving which becomes the physical basis for a continuing opiate addiction. Therefore, a prime purpose of any effective medication must be the relief of narcotic craving.

First they tried morphine maintenance, but this technique proved unsatisfactory. Although society might benefit from a reduced crime rate, consequent to such an approach, the morphine-maintained patients remained sedated, apathetic, and drug-oriented in their behavior and thinking. In essence, morphine maintenance did not qualify as good medical treatment because some of the incapacitating aspects of heroin addiction still affected the patients.

They then tried two methods of methadone maintenance. Initially, methadone was administered parenterally and given four times daily. Although the patients remained comfortable, they complained of being "human pin-cushions" and asked whether methadone could be given orally. Immediate dramatic changes were noted with the oral administration of methadone. The patients were no longer sedated or apathetic and their ever-present opiate craving was relieved without distorting affect or perception. Furthermore, the patients developed tolerance to the euphorogenic, sedative, and analgesic properties of methadone. When administered orally in gradually increasing doses, methadone ceased to act as a euphoria-producing narcotic, except perhaps in the earliest stages of stabilization. Double-blind studies demonstrated that, in addition to eliminating the craving for narcotics, methadone blocked the effects of heroin and other narcotics. On maintenance doses of between 80 and 120 mg. of methadone a day, patients became impervious to the narcotic, euphoric, and sedative effects of heroin and other narcotic drugs.

Because methadone is a long-acting drug with cumulative effects, these physiological properties are achieved with one daily oral dose after an initial stabilization period of about three weeks. And because stabilization on methadone induces a constant state of tolerance, the same amount of methadone can be prescribed over an indefinite period of time, although some may require minor adjustments in dosage.

Comprehensive medical and psychological tests have failed to reveal that chronic administration of methadone leads to any physical toxicity or consistent psychopathology caused by the medication. The majority of patients on methadone maintenance were found to be within the normal range of behavior. Common psychiatric diagnostic classifications for the drug addict, such as character disorder and sociopathic personality, were not generally applicable. Among those patients who had been characterized as sociopathic personalities before entering the methadone program, there appeared to be a diminution of acting-out behavior as measured by a decrease in criminality based on re-arrest records.

Langrod et al. report that 55 per cent of the methadone program patients at Harlem Hospital tested the methadone blockade with heroin after stabilization. Once the patients were satisfied that they could no longer feel heroin, their experimentation ceased. Methadone's blockade effect also aided in the extinction of conditioning, which contributes to heroin-seeking behavior. With the heroin craving relieved and the narcotic blockade established, the patients became amenable to further rehabilitative efforts.

On the basis of the first positive results, the pilot project was expanded in 1965 into a large-scale research program, using the facilities of the Morris J. Bernstein Institute of Beth Israel Medical Center in New York. The results of the pilot project were replicated on the larger scale.

An impartial committee and evaluation unit to verify the program's data and analyze the results was established in 1965 at the Columbia University School of Public Health and Administrative Medicine under the chairmanship of Henry Brill and under the executive direction of Frances R. Gearing. Gearing directs a research staff which prepares the program's data for Brill's evaluation committee. The committee summarizes the data and makes the appropriate recommendations for further research and program implementation. Because of the consistent success of the program over a six-year period, the evaluation committee recommended in 1969 that the methadone maintenance treatment program be expanded and that methadone programs that differ radically from the Dole-Nyswander model be treated as research studies with the necessary evaluation procedures.

By 1970 about 5,000 former heroin addicts were being treated in methadone maintenance treatment programs throughout the United States, Canada, and Europe. In New York City more than 2,200 methadone patients were in programs monitored by the Central Data System at Rockefeller University and the impartial evaluation unit at Columbia University. Major medical institutions in New York City, under the aegis of Beth Israel Medical Center and Bronx State Hospital, were developing additional programs based on the Dole-Nyswander model as the demand for this treatment by the addict population increased. About 6,800 hard-core heroin addicts were on waiting lists for New York City methadone programs and the New York State Medical Society had approved a resolution recognizing the Dole-Nyswander methadone maintenance program as a valid treatment for narcotic addiction.

Treatment Goals

The methadone maintenance treatment program has as its primary goal the productive social functioning of the addict in the community. This goal includes the voluntary retention of the patient in treatment; the increase in his socially productive behavior (employment and schooling), the cessation of criminal activity; and the curtailment of narcotic and other drug abuse, whether with heroin, amphetamines, sedatives, cocaine, or alcohol. Acceptable social functioning as the principal goal of addiction treatment constitutes a radical departure from the predominant abstinence orientation of other treatment programs.

Treatment success can be measured by comparing the patient's behavior before and after admission to the methadone program. In general, methadone patients reflect the wide spectrum of activities of the non-addicted population within the respective communities. Patients are assisted in coping with problems of everyday living, such as finding a job or a place to live. Some patients require assistance in re-establishing family ties that were broken as a result of addiction. Total dependence on the program for social relationships is not encouraged and the patient is assisted in developing a life of his own.

Entrance Criteria

When the program was begun, relatively strict criteria for admission were established in order to meet the research requirements. The heroin-addiction problem had to be isolated so patients suffering from physical and mental conditions that might obscure the research findings were screened out as carefully as possible. On this basis, patients with known mixed-drug abuse or alcoholism problems were not accepted and applicants suffering from complicating medical conditions, such as tuberculosis, cardiovascular disorders, diabetes, epilepsy, and psychosis, were also rejected. Since a new medical procedure was being tested, the possible effects of mixing methadone with such medications as diphenylhydantoin sodium, insulin, digitalis, and chlorpromazine were not known. A four-year history of narcotic addiction was stipulated. Age limits were set at between 21 and 40 years since it was felt that adolescents who were experimenting with heroin might eventually stop on their own. The upper age limit was fixed at 40 because of the hypothesis that older addicts might stop using drugs on their own.

Once the program demonstrated its effectiveness with addicts meeting the above criteria, the screening requirements were eased. The lower age limit was set at 18 with a two-year history of daily heroin addiction; the upper age limit was eliminated entirely, as many addicts over 40 applied for treatment. Patients with histories of mixed-drug abuse, mental illness, tuberculosis, and other complicating medical conditions were accepted and treated with considerable success. Methadone has been found to be medically safe and it does not interfere with other conditions or prescribed medications

Treatment Methods

The program consists of three phases, designed to provide a gradual re-entry into society. Phase 1 consists of the initial stabilization period of three to six weeks, and it may be completed on either an inpatient or an ambulatory basis. During this phase, the patient is introduced to the program, instructed with regard to his responsibilities, and assigned a counselor who may be a successful graduate of the methadone program. The counselor deals with the anxiety the patient may have regarding the effectiveness of the treatment and his ability to function in society. A research assistant who is a successful patient is assigned to every outpatient and works with the professional staff and patients. He also acts as a positive role model who offers new patients hope of ultimate success.

In the beginning of Phase 2, the patient reports five times a week to the outpatient clinic. He is assisted in finding his way back to conventional functioning through employment, education, the formation of new relationships, and counseling. If the patient shows that he is responding to the program and gives evidence of productive social functioning, he is allowed to report only three times a week, and, after six months, twice a week to pick up his medication.

Phase 3 patients are those who have shown progress in their rehabilitation that they can be trusted to come to the clinic just once a week to pick up their medication. Such patients should be free of all drug abuse and are expected to function as normal productive citizens. To enter Phase 3 the patient should have been functioning acceptably on the program for one year.

During all three phases, the patient submits to urine-testing whenever he reports for medication; the urine is tested for methadone, morphine (a metabolite of heroin), quinine, amphetamines, and barbiturates. The patient is given enough bottles of medication to last until his next clinic visit. On the days that he reports to the clinic, the patient must ingest his methadone under the observation of a nurse. In this way the patient demonstrates that tolerance to the medication is maintained and the possibility of abuse or diversion of methadone is minimized. The medication is dissolved in an orange drink to blunt the bitterness of the methadone and to render it noninjectable as a result of the medium's acidity.

Stabilization Procedure. Dole and Nyswander recommend that the initial dose of methadone be commensurate with the size of the patient's heroin habit at the time of his admission to the program. If the initial dose of methadone is too small, withdrawal symptoms may appear; if the dose is too high, the patient may become oversedated. The precise determination of the extent of the patient's heroin habit may present some problems because some patients tend to exaggerate it in order to receive more methadone. Patients who have been recently released from jail or otherwise detoxified obviously require smaller initial doses of methadone than the fully addicted patients.

The average patient can be started with twice-a-day doses of 10 to 20 mg. of methadone dissolved in orange drink. This dosage is increased every three days by adding about 10 mg. of methadone to either the morning or the evening dose until the patient's daily stabilization dose, generally from 80 to 120 mg., is reached. At this point the total daily methadone dose is held constant but the evening dose is reduced by 20 mg. every three or four days and the morning dose is increased by a corresponding amount. Once the patient is able to take his daily medication in a single dose, the stabilization process is considered completed. The total time required for this procedure is about three weeks.

During stabilization, a physician must regulate each patient individually since no precise correlations have been established between dosage levels and such variables as length of heroin use, sex, age, body weight, and psychiatric diagnosis.

Stabilization was first done on an inpatient basis. Then Brill and Jaffe successfully initiated stabilization on an outpatient basis with equally good results. The principal advantages of ambulatory stabilization lie in the elimination of hospital costs and the fact that employed patients need not lose time from work while being stabilized. In

1970, reports Gearing, about 75 per cent of all methadone patients in New York City were stabilized on an outpatient basis, with in-hospital stabilization being limited to patients requiring simultaneous detoxification from sedative drugs, persons with other complicating medical problems, and those who have no place to live. Stabilization may also take place while the heroin addict is hospitalized for surgery or for such medical problems as knife and gun wounds. Upon discharge from the hospital, he can be continued in a regular methadone program.

The procedure of stabilization is essentially the same for both inpatients and ambulatory patients, but ambulatory patients are usually stabilized at a somewhat faster rate. Since they are exposed to drugs in the community, they need a more rapid elimination of their heroin craving.

Group Therapy. Although methadone maintenance treatment relieves the craving for narcotics, some patients have personality problems that require intervention of a psychotherapeutic nature. Patients manifest their psychopathology in one or more of the following ways: (1) a continuing need for an altered state of consciousness achieved by the abuse of alcohol, amphetamines, barbiturates, cocaine, or hallucinogens; (2) an inability to adhere to a medical program which manifests itself in multiple-drug abuse designed to obtain relief from anxiety or depression; (3) deviant behavior or drug abuse resulting from an inability to give up addict friends or criminal associations or both; (4) continuing antisocial or drug-using behavior as a result of conditioning acquired through years of drug abuse; and (5) the emergence of problems that were formerly masked by the narcotizing effects of heroin, particularly problems related to marriage, work, and other interpersonal relationships.

In rare cases, psychotic patients who used heroin as a tranquilizing agent may have a recurrence of symptoms when they give up heroin. These patients should be the target group for psychotherapy in the methadone program. How well they respond depends on the applicability of the treatment given and on the patient's motivation for entering the methadone program. Therapists who have

worked with methadone patients in groups and in dyads report that the medication does not blunt or otherwise alter affect or anxiety level, perception, or mood. Furthermore, the resolution of the patient's psychiatric problems does not mean that his narcotic hunger will be abated if he is withdrawn from methadone.

At Bronx State Hospital in New York, two types of group therapy sessions are held: ward meetings and family therapy sessions with methadone patients and their spouses. Both are briefly described below.

Ward Meetings. Inpatient groups at Bronx State Hospital were formed for the express purpose of having the patients discuss their fears and anxieties about coping with the square world after their return to the community. All methadone stabilization patients on the ward are required to attend hour-long group meetings every day, Monday through Friday. Attendance at the meetings varies from 12 to 20 patients, depending on the ward census.

Patients who have reached the blockade level of methadone, after about three weeks on the ward, may be excused from group therapy if they are working outside. Because of the high turnover, the group frequently loses whatever feelings of closeness may have developed among the patients. Even if the patients have begun to confide in and empathize with one another, a new admission often prevents further discussion and self-examination because of the group's suspicions about the new patient's attitudes.

Group discussions revolve around ward responsibilities, i.e., around patients' cooperation with one another and areas of conflict due to personality differences. Group process techniques are used to help patients perceive how their behavior affects others.

The following topics of discussion come up repeatedly in the groups: (1) requests for more information and clarification about the effectiveness and side effects of methadone; (2) patients' ward work assignments, which are an occasional subject of disagreement among patients and staff; (3) patients' anxiety about returning to the outside community and the need to cope with the frustrating feelings they had been able to blot out by using heroin; (4) patients' concern about reuniting with and being accepted back by their families; (5) patients' positive and negative feelings about the staff; (6) patients' anxiety about their lack of education and basic job skills, which increases the difficulty of getting a job; and (7) patients' sexual problems.

Generally, methadone groups at Bronx State Hospital focus more on the above subjects and less on unconscious factors than do groups in abstention programs. The levels of discussion vary from group to group. Some groups spend most of their time complaining about the staff or certain patients who do not cooperate in ward assignments. Other groups are quick to develop a feeling of cohesiveness, which helps the patients gain empathy with one another and share their feelings about drug use and family life.

In a group patients are able to discuss fears and anxieties about a possible return to drug use and about the uncertainty of their acceptance back into the community. Many patients say they had blocked out doubts of abstaining from heroin but found solutions to questions raised by others in the group that they could apply to themselves.

Sometimes, patients who have previously been in therapeutic communities try to encourage the confrontation approaches found in those communities rather than the more permissive techniques used in the methadone program, where confrontation techniques are used sparingly.

The role of group therapy for newly admitted methadone patients is shown in these cases:

Bruce, a 32-year-old white man, had used heroin for 17 years. His problems revolved around his mother's domination of him and his subsequent rejection by his wife, who had taken him to family court for nonsupport. In the therapy group, Bruce gained greater insight into his problems by examining his dependent relationship with his current common-law wife. He saw that he needed to become more assertive and to gain recognition in the group, where his self-esteem improved.

Marty, a 37-year-old Negro married man who was almost illiterate, had made large sums illegally while a narcotic addict. In the group he was able to uncover his feelings of inadequacy and doubts about his ability to cope with the legitimate labor market. Marty was reassured by other patients who faced similar problems. When he left the hospital after being stabilized on methadone, he accepted employment as a porter for considerably less money than he could make illegally but he seemed to enjoy working and not being dependent on heroin.

Carmen, a 26-year-old Puerto Rican woman, was admitted to the program and, after being provided with concrete social services, was able to function as a homemaker for a period of 18 months. The group assisted her by making suggestions and helping her decide how she could manage with her newborn baby in the community. After her discharge from the hospital, she did very well until her husband, a heroin addict himself, was discharged from prison. At that point Carmen, who had been diagnosed as schizophrenic, began to deteriorate under the stress of her husband's acting-out behavior. She resumed the use of barbiturates to cope with her anxiety. Although she received counseling, she could not come to a decision about the future of her marriage, which was a sadomasochistic relationship.

Bruce and Marty were able to take benefit from short-term group therapy on the ward. Carmen, on the other hand, represents the minority of patients who require intensive therapy in a more structured setting.

Family Therapy Sessions. Some married methadone patients face problems that are amenable to therapy. For example, the nonaddicted spouse accustomed to the addicted partner's passivity may feel threatened by the patient's recently acquired independence. In such instances, the nonaddicted partner's dominant role may be undermined by the patient's normal behavior.

Another frequent problem occurs when a patient has difficulty in facing and accepting his marriage partner. When addicted to heroin, the patient may have accepted or adapted to the behavior of his spouse because of an altered state of perception. But once properly stabilized on methadone, the patient is in a position to assess realistically his partner's strengths, weaknesses, and needs. The patient may now find himself in a relationship he perceives as no longer compatible.

Family therapy groups meet once or twice a week under the direction of a social worker and with a paraprofessional counselor serving as a co-therapist. Groups consist of two or three married couples, with the male partner usually being the ex-addict.

Like the ward groups, family therapy groups deal specifically with problems facing the patient during the initial period of adjustment to treatment. After he has adjusted to treatment, the patient may manifest neurotic or other symptoms unrelated to the program, his addiction experience, or the medication. In such cases, the patient is urged to enter an individual or group therapy program offered to the nonaddicted persons in the community.

Results

The methadone maintenance program is the only treatment program for opiate addiction to undergo an impartial evaluation. Its results have been evaluated by a committee composed of physicians, sociologists, and psychologists under the auspices of the Columbia University School of Public Health and Administrative Medicine. The evaluation committee submits semiannual progress reports with recommendations to the methadone maintenance treatment program's funding agency, the New York State Narcotic Addiction Control Commission. This evaluation summarizes and documents all data pertaining to retention of patients, discharges, employment, education, criminality, other drug abuse, and medical safety. Data designed to measure the effectiveness of treatment have also been collated and analyzed by the central data system at Rockefeller University, thus providing an additional on-going check of the program.

Langrod et al. interviewed in depth 102 methadone patients at the Harlem Hospital unit, asking about their attitudes toward the program and themselves as methadone patients, their adjustment in the community as ex-addicts, and their abuse of other drugs. The interviewers also assessed the patients' affect. Preliminary data indicate that 76 per cent of the 102 patients viewed themselves as ex-addicts. According to interviewers' evaluations, 74 per cent of the patients did not appear to be high at the time of the interview; those that did appear to be high were either in initial stages of stabilization or were abusing other drugs and alcohol.

Gearing found that approximately 82 per cent of the 2,205 patients admitted to the program over a six-year period have remained in treatment. No sex differences in relation to program retention were noted.

The mean age of patients in the program is 33.1 years and about one-third of the group was between the ages of 19 and 30 at the time of admission. About 85 per cent of the patients are male and about 15 per cent are female. The average patient has a 12- to 13-year history of heroin addiction. The program's ethnic distribution follows essentially the same ethnic breakdown of the New York City Narcotic Register: black, 41 per cent; white, 39 per cent; Puerto Rican, 19 per cent; other, 1 per cent.

After the patients have been in treatment three months, about 70 per cent of them are employed, in school or, in the case of women, functioning as homemakers. Of the patients inducted on an outpatient basis, about 70 per cent are employed at the time of admission to the program. Only 30 per cent of those who are inducted on an inpatient basis are employed when admitted. The percentage of all patients employed, in school, or functioning as homemakers increases with their length of time in treatment. The highest increase in employment occurs within the first six months of treatment. The patients' increased productivity contrasts sharply with a corresponding decrease in financial dependency.

Dole et al. (1968) found that, of the first 723 male methadone patients admitted to the program over a 42-month period, about two-thirds of those who remained in the program (from which about 12 per cent were discharged) were employed or in school or both after three months of treatment. Prior to admission, only 15 per cent had consistent employment, and 85 per cent were leading lives of serious financial dependency, crime, and vocational failure. About 2 per cent of the employed patients were working within the program. The other employed methadone patients held a variety of jobs, ranging from the professions to skilled and unskilled jobs. Patients were encouraged to seek employment outside the addiction field in order to minimize their dependence on the program.

Joseph and Dole report a significant drop in criminality as patients remain in the program. Between January 1964 and May 1968, there was a 90 per cent drop in criminal convictions per 100 man-years after treatment

Table 2. *Criminal Convictions of 912 Methadone Patients*

Convictions	Before Admission	After Admission (939 Patient-Years)*
No.	4,500	51.0
Rate per 100 Man-Years	52	5.8
Persons Convicted (%)	91	5.6

* The term patient-years represents the total time in treatment for a group of patients. For example, if 80 patients are in treatment for two years, then the time would amount to 160 patient-years.

Table 3. *Reasons for Discharge from Methadone Program*

Reason	Men (% of 343)	Women (% of 62)
Arrests	22	14
Drug Abuse, Nonnarcotic	30	28
Alcoholism	18	28
Death	6	9
Medical and Behavior Problems	3	8
Voluntary Departures	21	13

for 912 patients admitted to the methadone program (see Table 2). (A rate per 100 man- or patient-years is the number of events (e.g., arrests, deaths, clinic appointments, etc.) that would be assigned to every group of 100 patients within the total patient population over a one-year period or to every group of 50 patients over a two-year period. The rate calculation is based on the number of events which occurred over a specified time period in the total patient group.)

Prior to admission to the methadone program, patients were mainly convicted for serious felonies and misdemeanors. The convictions represented only a fraction of the crimes committed, since addicts commit many crimes for which they are not apprehended. On the other hand, after admission to the program, a majority of those arrested were charged with minor misdemeanors or less serious offenses. Crime statistics from other methadone programs throughout the United States and Canada support the conclusion that the crime rate among methadone-treated patients decreases after they enter the program.

This sudden and dramatic decrease in criminal behavior after methadone treatment clearly demonstrates that, in numerous cases, the addict's criminal activity results from his heroin-seeking behavior and is not necessarily a manifestation of a sociopathic personality or character disorder.

Treatment Failures and Discharges. The principal reasons for discharging patients from the program are presented in Table 3. According to Joseph and Dole, about 18 per cent of all patients admitted to the program between January 1964 and September 1969 were discharged and 3 per cent of the patients left voluntarily; 1,800 patients remained in treatment.

The death rate for patients in the methadone program is about one for every 100 patient-years, about 1.5 per cent of all admissions. Joseph and Dole note that none of the patient deaths are attributable to methadone toxicity. The patients' autopsy reports revealed that deaths resulted from natural causes, such as disease, accidents, and infections.

The remaining discharges, about 15 per cent of all admissions, must be regarded as treatment failures. Patients who fail on the program are those who, despite the abatement of their narcotic hunger, present such problems as severe behavioral disorders, criminal activity, abuse of other drugs or alcohol, or problems the program is not fully equipped to deal with.

Factors such as sex and ethnic background do not significantly affect the probability of a patient remaining in the program. But patients less than 30 years of age show a slightly higher probability for remaining in treatment than do those over 30. Those over 30 may have been using heroin longer and are, therefore, more damaged both socially and psychologically by the prolonged addiction experience. If this theory is confirmed, methadone treatment should start as soon as possible after ,ne onset of addiction if optimal results are to be achieved.

Drug abuse and alcoholism account for about 50 per cent of all discharges. Among black patients, alcoholism is the major reason for discharge. Other drug abuse is the dominant factor in the discharge of white and Puerto Rican patients. Terminations related to alcoholism and drug abuse usually occur in the second and third years of treatment. The program tries to offer services that focus on multiple-drug abuse problems, so it allows a long time for a patient to respond before he is discharged. Beth Israel Medical Center reports that discharges are correlated with poor health and social functioning.

Medical Effects. Wallach et al.'s study of 83 premenopausal female methadone patients shows that 82 resumed normal menses after they began methadone treatment. While they were addicted to heroin, these women reported irregular or suppressed menses.

Female patients are able to go through normal pregnancies and deliveries without reducing their dosage of methadone. Although two out of the eight infants born to such women were given phenobarbital to alleviate possible withdrawal symptoms, the infants, as a group, showed minimal evidence of withdrawal syndrome. More sophisticated methods than clinical observation for detection of possible withdrawal symptoms are currently being investigated. The remaining six infants needed no withdrawal therapy.

Babies born to methadone patients have normal Apgar scores and body weight, and no effects of methadone toxicity have been found. Follow-up studies of these infants over periods of up to three years have shown no abnormalities resulting from the mother's being treated with methadone during pregnancy and delivery. All evidence indicates that there are no medical condraindications in treating a pregnant addict with methadone.

A few male patients have complained about a decrease in libido during the initial phase of treatment, but libido and sexual functioning are restored to normal within a period of a few days to several weeks, depending on the patients' tolerance to medication. Lowinson reports that tests of heart, liver, kidneys, endocrine glands, neuromuscular coordination, lungs, and bone marrow have shown normal values. Constipation has been a long-range side effect for some patients but this condition can be treated medically and usually subsides as treatment progresses. And some patients have complained of excessive sweating, especially during hot weather.

On the basis of such reports, the manufacturers of methadone are now in the process of applying for a Food and Drug Administration reclassification of the drug to allow its use as maintenance medication in the treatment of opiate addiction. At present, methadone is licensed only for analgesic and detoxification purposes. Use for maintenance purposes is approved on a research basis only.

CONCLUSION

Patients, irrespective of their motivation, do not respond to inappropriate treatment techniques. Existing data indicate that group therapy without proper medication is ineffective for the majority of patients in controlling narcotic craving, especially in the addict who has returned to the community. Those who remain in a drug-free cloistered setting, such as Synanon and other therapeutic communities, may suppress the craving and permit the discharge of the related anxiety in encounters, confrontations, and group pressures. But statistics reveal that the majority of addicts, even those who were highly motivated at first, leave the therapeutic communities and start using heroin again.

Although therapeutic communities are not effective in abating opiate hunger in an appreciable number of addicts, they may effect an attitudinal change, although this claim has not yet been statistically documented. Therapeutic communities may also play a role in the treatment of those patients who reject methadone maintenance, who abuse nonnarcotic drugs, and who present acting-out disorders.

Therapeutic communities are not recommended for and may be harmful to the psychotic or borderline patient because they deliberately break down defenses, which may precipitate a psychotic episode, especially in the absence of trained professionals. Group therapy in abstention-oriented programs, especially those that use marathon and encounter techniques, must be evaluated for psychiatric safety and for effectiveness in returning addicts to the community as normal, functioning people.

For the addicted psychotic, a combination of classical group therapy, coupled with methadone maintenance and appropriate psychotrophic drugs may be a viable approach. Either group or individual therapy can be used with nonpsychotic methadone patients who require psychiatric support. Plans are now being made to establish a therapeutic community for the marginally adjusted methadone patients.

The effectiveness of any group therapy program for addicts must be measured against a baseline of treatment results in a methadone maintenance therapy program. Methadone maintenance is a validated treatment for the intractable opiate addict. The successful results of this approach, as measured by retention of patients, decrease in crime and drug abuse, and increase in productivity, have been impartially evaluated and documented. Wherever the Dole-Nyswander protocol has been properly implemented, the results have replicated the original New York City model.

REFERENCES

Bassin, A. Daytop Village. Psychol. Today, *2:* 48, 1968.

Blachly, P. H., Pepper, B. J., Scott, W., and Baganz, P. Group therapy and hospitalization of narcotic addicts. Arch. Gen. Psychiat., *5:* 393, 1961.

Brett, S. R., and Villeneuve, A. Evaluation of group therapy policies with hospitalized drug addicts in the narcotic unit at Central Islip State Hospital. Psychiat. Quart., *37:* 666, 1963.

Brill, L., and Jaffe, J. The relevancy of some newer American treatment approaches for England. Brit. J. Addict., *62:* 375, 1967.

Calof, J. *A Study of Four Voluntary Treatment and Rehabilitation Programs for New York City's Narcotics Addicts.* Community Service Society of New York, New York, 1967.

Calof, J. *Lifeline to Tomorrow: A Study of Voluntary Treatment Programs for Narcotics Addicts.* Community Service Society of New York, New York, 1969.

Casriel, D. *So Fair a House: The Story of Synanon.* Prentice-Hall, Englewood Cliffs, N. J., 1964.

Casriel, D., and Deitch, D. New success in cure of narcotics addicts. Physician's Panorama, October 1966.

Cochin, J., and Kornetsky, C. Development and loss of tolerance to morphine in the rat after single and multiple injections. J. Pharmacol. Exp. Ther., *145:* 1, 1964.

Collier, W. V. *An Evaluation Report on the Therapeutic Program of Daytop Village, Inc.,* Daytop Village, New York, 1970.

Densen-Gerber, J., and Murphy, J. P. The therapeutic community approach by both professionals and ex-addicts to the treatment of narcotic addiction. In *Bulletin of Committee on Problems of Drug Dependence,* pp. 5679–5690. National Research Council, Washington, D. C., 1969.

Dole, V. P. Biochemistry of addiction. Ann. Rev. Biochem., *39:* 821, 1970.

Dole, V. P., and Nyswander, M. A medical treatment for diacetylmorphine (heroin) addiction. J. A. M. A., *193:* 646, 1965.

Dole, V. P., and Nyswander, M. Heroin addiction: a metabolic disease. Arch. Intern. Med., *120:* 19, 1967.

Dole, V. P., Nyswander, M. E., and Kreek, M. J. Narcotic blockade. Arch. Intern. Med., *118:* 304, 1966.

Dole, V. P., Nyswander, M., and Warner, A. Successful treatment of 750 criminal addicts. J. A. M. A., *206:* 2708, 1968.

Einstein, S., and Jones, F. Group therapy with adolescent addicts. In *Drug Addiction in Youth,* p. 132, E. Harms, editor. Pergamon Press, New York, 1965.

Eisenman, A. J., Sloan, J. W., Martin, W. R., Jasinski, D. R., and Brooks, J. W. Catecholamine and 17-hydroxycorticosteroid excretion during a cycle of morphine dependence in man. J. Psychiat. Res., *7:* 19, 1969.

Gerard, D. L., Lee, R. S., Rosenfeld, E., and Chein, I. *Post Hospitalization Adjustment: A Follow-up Study of Adolescent Opiate Addicts.* New York University, New York, 1956.

Gewirtz, D. Methadone maintenance for heroin addicts. Yale Law J., *78:* 1175, 1969.

Himmelsbach, C. K. Studies on the relation of

drug addiction to the autonomic nervous system: results of cold pressor tests. J. Pharmacol. Exp. Ther., *73:* 91, 1941.

Himmelsbach, C. K. Clinical studies of drug addiction. Physical dependence, withdrawal and recovery. Arch. Intern. Med., *69:* 776, 1942.

Johnston, M. An experiment in group psychotherapy with the narcotic addict. Amer. J. Psychother., *5:* 24, 1951.

Joseph, H., and Dole, V. P. Methadone patients on probation and parole. Fed. Probation, *34:* 42, 1970.

Kramer, J., Bass, A., and Berecochea, B. A. Civil commitment for addicts: the California program. Amer. J. Psychiat., *125:* 816, 1968.

Langrod, J., Lowinson, J., Brill, L., and Joseph, H. Methadone maintenance from research to treatment. In *The Treatment of Drug Addiction and Drug Abuse*, L. Brill and L. Lieberman, editors. Behavioral Publications, New York, in press.

Laskowitz, D., Wilbur, M., and Zucker, A. Problems in the group treatment of drug addicts in the community: observations in the formation of a group. Int. J. Addict., *3:* 361, 1968.

Lowinson, J. The methadone maintenance research program. In *Rehabilitating the Narcotic Addict*, p. 271, S. B. Sells, editor. United States Government Printing Office, Washington, D. C., 1967.

Markoff, E. L. Synanon in drug addiction. Curr. Psychiat. Ther., *9:* 261, 1969.

Martin, W. R., Wikler, A., Eades, C. G., and Pescor, F. T. Tolerance to and physical dependence on morphine in rats. Psychopharmacologia, *4:* 247, 1963.

Nyswander, M. E. *Drug Addict as a Patient.* Grune & Stratton, New York, 1956.

Ramirez, E. Addiction Research Center Bulletin No. Four. Puerto Rico, 1961.

Ramirez, E. The mental health program of the Commonwealth of Puerto Rico. In *Rehabilitating the Narcotic Addict*, p. 171, S. B. Sells, editor. United States Government Printing Office, Washington, D. C., 1964.

Rosenthal, M. S., and Blase, D. V. Phoenix Houses: therapeutic communities for drug addicts. Hosp. Community Psychiat., *20:* 27, 1969.

Sears, V. *Description of the Topic House Program.* Nassau County Drug Abuse and Addiction Commission, Mineola, N. Y., 1968.

Trussel, R. E., Alksne, H., Elinson, J., and Partick, S. *A Followup on Treated Narcotic Users.* Report of the Columbia University School of Public Health and Administrative Medicine, New York, 1959.

Wallach, C., Jerez, E., and Blinick, G. Pregnancy and menstrual function in narcotics addicts treated with methadone. Amer. J. Obstet. Gynec., *105:* 1226, 1969.

Warner, A., and Dole, V. P. The operation of the data system in the methadone maintenance treatment program for heroin addiction. Amer. J. Public Health, in press.

Wikler, A. Conditioning factors in opiate addiction and relapse. In *Narcotics*, p. 85, D. M. Wilner and G. G. Kassebaum, editors. McGraw-Hill, New York, 1965.

Zucker, A. H. Group psychotherapy and the nature of drug addiction. Int. J. Psychother., *11:* 209, 1961.

3

Group Therapy with Alcoholics

Aaron Stein, M.D. and Eugene Friedman, Ph.D.

INTRODUCTION

Group psychotherapy as a form of treatment for alcoholism was first used in the mid-1930's. The formation of Alcoholics Anonymous at that time led to the development of one of the most effective means of helping alcoholics control their drinking. The success of Alcoholics Anonymous and other group therapeutic methods was acknowledged as early as 1943 by Thomas in his review of the literature on group psychotherapy. Since that time, all types of group therapeutic approaches have been widely used to help patients with alcoholism deal with their illness.

Except for a few patients whose personality and psychological difficulties made them suitable for some kind of individual psychotherapy, most alcoholics do not respond favorably to individual therapy. This fact, together with the success of group therapeutic approaches like Alcoholics Anonymous has led to an increasing use of group psychotherapy in the treatment of patients with alcoholism. As the use of group psychotherapy has increased, numerous workers have confirmed the usefulness of various types of group psychotherapeutic approaches. Group psychotherapy is, in most instances, the treatment of choice for the psychological problems of the alcoholic.

The personality structure and the nature of the emotional and psychological difficulties of the alcoholic are of the type that can be most effectively treated with group psychotherapy. Certain dynamic features of group psychotherapy, particularly the nature of the transference to the therapist and the interaction with peers in the group, make it specifically useful for the kind of patient who usually develops the illness characterized by alcoholism.

Various special techniques of group psychotherapy have been used with alcoholics. Both Walton and Strayer found prolonged group psychotherapy—lasting several years —most useful. Scott used the technique of having each member of the group take turns in being intensively questioned by the other members. Williams held dinners at monthly intervals for alcoholics who had been discharged from a hospital and followed these dinners with group therapy sessions. Esser devised a technique in which the group therapy discussion centered around and was limited to one question raised by the group therapist. Fox, Cabrera, and Weiner, among others have used psychodrama combined with group psychotherapy.

Many workers have combined individual and group psychotherapy in the treatment of alcoholics. Paley, Heath, and Wallerstein are some who have described the use of hypnosis combined with group therapy. And some workers have combined group therapy with aversive drug therapy and even with LSD.

Most of the literature dealing with the use of group psychotherapy in the treatment of alcoholism states that favorable results were obtained. But many of these reports give little supporting data; usually they simply state that group psychotherapy was used in the treatment of patients with alcoholism and that good results were obtained. But a few workers have used objective evaluative methods and control groups. And several have reported poor results.

Relatively few reports discuss the group dynamics involved. Among those that do, Allison reports that he used a nondirective approach to overcome the patients' passivity. Pfeffer et al. describe how the group psychotherapy diluted the intensity of the transference to the therapist and diverted it toward the other group members, enabling many alcoholic patients to tolerate the treatment. Usdin et al., describing the use of group psychotherapy with the aversive disulfiram, felt it had significance for the patients as the oral incorporation of superego aspects of the leader. Stewart deliberately fostered identifications in the group to develop empathy and positive values. Greenbaum focused on transference. Lindt feels that, through projective identification with another group member, the alcoholic fulfills his own rescue fantasy. Forizs, Shulman (1950), Scott (1963), and Fogarty found the interaction, the changing of roles, and the identifications in group psychotherapy especially useful in dealing with the alcoholic's passive hostilities.

Several reports discuss the considerable value of group psychotherapy for the wives of alcoholic patients. Both Preston and Scott (1959) used joint interviews with husband and wife as well as group psychotherapy for the wives and found this method very helpful. Ewing et al., Gliedman et al., and Macdonald found that the wives of alcoholics tended to be depressed and irritable and often showed severe mental and emotional disturbances as their husbands improved. Group psychotherapy was most useful in dealing with these difficulties.

THE NATURE OF ALCOHOLISM

Social, legal, and medical attitudes toward the alcoholic have been gradually, but definitely, changing. Essentially, the change consists of an abandonment of the critical, judgmental, and moralistic disapproval of the alcoholic and a new recognition that he is afflicted with a chronic and complex type of illness. Various legal authorities, courts, and social agencies have accepted this new concept in their approach. Medical organizations and institutions have also used the new concept and have initiated specific measures to provide effective treatment for the patient with alcoholism.

This new concept of alcoholism as a highly complex illness is best summarized by the following definition, which is taken from the American Medical Association's *Manual on Alcoholism:*

Alcoholism is an illness characterized by a preoccupation with alcohol and loss of control over its consumption such as to lead, usually, to intoxication, if drinking is begun; by chronicity; by progression; and by tendency toward relapse. It is typically associated with physical disability and impaired emotional, occupational, and/or social adjustment as a direct consequence of persistent and excessive use of alcohol.

The number of people with alcoholism problems in the United States today is quite large, somewhere in the neighborhood of four to six million. And the medical, social, and economic difficulties stemming from the problems of excessive use of alcohol are vast and of the utmost seriousness.

Many possible causes have been suggested, including hereditary factors and such metabolic disturbances as endocrine deficiencies, glandular dysfunction, and enzyme disorders, particularly in the central nervous system. Sociological factors have always been considered of great significance in the origin and development of alcoholism. The prevailing social and cultural attitudes toward the use and abuse of alcohol have had a great deal to do with former legal and medical attitudes. Some of these cultural and social attitudes still prevail and need to be considered in some of the treatment approaches to this condition. But generally considered to be of primary importance are psychological and psychopathological factors. The modern concept of alcoholism is that it is an illness caused by the complex interaction of many physiological, psychological, and sociological factors.

The Role of Personality

The personality structure is a major factor in the development of alcoholism. No specific type of personality structure is characteristic of alcoholics only, but most workers in the field feel that certain types of personality and character disturbances occur frequently in alcoholics. These personality and character deficiencies stem from traumatic defects that have led to an arrest of personality development or to a regression to earlier levels of development.

Patients with alcoholism problems can be divided into two classes, according to Knight: (1) essential or primary alcoholics, and (2) symptomatic or reactive (secondary or neurotic) alcoholics. The essential type of alcoholic tends to have a severe character or even psychotic type of disorder. The secondary or symptomatic type of alcoholic has progressed to a more integrated personality and character, but under the impact of emotional conflicts he tends to regress to earlier levels of personality and character development, particularly when he has engaged in heavy drinking. This distinction between neurotic and psychotic disturbances helps in determining the treatment needed.

The personality structure of the severe alcoholic—probably of the essential type—is described by Feibel as archaic, fixated at an early infantile level with primitive and unstable defenses and inadequate reality-testing. Despite these similarities to the psychotic, most alcoholics, says Feibel, have not completely relinquished their contact with reality. Although the ego is weak, it does continue to function to some extent. These patients show a marked tendency toward regression; strong denial of unpleasant external or internal realities; the acting out of aggressive and sexual instinctual impulses, particularly under the influence of alcohol; blackouts; massive amnesias, which are probably a severe form of denial; marked dependency on the environment and the people in it in terms of their estimate of themselves and their functioning; a harsh superego that leads to fear and guilt, projection onto the environment,

further guilt and depression, and self-punitive and self-destructive consequences; and, finally, a marked tendency to introjection and projection of a primitive type. These personality characteristics, Feibel states, need to be considered in the choice of treatment.

Pfeffer also thinks the more severe type of alcoholic has remained relatively fixated at an early developmental level. Difficulties in infancy or in the early stages of development, frequently caused by inconsistent maternal attitudes, lead to traumatic fixation at these early levels and inability to withstand the tensions associated with the lack of fulfillment, particularly of oral needs. These patients exhibit the self-centered, spoiled child, or infantile type of character disturbance. They show an inability to withstand frustration of any type of need. Frustrations manifest themselves in tensions, which are felt as intolerable psychic pain, and focus the patient's attention on an immediate need for relief. Characteristically, these feelings are variations or equivalents of depression, often with paranoid coloration. They are an expression of tensions resulting from underlying conflicts connected with oral, aggressive, and sexual needs. These patients turn to ingestion of alcohol for relief and thereby accomplish a momentary satisfaction of their need as well as relief from the tensions associated with the painful awareness of superego restrictions and the demands of reality.

Pfeffer states that these patients are markedly egocentric or narcissistic; their main concern is with the satisfaction of their own needs and pleasures. Their relationship to others is on a narcissistic level, without any real emotional involvement. Others are considered to be the suppliers of needs or love, support or admiration, and they are not seen as individuals in their own right. Any failure of the environment or the people in it to satisfy the infantile needs of the alcoholic results in tension and pain, rage and depression, and the seeking of relief through further ingestion of alcohol. The strictures of a primitive and harsh superego further increase the depression, sense of guilt, and fear of punishment from the environment, leading to self-destructive behavior and suicidal tendencies. The relationship to the environment and the people in it is pathologically immature and excessively dependent. In order to function, the alcoholic requires the support of a structured situation and the directions and expectations of those in his environment.

In his work with alcoholics in an industrial setting, Pfeffer found that many were very constricted and rigid people, lacking in insight and presenting a picture of considerable limitation of interest and activity. They were very anxious people, who resisted any awareness of underlying feelings of tensions or conflicts. This resistance led to a restriction of ego functioning, so that they were not aware of emotional or other factors related to underlying feelings in the environment and in the people in it. They were so fearful of their instinctual needs and of fantasies connected with them that they would resort to massive denial, further limiting their emotional and intellectual functioning. They were truly dependent on their environment, and they used the structure and expectations of the environment and the people in it to guide them into the type of functioning they felt was expected of them. This rigid type of personality constriction and defensive denial of underlying thoughts and feelings presents problems in the choice of psychological treatment.

Psychoanalytic Theories

The addiction to alcohol, which constitutes the problem of alcoholism in susceptible persons, is considered psychoanalytically to be a dependence on a substance—in this instance, alcohol—to provide pleasure on one hand and relief from psychic pain, anxiety, and depression on the other hand. Addiction to alcohol represents a compromise that protects the individual from psychosis, antisocial behavior, and suicide. Addictive acts, like compulsive drinking, are repetitive and adaptive attempts to actively master a painful situation that had previously been suffered passively. Some authors relate such attempts to counterphobic attitudes.

A failure in development leads to the regressions exhibited by the alcoholic. The earlier the developmental failure occurs, the more severe the disturbances in behavior and personality. Patients in whom traumatic occurrences led to a fixation in the early infantile stage of development constitute the essential or primary alcoholic in Knight's classification. This type of person has the most severe disturbances, a poor prognosis, and great difficulty in treatment. Persons who have matured to a greater extent but have regressed under the influence of traumatic events exhibit some of the earlier personality or behavioral characteristics, but these are temporary, with fewer defects in the ego. For this secondary or neurotic type of alcoholic, the developmental failure is not as severe, the prognosis is better, and various types of treatment are possible.

Mismanagement in infancy and childhood is considered by all to be a predisposing element in the genesis of alcoholism, particularly when the mother or other parental figure is inconsistent, alternating between the extremes of overindulgence and excessive punitive frustration. In addition, disturbances in the parents and psychological difficulties in relationship to the parents further predispose the child to the development of personality defects and to the use of compulsive drinking to deal with them. A frequent finding is an overindulgent, seductive, or inconsistent mother and a weak or absent father. Identification with an alcoholic parent or other relative is another factor in the predisposition toward alcoholism.

Identification with rigid superego attitudes and excessively regressive, punitive behavior on the part of the parents leads to the development of a rigid, primitive, harsh type of superego in the person who later develops alcoholism. He develops an ability to handle aggressive drives directed toward the environment—in this instance, the parents—and a tendency to turn these drives toward himself, leading to self-destructive, depressive, and frequently suicidal impulses.

Fixation at the oral stage of development

leads to an insatiable need for gratification, poor tolerance, narcissism, and a tendency to use such primitive defensive mechanisms as denial and projection. A marked tendency to paranoia and depression also characterize this stage. The essential or primary alcoholic remains fixated at this stage.

If traumatic events result in the person becoming fixated at the anal stage, he may display aggressiveness, cruelty, obstinacy, rebelliousness, a drive for mastery, and tendencies toward paranoia and homosexuality. These patients have developed further in their personality than the essential or primary alcoholic and tend to be in the group of secondary or neurotic alcoholics, who have a better prognosis.

Those who have developed to the phallic-oedipal stage show somewhat different types of deficiencies. They show ambivalence toward people of the opposite sex, a tendency to develop hysterical symptoms, and a hysterical type of character. A tendency toward jealousy, impotence, and marked conflicts with authority figures also result.

In early work with alcoholics, analysts hoped to find some single cause for the development of alcoholism, but their hopes were not fulfilled. Nowadays, most analytically oriented workers in the field of alcoholism believe that a multiplicity of factors and symptoms, arising as a result of developmental failure, need to be considered in understanding and treating any particular case.

Defective ego functioning makes it impossible for the alcoholic to use the knowledge gained from experiences in later life to help overcome the infantile fixations that result in the symptom of alcoholism. This inability is found even in persons in whom a part of the ego has gone on to develop so that they are able to achieve considerable success in their field of endeavor. Another aspect of faulty ego integration in such people may be the inability to organize perceptions and thinking in an effective fashion.

Witkin (1965) suggests that alcoholics for the most part are markedly field-dependent and that those few that are not probably differ with regard to the dynamic route leading to symptomatic drinking. He characterizes field-dependent individuals

as global and diffuse in their personality organization and concomitantly poorly integrated. He cautions, however, that field dependence is not indicative of psychopathology but rather of the form it will take. For example, a field-dependent schizophrenic will more likely be catatonic and a field-independent schizophrenic will favor paranoid symptoms. Similarly, field-dependent individuals will tend to develop neurotic and behavioral symptoms in the oral sphere, such as obesity and alcoholism. These persons will tend to depend on the external world—people and objects—for a considerable amount of their ego functioning. It is of interest that workers such as Witkin and Karp report that a number of alcoholics do exist who are not field-dependent. Karp reports that alcoholics who are field-independent tend to remain in psychotherapy longer than those who are field-dependent. Witkin feels that the proportion of field-independent alcoholics is relatively small but Burdick (1969) reports that middle- and upper-income alcoholics as a group tend to be field-independent. Friedman found a correlation between field dependence, occupation, and educational achievement among alcoholics receiving psychotherapy.

These findings suggest that no single factor is sufficient to establish a relationship between a personality measure—such as field dependence—and a symptom, but that such measures are of inestimable value when used as additional data in aiding diagnosis and in the planning of the treatment.

The field-dependent/field-independent continuum parallels to some extent the approach cited above on the relationship between levels of fixation and personality organization. Indeed, diffusely organized individuals will tend to be infantile and narcissistic while those who are more obsessional in their character organization will tend to be more differentiated and better organized.

Some older theories related alcoholism to the need to discharge tensions and to seek pleasure in satisfying instinctual drives. Now, it is felt that the person with an addiction problem is seeking some type of stimulation to provide pleasure, gratification, and relief from tension. Some new work in the field of psychoanalysis and experimental psychology suggests that the alcoholic seeks pleasure in mastering the environment; pleasure in stimulating, repetitive, and threat-producing behavior; and pleasure derived from certain types of repeated stimuli and sensory perceptions. Some new work is also related to the concept of the depletion of psychic energy, something that revives Freud's old concept of actual neuroses. Included in these analytic explanations for the predisposition to drinking are some of the older concepts of the inner-directing of the aggressive drives, leading to depression and suicide as a result of the need to avoid the harsh strictures of a primitive superego. The concept of an alimentary craving or oral type of release and satisfaction has been developed by several workers.

Others have combined several features of the above concepts in the following formulation of the dynamics of alcohol addiction. In any susceptible individual who develops alcoholism, they find a decreased ability to handle pain and a defective functioning of the ego. The painful affect is felt as a "somatic anxiety equivalent" that is associated with depression and a decreased capability to be consciously aware of the affect. To deal with the pain and his anxiety at his regressed level of development, the patient seeks a benign introject. Alcohol is used as this introject, but it may be experienced as both loved and dangerous. In essence, this ambivalence represents a failure of normal object representation as well as a failure in self-representation. Alcoholism becomes an object that is ambivalently cathected. There is a regression to a near-psychotic level of psychic function, utilizing introjection and projection as the main defense mechanism. Chafetz also feels that alcohol represents an ambivalent type of object introject that must be replaced in treatment.

TREATMENT

Alcoholism is the result of a number of physiological, constitutional, and environmental factors; the intrapsychic state of the patient; and his relationship to an interaction with his family, working associates, and other neighborhood, social, economic, cultural, and religious groups. It is a complex, chronic disease, marked by remissions and exacerbations that can occur at any time, frequently without any discernible reason. The alcoholic almost always has a serious personality disorder and often shows severe psychopathology. He is unusually susceptible to disturbances—even slight ones—in his social, personal, and emotional adjustment, and a disturbance can trigger a flare-up of his symptoms of alcoholism.

The attitude of the alcoholic and of his immediate family toward the treatment of his condition is complicated and ambivalent, especially in regard to any type of psychological or psychiatric treatment. As a result, the patient often acts out with his family to make his approach to treatment very difficult. Even if such a hard-to-reach, poorly motivated patient does begin treatment, he frequently drops out after a short period, before any type of psychological or psychiatric treatment can demonstrate its effectiveness.

All the difficulties that the alcoholic presents at the beginning of treatment and during treatment are manifestations of his resistance to facing his emotional tensions and conflicts. Accordingly, the difficulties connected with having the alcoholic patient come to treatment, enter into it, and remain in it must be dealt with as important parts of all treatment procedures. The therapist must deal with the same emotional factors, difficulties, and resistances that, in another area, produce drinking. The patient's personality, needs, tensions, and conflicts directly affect the way he handles the approach to treatment. All those who come into contact with him must recognize this connection and be prepared to work with it.

More specifically, the alcoholic is a sick, immature person who has incorporated into his personality—and, therefore, into his approach to any person or any situation in which he finds himself—various types of regressive and unhealthy personality and character traits. He may be overly aggressive or overly passive, overly dramatic or hysterical, overly demanding or overbearing.

He may be extremely shy and tense, or overly talkative and euphoric. Anxiety, fear, suspicion, resentment, and various types of exhibitionistic, seductive, and defiant behavior and reactions are present from the very beginning of the contact and are exhibited in an extreme and intense fashion, without any realistic reason.

Very often the alcoholic, when he first seeks treatment, does so as a result of some crisis due to an increase in his symptoms or as the result of difficulties with his family, employer, or such authority figures as the police. Quite frequently, the initial request for treatment is made by someone else—his spouse, parent, doctor, lawyer, or employer—which aggravates and intensifies the patient's tension and resistance to treatment.

Because of these complicated factors special procedures must be employed to get the alcoholic into treatment. The initial approach must include an attempt to secure maximal emotional involvement of the patient at all levels, constant emotional support and acceptance of the patient, and a flexible approach in dealing with the patient from the beginning of the contact.

A team approach is often used to bring the alcoholic into treatment and keep him there. Members of the treatment agency meet frequently and engage in group discussions that enable them to ventilate and become aware of their own feelings toward these difficult patients as well as to devise suitable techniques for reaching them.

Value of Group Psychotherapy

Experience over the years with various types of psychotherapeutic approaches to the alcoholic has clearly indicated that the group approach is, on the whole, more effective than the individual approach. Specifically, the dynamic factors in group psychotherapy make it useful in the treatment of the alcoholic.

Transferences. The alcoholic's narcissistic and primitive object relationships, with their marked ambivalence and inability to tolerate frustration and their depressive and paranoid elements, result in a primitive type of transference in individual treatment, which makes the therapist's task extremely difficult. With the essential or primary type of alcoholic, the usual type of individual psychotherapy is almost impossible because of the patient's marked ambivalence and rage if any frustration is encountered. Many workers feel that some gratification of the alcoholic's needs, either in a hospital or by some special techniques outside, is absolutely necessary in the individual treatment of such patients.

In group psychotherapy, however, the ambivalence and the resultant hostile, competitive, and aggressive tensions related to the transference to the therapist are markedly lessened. Because other group members are present, the relationship to the therapist is inhibited and, therefore, diluted or diminished in intensity. The transference is diverted to the other group members, causing a further diminution in the intensity of the relationship to the therapist. The tensions and conflicts the alcoholic feels because of his impulses are deflected into the transference manifestations directed toward the other members of the group. To the ambivalent, anxious, and guilt-ridden alcoholic, this type of transference is far less threatening than the transference to the therapist. This diminution of the intensity of the transference to the therapist and the deflection of the transference feelings onto the other group members make it possible for many alcoholics to enter into a therapeutic relationship that would be too threatening on a one-to-one basis.

The deflection of the transference onto the other patients in the group leads to intragroup tensions and interactions. Patients direct toward each other the infantile impulses connected with the transference, seeking gratification from each other as multiple, transient transference objects.

A kind of therapeutic acting out occurs in the group. In individual psychotherapy, the therapist does not usually respond to transference manifestations of the patient. But in a group, the initial, unconscious response of one patient to another's transference manifestations is seen clearly and effectively and can be used in a therapeutic way. Personality defects and character disorders are clearly and quickly brought out by this type of interaction.

Identifications. The alcoholic's aggressive, ambivalent impulses and the presence of a harsh superego make him anxious and fearful of expressing verbally any of his aggressive, sexual impulses and fantasies. This is particularly true in individual psychotherapy, where the therapist is seen as a harsh, restrictive, punitive superego figure. In a group, however, the therapist is seen as a more tolerant and permissive figure, and the patient identifies with him, replacing his own harsh superego with the idealized figure of the tolerant therapist. In a group composed of alcoholics, the fact that all have the same difficulties and share the same weaknesses and feelings aids in the identification with the other members of the group and helps the alcoholic to overcome his guilt and to express feelings connected with forbidden instinctual impulses.

Massive denial is the alcoholic's most common mechanism of defense. It is frequently associated with defects in ego awareness and perception. In individual therapy, his defense mechanisms are extremely difficult to deal with. But in a group, the alcoholic hears others bring out some of the things he feels, he identifies with them, and he hears them point out the thoughts and feelings he displays. As a result, he quickly drops these primitive methods of defense.

The identification with the other patients and their active interest and support help the alcoholic withstand some frustrations, delay gratification, and become aware of underlying feelings and tensions. In group psychotherapy, as in Alcoholics Anonymous, the other members help the patient control his drinking. In addition, group psychotherapy provides even more specific forms of ego support. For instance, the group members point out restrictions in the patient's ego functioning—his limitation in perception and awareness of things outside of himself, his difficulty in reality-testing. With the support and help the group offers, the patient can start to deal with these things.

The emotional ties between the members of the group consist largely of a number of identifications. They share a common object —the leader or therapist—and they set him up as a narcissistically invested idealized image. In Freud's terms, they set him up in place of their ego ideal and consequently identify him with themselves and with one another.

Types of Group Therapy

A wide variety of group therapeutic approaches are used in the treatment of alcoholics. The approach used in a particular case depends on the needs of the patient, the severity of his illness, the kind of treatment selected, and the site of the treatment— whether it is in a general hospital, state hospital, half-way house, or outpatient clinic.

Three types of treatment groups have been described by Foulkes and Anthony—activity group, therapeutic group, and group psychotherapy proper.

Activity Group. An activity group consists of a group of people engaged in a common activity, such as crafts or sports. Here the nature of the activity is deemed to have a therapeutic effect on the group. Activity groups can be used with outpatients, patients in partial hospitalization centers, and inpatients. The activity involved—work projects, occupational therapy, recreational therapy, dance, music—is used to activate and resocialize the withdrawn and isolated patient. One of the important benefits provided by various half-way houses, partial hospitalization units, and Alcoholics Anonymous meetings is the opportunity for patients to re-establish social relationships with other people.

Therapeutic Group. The specific task of this group is of secondary importance; active participation in the group is the main therapeutic agency. The interaction among the members of the group is therapeutically useful, with each member trying to find a role to fill in the life of the group. Therapeutic groups are widely used in partial hospitalization units and inpatient facilities in the form of patient governments and patient-staff groups. The use of such groups in correctional facilities, Salvation Army centers, and certain facilities for released offenders is one of the newer and more promising developments in the treatment of chronic alcoholics who require repeated hospitalization or who have run into legal difficulties.

Although the discussion in these therapeutic groups deals with conscious emotional attitudes, it is not directed toward increased self-awareness or toward self-investigation, and interpretations of unconscious psychopathology are not fostered. Instead, interaction in the therapeutic group helps the patients become aware of some of the attitudes and reactions they show and of some of the feelings connected with these reactions. The therapeutic effect is largely the result of the staff and the other members acting as good parental figures and good siblings who help each member move toward better control and integration, better participation in the group, and better socialization with the other patients. Despite its limitations, the therapeutic group is a useful therapeutic tool in overcoming the isolation and withdrawal of many severely ill patients, including many with alcoholism problems.

Didactic Discussion Group. In this type of group, which is also known as the classroom type of group therapy, the leader provides some didactic material or information of an educational sort and then guides the group into a discussion of the issues raised by the material. It is useful in setting up various types of orientation groups in treatment centers. It is particularly useful in acquainting the relatives of alcoholics with the nature of alcoholism, the psychological factors involved in the illness, and the best methods for dealing with alcoholic patients. Didactic types of group discussion have also been useful in the rehabilitation of alcoholics, particularly in group vocational counseling.

A related form of didactic discussion group, combined with a structured type of interaction, is found in psychodrama and other group therapies that use role-playing techniques. The interaction does provide some emotional release, but, essentially, these groups use the interaction to bring up material with which to educate the patient about the nature of his emotional responses. Psychodramatic techniques might be used to help the relatives of an alcoholic work out

their feelings and attitudes toward the patient returning home from a hospital.

Alcoholics Anonymous. A.A. is a self-help organization that has considerable success in helping alcoholics abstain from drinking. It does not claim that its type of group meeting facilitates personality change. It is, essentially, a selected group of people who regard themselves with considerable pride as members of an outcast elite, the aristocracy of the rejected. By acknowledging their failure, they develop a sense of unity and pride and foster a high *esprit de corps* which facilitates a self-help program.

A.A. makes use of deeply religious attitudes and approaches, which repel some alcoholics. A.A. also prides itself on achieving abstinence without the help of psychotherapy, which has made for difficult relationships at times with mental health professionals. A more important result of A.A.'s pride in doing without psychotherapy is that it fosters denial of psychiatric illness, something that is in contrast with A.A.'s helpfulness in overcoming the denial of illness connected with drinking. Because of the strong religious coloring of A.A.'s approach and activities, its group meetings have been variously known as inspirational-supportive, repressive-inspirational, and directive-supportive.

The group meetings are nominally leaderless in the sense that no leader is formally designated. However, as is true with most so-called leaderless groups, one or more participants usually serve as leaders. The meetings do have some structure, opening and ending on a semi-religious note. Like revival meetings and such religious groups as The Emanuel Movement and the Oxford Movement, A.A. meetings use public self-revelation. They are similar to the large group therapy meetings led by Marsh in the early days of group psychotherapy. The A.A. meetings focus on discussion of various approaches to the control of drinking. In this sense, they may be considered a didactic type of group discussion. A large part of the group meetings is devoted to helping the members abstain and to devising techniques to abstain from drinking. In this sense, the A.A. meetings are repressive and directed toward self-discipline and self-control with regard to drinking.

Dynamically, the most important point about A.A. fellowship is that it fosters interdependency among the members. Newcomers are taken over and helped by the older members, who make themselves available to educate and support new members in moments of crisis. In this they function somewhat like groups devoted to helping patients face various types of illness, such as ileostomy clubs. As a result, A.A. sets up a new type of interpersonal relationship, a submissive and dependent one, which the religious attitude of the group helps to foster. It uses the social relationship to help members establish new emotional ties to fellow members. And because of their focus on the need to abstain from drinking, A.A. members help set up a substitute neurosis—a compulsion and a set of activities connected with it to help them abstain.

The major usefulness of the A.A. meetings is that they help the new member overcome his denial of the fact that his excessive drinking constitutes an illness and may be a reality problem. They also help him face the reality of the effects of his drinking on the external environment and its relation to internal psychological difficulties, although in A.A. this last point is focused on much less than in group psychotherapy proper. Most important of all, A.A. provides support during the crucial time of the patient's entering into the therapeutic atmosphere of the meetings, and it helps him control his drinking.

The chief therapeutic effect results from the members' interactions. They provide support and gratification for each other in terms of infantile needs.

New Techniques. In certain new types of group therapy techniques, interaction is heightened and focused for the purpose of expediting and facilitating the therapy discussion.

One type is the aggressive-confrontation technique used in the treatment of addiction. The intense group discussions are designed primarily to make the members acknowledge their addiction and to deal with it. The meetings, despite their intensity and supposed freedom and frankness, deal largely with superficial and conscious emotional attitudes. As in A.A., the member interactions provide the therapeutic benefit. When this type of group support and interaction is provided in a live-in facility—such as a half-way house, a partial hospitalization center, or a residence like Synanon—additional support is provided because the members live closely together and constantly interact, which gratifies the need for attention and active support. Blum and Blum strongly urge that this type of live-in facility be applied more extensively to the treatment of certain chronic types of alcoholism.

Another well-known new type of group therapy is the marathon group, which meets for 36 to 72 hours in more or less continuous session, with the idea that the continuous action will speed up the intensity and the value of the therapeutic discussion. Various other techniques have been used to heighten the interaction, such as the nude marathon, the marathon focusing on sensory exercises, and the marathon designed to heighten aggressive interaction through role-playing.

Since the underlying, unconscious aspects of the interactions involved are not interpreted, these active types of groups primarily gratify unconscious infantile transference needs, providing relief and support for members of the group. The members act as group parents, good teachers, and good siblings for one another and supply the external gratification and support that help to control, at least for a while, the painful difficulties arising from unconscious conflicts. Obviously, the patient may get some relief as a result of the diminution in intensity of certain symptoms, and the support of the group may encourage some strengthening of the defenses. The usefulness of such external support and relief cannot be denied. However, one must question some of the claims for extensive personality change made by proponents of the active interaction groups. And although the leader's active manipulation and the other members' deliberate pressure may at times facilitate better social integration, they may at other times be ill-advised and cause serious disturbance in some members of the group, as has been reported in the literature.

Group Psychotherapy Proper. Here the group meets for the treatment of the individual members of the group and for the purpose of uncovering and dealing with the individual member's psychopathology. The group relies on verbal communication only, each individual member is the object of group treatment, and the group itself, through group interaction, is the main therapeutic agency.

Traditional Group Psychotherapy. In this type of group psychotherapy, sometimes called intensive group psychotherapy or analytic group psychotherapy, conditions are set up to facilitate interaction and freeflowing discussion among members of the group so as to uncover the members' unconscious conflicts and resistances. These resistances are interpreted to a considerable degree, although the analysis is never as intensive as in individual psychoanalysis.

Supportive Group Psychotherapy. In modified or supportive group psychotherapy, less of an attempt is made to uncover resistances and psychopathology. Areas related to the transference to the therapist and other members are left uninterpreted; therefore, certain transference needs or infantile object needs are gratified, which provides the group members with a great deal of support.

Group Counseling and Group Guidance. Group counseling is directed toward helping the members solve immediate realistic problems; it is short-term therapy and the group counselor is quite active. In group guidance, a longer type of modified group psychotherapy, the attitudes and feelings involved in the group members' problems are exposed for consideration and evaluation, but the unconscious psychopathology is not exposed. Most group psychotherapy practiced today is some form of group counseling or group guidance.

CLINICAL ASPECTS

Group Therapy Approaches

The first contact with the alcoholic patient is difficult and, most important, special techniques need to be used. These techniques include joint interviews, family therapy meetings, and the setting up of such special groups as orientation groups. Of special importance is the setting up of staff meetings to help the staff in dealing with these difficult patients.

Staff Meetings. The discussion of how to handle problems presented by patients with alcoholism has recently been emphasized. When these staff meetings permit the staff to indicate some of their troublesome feelings about dealing with alcoholics and their anxiety and frustration because of the limitation in what can be done with such difficult patients, the meetings not only become a useful way of coordinating staff activities but also provide a useful outlet for some emotional tensions. The staff meetings also permit an interchange of views and enable the staff to come to a clear understanding of the dynamics involved in treatment. The staff can, for example, come to an understanding of their own identification with a patient's feelings and of their going along with the patient's acting out.

A former patient called the clinic in great agitation and despair because his wife had turned him out into the street penniless and told him that he should go to the clinic for help. He sounded so depressed and so agitated that the staff became quite fearful and urged him to come to the clinic at once. When he arrived, it was obvious that he had been drinking and that he was extremely anxious, agitated, and depressed. The situation, on the surface, clearly indicated that he had no resources of any kind and that his wife had "kicked him out" and did not wish to have anything further to do with him because of his continued drinking and inability to work. He was seen by the social work aide who was on reception that day and also by his former social worker. Both were impressed by the patient's agitation and depression and by his statement that "Life is not worth living." They became fearful of a possible suicide attempt and felt that emergency hospitalization was indicated.

They asked for a meeting to discuss the situation with the director of the clinic. At the meeting it became clear that this type of incident had occurred frequently, was part of an acting out by the patient and his wife, and usually subsided quickly. The director encouraged the staff members to express their feelings and then helped them to formulate a therapeutic approach to the problem. The staff members saw the patient again and decided that his depression was not really severe. They then helped him to understand the realistic help the clinic could give him, such as referral for lodging, funds, and work. They also helped him to see the need to work things out with his wife and offered to make arrangements for joint interviews, which both the patient and his wife accepted. A constructive and realistic working out of their difficulties then became possible.

Another patient was referred by his supervisor in a governmental agency, where he was in danger of losing his job. The patient came to the clinic reluctantly but did cooperate in treatment. After a short time, his supervisor demanded that the patient be given an attendance slip each time he came to the clinic. The patient objected strongly, showing his anger at his supervisor. The staff went along with him because of their anger at the demanding attitude of the supervisor.

The matter was brought up at a staff meeting, and the staff members were encouraged to bring out their feelings. After some discussion, it became clear that they were identifying with the patient's anger at his supervisor and that this situation had become a vehicle for their frustration concerning the treatment of this rather difficult patient. A plan was worked out for the social worker to visit the supervisor and explain to him the workings of the clinic, the treatment method, and its relation to attendance slips.

During the visit it became apparent that the patient's provocative attitude and the supervisor's anxiety and insecurity were involved. The social worker helped the supervisor to work out a realistic method of dealing with this type of problem. The supervisor was grateful and impressed and later cooperated with the clinic in regard to this patient and others in a helpful fashion.

Joint Interview. This approach is useful to define the conflicts between husband and wife that contribute to alcoholism, as the following case illustrates.

The patient, a man in his late thirties, had a long history of drinking and psychopathic and violent behavior. He came to the clinic, at his wife's insistence, because of his heavy drinking, which dated from the time of their first child's birth. The patient was cooperative, but there was great tension between him and his wife. Because the patient showed some paranoid tendencies, the staff decided to see husband and wife together. At the joint interview it became clear that the birth of the baby had made both of them anxious and depressed, particularly in relation to violently ambivalent feelings concerning the child and each other. The interviewer cautiously explored these feelings and offered help to the wife, which she eagerly accepted. The joint interviews were continued until both husband and wife were settled in group therapy in different groups. The joint interviews lessened the tension between them, enabling the husband to stop his drinking and enabling both of them to start working out their difficulties in a constructive and realistic fashion.

Family Therapy. The use of family therapy in the treatment of an alcoholic is frequently helpful, since the family is always involved in and affected by the drinking problem.

A 19-year-old was referred to the clinic by one of his teachers who had become aware of the young man's drinking. The patient came very reluctantly. He was the adopted child of a couple in their fifties who had a son of their own of about 20. The patient had petit mal seizures and was short and thin compared with his stepbrother, who acted provocatively toward the patient. The parents were anxious about the patient and tended to baby him and be overprotective, alternating this behavior with violent quarrels, threats, and punishment, such as cutting off his allowance.

The patient was a sulky, dull young man who had little awareness of his emotional difficulties and was not well-motivated for treatment. The clinic staff felt that working with the family might help, and family therapy was begun. The older brother came once and confirmed the parents' inconsistent attitude; the therapist helped the brother to see his own provocative attitude to some extent. In the treatment sessions the parents were able to ventilate some of their feelings, and the nature of their pathological interaction with the patient became clear. The patient was able to express some of his resentful feelings, and a more useful method of discussing things with the parents was worked out. After several family sessions, the patient entered a group, and the parents continued to meet with the family therapist. The tension at home lessened markedly, with a considerable diminution in the patient's drinking.

Orientation Group. This short-term, active, reality-focused form of group counseling has been used with waiting-list and screening or diagnostic groups. It often helps patients enter into treatment by giving them some idea of what it is about and by letting them know that other patients have the same difficulty. The orientation group approach offers the staff a chance to explain how the clinic and the treatment work and to find out which patients are motivated for treatment and which will continue to come—a point of considerable importance with alcoholics.

In one clinic, an orientation group was set up with a social worker as the group therapist and a social work aide as a resource person and co-therapist. As new applicants came to the clinic, they were assigned to the orientation group while they were being worked up and pending their assignment to a specific type of treatment group. In this way, the orientation group served as a holding group. The number of patients in the group was usually ten to 12. The group leader at each weekly meeting gave a brief talk about the clinic, alcoholism, and treatment and then actively led the group discussion. As patients were assigned to treatment groups, they left the orientation group. New patients were then added to the orientation group; new patients were also added if patients dropped out of the group.

The orientation group gave patients an opportunity to ask questions and express doubts about the nature of the clinic's work and the usefulness of psychotherapy, group and individual, in the treatment of their condition. This led to a discussion of the nature of alcoholism and the usual questions about chemical and nutritional factors. The patients also exchanged experiences they had had in trying to stop drinking and discussed the usefulness of the A.A. approach.

The orientation group was most useful in indicating which patients would continue to come to treatment and which would drop out. Patients who were not properly motivated or who for some other reason would not continue treatment did not return to the orientation group after one or two visits. But patients who indicated in the orientation group that they needed more time to discuss their difficulties and feelings more intensively were found to be ready and motivated to go into either individual or group psychotherapy. It was even possible to determine, to some extent, which patients would be able to work best with a group approach and which needed an individual approach.

For some patients, attendance at a few orientation group sessions gave them so much understanding of their condition that they did not feel the need for more prolonged treatment. And surprisingly, the structured atmosphere and the guarded contacts in the orientation group were suitable for some chronic and severely ill patients

—the primary type of alcoholic. They continued to attend these meetings, though somewhat irregularly.

A Successful Use of Group Therapy

Robert, a married man in his thirties, was referred to group psychotherapy because of persistent heavy drinking, dating back to the age of 16. The amount of drinking began to increase about two years before he entered treatment, and during the most recent six or seven months his drinking bouts had become almost nightly occurrences, leading to many quarrels with his wife. As a result of pressure from her, he sought treatment.

Background. Robert was an only child. His father had been a foreman in a factory and was a quiet, tense man who had developed ulcers a number of years before. He did not drink, but there was considerable drinking in his family. The patient's mother had high blood pressure and had always been a nervous, anxious, and domineering woman. When Robert was an adolescent, she was hospitalized a couple of times because of depressive episodes. She was an extremely difficult person to get along with—always quarreling with Robert and his father, accusing them of various types of bad behavior, and blaming them when she became upset. Robert and his mother had always been very close, although the relationship was difficult. She had a severe depressed reaction when he got married.

Robert's development and early history were essentially normal. When he was 12 years old, he began to engage in homosexual activities with an older boy, and this relationship continued until he left home to go to college. There he began to drink because of social tension and loneliness related to leaving home. He continued his homosexual activities in college but only after he had been drinking. This pattern of engaging in homosexual activity after drinking continued, with some slight increase in frequency, up until the time he met his wife. In college he also went out with girls and had heterosexual relations, although not frequently. After graduating from college, he worked in the advertising field in various cities and finally came to New York two years before entering treatment.

He met his wife some five years before entering treatment, began to have sexual intercourse with her, and found the relationship quite good, both generally and sexually. When he entered treatment, they had been married four years and had two children, a girl of two and a boy of seven months. The birth of the girl coincided with the move to New York, and the birth of the boy coincided with the pressure of a new job. Each time, the patient's drinking increased, and he began to have difficulties with his in-laws, leading to tension and frequent quarrels with his wife.

He would drink heavily two or three times a week and, about once a week, get into a fight with his wife, leave home, stay out all night, and usually engage in a homosexual affair.

The increasing concern of his wife and her alarm and bitterness about his behavior finally led him to seek treatment. His wife also drank, which she attributed to her anxiety and depression concerning his drinking and behavior. She was quite tense and found the children difficult to handle, which she attributed to her husband's lack of cooperation.

Approach to Therapy. A psychiatrist saw Robert a few times and determined that he was tense, ill-at-ease, and anxious in one-to-one psychotherapy. Most important of all, Robert found it extremely difficult to talk. He would repeat the story of the tension, the drinking, and the quarrels with his wife, but he seemed unable to discuss the feelings and conflicts involved in these situations. He became quite discouraged in the diagnostic individual sessions and wondered whether he would be able to talk enough in individual psychotherapy.

Because of the patient's rigid, tense personality and his intolerance of any frustrations, and because he did not seem to be aware of underlying emotions and tensions, the psychiatrist felt that a group therapy approach might be useful. He referred the patient to another psychiatrist, who confirmed the evaluation and decided to place Robert in group therapy combined with individual sessions as needed. Robert was obviously relieved when these suggestions were made, and he again expressed his concern that he might have great difficulty talking in individual therapy.

The Group Members. Robert was placed in a group with five other people—two men and three women. They had fairly severe character disorders, with tension and depression in interpersonal relationships and a tendency toward chronic anxiety and depression. One of the other men in the group drank a good bit but considerably less than Robert did. All the patients in the group, except for Robert, had had considerable individual therapy, which had helped allay certain acute symptoms of depression and anxiety and had given them some insight into the nature of their underlying tensions and conflicts. But the individual therapy had not helped them deal with certain character disorders and with their conflicts and tensions centered around the transference in individual therapy. For these reasons, they were assigned to a group. And it was felt that their difficulties were sufficiently similar to Robert's that he and they might help one another uncover and work out their difficulties.

Putting an alcoholic into a group of patients without alcoholism problems has advantages and disadvantages. The chief disadvantage is an obvious one: Since the other patients do not have the problem of alcoholism, they discuss other things, and there is less exposure of the nature of the alcoholism problem. On the other hand, alcoholics sometimes use the focus on alcoholism problems as a form of resistance. By avoiding these problems, the group can focus on underlying emotional problems, tensions, and conflicts.

Brief descriptions of the other members in Robert's group follow:

Boyd. Boyd was a 54-year-old man who worked in the publishing and advertising fields. He had a history of fairly severe drinking at times but not to the extent shown by Robert. Boyd had been divorced for a number of years and had two grown children. He had periods of extreme tension and anxiety, during which he tended to become agitated and to show various psychosomatic difficulties, such as diarrhea and headaches. At one time he used to deal with these periods of tension and depression by getting drunk and going on a binge or getting involved with prostitutes. This pattern had subsided in recent years. He had had many years of individual therapy with different therapists, with some benefit. His main difficulty arose from recurrent episodes of depression and anxiety, with a tendency to withdraw and an inability to work when he felt this way.

George. George was a 49-year-old executive in a firm that manufactured men's furnishings. He had never married, although he had been engaged for a short period many years before. His main complaint was recurrent anxiety and depression, marked impotence, and marked anxiety connected with his impotence. He had had many years of individual therapy, with some benefit.

Lillian. Lillian was a 48-year-old married woman with two grown daughters. She had been in individual treatment for a number of years because of hysterical symptoms and periods of acute anxiety and depression. She had many marital problems. Although intellectually interested in feelings and emotions, she was a rigid, tense, ladylike person with little awareness of her feelings.

Mara. Mara was a 39-year-old married woman with four children. She had problems of depression and some anxiety related to severe marital difficulties. Several years of individual therapy had helped her acute symptoms, character disorder, and persistent acting out, but it had not helped her marital relationship to her physician-husband. In addition, in individual treatment she maintained a masochistic, whining, little-girl attitude toward the therapist that had resisted all attempts at interpretation.

Rita. Rita, a 38-year-old teacher, had been married twice and had no children. She had been in analytic therapy for a long time. She had improved a great deal, but she still had marked difficulty in any kind of significant relationship, whether personal or professional.

The Group Sessions. The group, from the first, functioned quite well. All the members were intelligent, articulate people and were interested in trying to understand their difficulties and how to deal with them. They showed, at first, an understandable reluctance to expose themselves, but this reluctance was rapidly overcome. The group went through the usual initial phase of group therapy, in which there is much intellectual, analytical discussion of difficulties and little real interaction with each other. They were therapist-centered for many months, each patient bringing up his own difficulty, describing it in a characteristic style, and trying to obtain the therapist's intervention in various ways. When the members discussed one another's problems, they did it in an intellectual, analytical manner, with little acknowledgment of their feelings about each other or reactions to each other and with little interaction except on an intellectual, analytical level. The therapist repeatedly pointed out this fact, and the group began to recognize and deal with this and other forms of resistance.

In the initial phases, three patients—Robert, Boyd, and Mara—spoke a great deal; the other three remained comparatively silent. The sessions at the beginning consisted of one of these three talkative patients presenting a long, detailed story of difficulties with people, while the other members listened and asked some questions, without presenting much about themselves. Then, the group would become aware of what was going on or else the therapist would intervene, and the next person would take up the task of presenting his material while the other patients listened and asked questions. The therapist helped the patients realize that this pattern was a form of resistance, and gradually they began to change.

The therapist also helped the group see that they presented their stories in a characteristic way and got the other group members to respond characteristically. For example, Boyd would present his story in a dramatic, gruff fashion and he always turned out to be a bad little boy who acted wildly. The women in the group frequently indicated disapproval of his provocative account. In this way, the character disorders of Boyd and the women in the group were clearly brought out, and a transference interaction occurred. The therapist helped the patients recognize this pattern and gradually they changed the manner in which they presented themselves and recounted their difficulties.

Robert took part in this repetitive approach to bringing out material. Repeatedly, he presented stories of difficulties with his wife and his in-laws, in such a fashion that he always appeared to have acted in a violent, irresponsible, emotionally and mentally disturbed fashion. Many of the stories ended with his stalking out of the house, getting drunk, and staying out all night. At first, the group reacted in a predictable fashion. The two men would support him in his anger toward his wife, and the three women, particularly Lillian, would be extremely critical and would point out how badly he had behaved and how disturbed his attitude, feelings, and behavior were.

The therapist repeatedly called the group's attention to this type of interacting and indicated that they would have to help each other work these reactions and interactions out. The group went through a period of anger, defiance, and rebellion toward the therapist for his frustrating attitude and his opposition to their childish, demanding behavior toward each other and toward him. After this angry, rebellious phase had subsided, the members began to confront each other with the resistive aspects contained in their provocative, demanding attitudes. The therapist would repeatedly get the group to help each other face why they had to present themselves as "bad little boys" and "whining little girls" and why they had to discuss their difficulties in a provocative fashion that elicited angry or disapproving comments from the rest of the group. He also helped them become aware of the nature and significance of their interactions.

On one occasion, Boyd was ten minutes late in coming to the session and appeared depressed and preoccupied. The group ignored his lateness. During a pause, the therapist indicated to the group that they had not discussed Boyd's lateness, and they asked him about it. After a brief, half-hearted attempt to offer excuses, he said he hadn't felt like coming. He went on to say, somewhat timidly, that he didn't seem to be getting anything out of the group and that the time and money were wasted. The other members attempted to reassure him, remarked about his depression, and urged him to talk about it. The therapist intervened and pointed out that they were not listening to his complaints about the group and that it might be helpful to do so.

Boyd began to speak with some bitterness, indicating that the group didn't seem to help. Even when he brought up something, he said, no one paid much attention to it. At this point, one of the members said:

You mean two weeks ago, when you mentioned that your aunt had cancer and that your mother kept calling you?

Another man said:

The group can't take away your aunt's cancer, but if the cancer and your mother's reaction are depressing you, we can help you talk about it.

At this point Mara began to laugh somewhat hysterically and said it sounded funny to say the group couldn't take away the cancer. Boyd acknowledged that he had been very upset by his mother's constant calls and depression and by her fearful and characteristic expressions of concern for the aunt, herself, and him. He was sitting opposite Mara and looked at her as he spoke.

Mara had been sitting very tensely, and at this point she put her hand to her mouth and looked at Boyd in a frightened fashion and began to cry. The others asked her what was the matter and she said in a tearful voice that she was afraid for Boyd. He was so depressed; maybe something would happen to him. The others asked, "What?" and she said, "Suicide."

The group became silent for a few moments, and then they began to argue with Mara and question Boyd about how badly he felt. At first, he seemed bewildered, but then he began to speak with increasing assurance. Looking at Mara, he stated that he was depressed but not that badly.

There was a pause, and then the therapist asked the group to discuss the interaction between Boyd and Mara. After pointing out Mara's excessive concern, one woman said,

"She sounded like an overanxious mother." At this point, Boyd gasped and said:

She sounded like my mother. When I was telling how depressed I was, I felt helpless and was looking at her the way I look at my mother. She got scared and upset about me, just like my mother.

In this way, the group began to abandon some of their provocative, resistive, and characteristic ways of expressing themselves and interacting with each other, and they helped each other get to the more specific things that were bothering them.

Robert began to speak more clearly of his great anger toward his wife, and several significant things emerged. He felt she was not handling the children or her household duties well, and her failure as he regarded it angered and frightened him. It angered him because it meant that she could not give him the attention and comfort he desired. It frightened him because it reminded him of his sick mother and brought out the fear that his wife, also, was mentally sick. He began to see that his wife's involvement with her family was excessive and that in relation to them she acted like a guilty little girl. This attitude had led her into going along with her family in blaming her husband for whatever went wrong, which was similar to what his mother did. His mother constantly called him, criticized what his wife was doing, and blamed her for everything that went wrong. Robert had gone along with his mother's criticism, which was part of the reason for his anger and for his acting out in provocative style—drinking and leaving the house.

Robert also revealed that his wife had not been able to have an orgasm. He felt angry toward her and also anxious because he felt it showed something was wrong with him sexually. This difficulty, together with his clinging to his mother emotionally, had a great deal to do with his drinking and with his homosexual activities.

As the group progressed in this middle-therapeutic phase of group therapy, they were able to help Robert see the underlying demanding and angry nature of his feelings toward his wife. They also helped him acknowledge these attitudes by showing him that similar attitudes—angry, demanding, and provocative—were present in the other group members.

On one occasion, Robert came late to the group meeting after having missed the previous session. When the group asked him why he had been absent, he indicated that he had been having a difficult time at work because of excessive demands by his immediate supervisor. The group then went on to speak of other things, and Robert remained silent, obviously withdrawing from the group discussion, fidgeting, looking depressed and angry, and glancing at the clock. The group continued to discuss other matters, and no one made any comment about his obviously angry, impatient, withdrawn behavior. Finally, the therapist called the group's attention to Robert's behavior. When they asked him about it, Robert began to say angrily that the group hadn't paid any attention to what a rough time he was having, that he was angry and disappointed, that he wasn't getting anywhere in the group and maybe he should leave.

He also said he felt this way at work. He had worked very hard and had done a good job, but his supervisor never seemed to be satisfied. When he tried to tell his supervisor how difficult matters were, the supervisor paid no attention and went on to something else. When he had indicated to the supervisor that he was dissatisfied and might leave, the supervisor had said that was up to him. Robert had been furious at this rejection. He had been accustomed to something different. If he was ever absent or late, everyone would be concerned and comforting. If he indicated that he wanted to leave a job, everyone would beg him to stay because they thought he was "such a terrific guy."

This last remark, as the therapist noted, related to his feelings about his marriage and his wife. One of the reasons he frequently provoked a quarrel and threatened to leave her was that he wanted her to say "what a great guy" he was; he wanted her to cry and beg him not to leave. The group members pointed out to Robert the provocative nature of this demanding behavior and his great need for special attention and comfort. And eventually they related this behavior to themselves.

Therapeutic Effects. In the group,

Robert was able to see the nature of some of his underlying demanding and angry feelings and especially how they were related to his feelings about his marriage and toward his wife. During the time the group was helping him to see this relationship, he began to discuss things somewhat more clearly with his wife, and his tendency to act out by drinking and leaving the house began to subside. At this point, he became aware that his wife was quite tense, anxious, and depressed, and he was able to discuss his anxiety, fears, and anger about his wife in the group. The group helped him deal with these feelings, and he was able to suggest to his wife that she also seek psychotherapy. She gladly accepted this suggestion and began treatment. After a few weeks in treatment, she was able to indicate to him that she had been extremely anxious and depressed since the birth of the children, when she had felt the demands made upon her were too great for her to bear, and that during this time she felt that he had not been understanding or helpful.

At this point, a significant breakthrough occurred in the relationship between Robert and his wife, and he discussed the change in the group. While discussing his previous quarrels and his drinking, the group asked him why his wife didn't challenge him on his behavior. He then revealed that she drank almost as much as he did and that she usually contributed to the quarrels by responding in a way that encouraged him to leave. The relationship of this kind of behavior to his wife's own problems and how the two of them had interacted so as not to face their feelings was brought out in the group discussions, enabling Robert to see what the difficulty was. The group explored in some detail the relationship of their behavior to their feelings of anxiety and anger and frustration, to their need for special attention and comfort, and to his sexual difficulties.

Most important, the quarrels at home and Robert's drinking began to subside considerably, and the times when he would angrily leave the house and stay out all night became less frequent. The group helped him by pointing out how he could discuss matters quietly with his wife and how the two of them could try to work out their difficulties instead of continuing to quarrel until he left the house.

The group's interactions helped in the emergence and working through of many important tension conflicts. For instance, an angry interchange took place between George and Robert. George was describing how he had felt out of place, depressed, and rejected at a party when a couple of women he approached had not shown very much interest in him. Robert impatiently interrupted, saying that he didn't come to the group to listen to cocktail chatter; he had important problems, personal problems. George said that his problems were just as important as Robert's, and an angry interchange occurred. Later, other members of the group pointed out to Robert his demanding attitude and commented especially on how angry he had been when someone else was receiving the attention he wanted for himself.

This comment and the group's clear indication of how angry he had been made a great impression on Robert. For the next few sessions he was quiet and somewhat withdrawn in the group. When pressed, he finally said he was bothered and frightened by the group's pointing out how angry he had become, because it made him think that there was something wrong with him. Mental illness was associated in his mind with wild anger, loss of control, and breakdown—things his mother had been pointing out to him. At the same time, he recognized how resentful he had been toward members of the group for pointing out his anger, even though they did help him see how his anger carried over into many of his relationships without his realizing it. As a result, he began to recognize the upset and anger connected with his wife more readily and more clearly, and he was able to control his speech and behavior toward her. Quarrels became even less frequent, and the couple began to work out some of their difficulties through constructive discussion.

In another episode, Robert and Boyd were discussing presentations they had to make to their respective bosses. They supported each other in the hostile, angry, and competitive feelings they expressed toward their bosses, and both indicated that in their presentations they were going to try to show the bosses up. Lillian, the disapproving mother-like figure, cautioned them about showing their hostility too openly toward their bosses. Both men became quite angry, and Robert denounced her for discussing things she knew nothing about and for unjustly accusing them of bad feelings and bad behavior. As Robert said to Lillian:

What do you know about this stuff? Where do you get off telling me what I should do?

In the interchange that followed, it became clear that Robert was acting as a defiant little boy, extremely angry at being criticized, and that Lillian was acting like a critical, disapproving mother, as the group pointed out to them. Robert then produced some significant material relating to his mother and her extremely critical—at times destructively critical—attitude toward him.

The relationship between his mother's attitude and the anger he felt when his wife disapproved of something he said or did became very clear. Then Robert, with the help of the group, began to speak of his anger toward his wife for what he felt was criticism implied in her not being satisfied sexually. A great deal of material and some working out of feelings evolved as a result of this discussion in the group.

At this writing, Robert is continuing treatment, going into his third year with the group. His situation is considerably improved. His drinking has lessened considerably. Except for one drink before dinner and a few drinks when there are guests at home, the prolonged, continued drinking has subsided. He and his wife are getting along much better. The long quarrels of the past, with the patient leaving the house, have stopped altogether. The quarrels are now occurring with less frequency and intensity and are worked out by discussions between the patient and his wife. The group helped him to proceed in this more realistic, adult fashion, and his wife was helped by her own therapist. His therapist has seen Robert individually from time to time to go into more detail concerning his difficulties. In the individual sessions, Robert has continued to be somewhat hesitant. Although he is cooperative he

obviously does not present his feelings with the same intensity and freedom as in the group. His attitude toward the therapist is essentially a polite and somewhat submissive one. In the group, he is much more outspoken; his productions are much more full of feeling and much more intense; and he interacts with the other patients with a great deal of freedom—with anger, demands, and criticism.

Reasons for Success. Group therapy enabled Robert to overcome the hesitancy and submissiveness that interfered with his free communication in individual therapy. The nature of the relationships in the group facilitated his lessening the intensity of the relationship to the therapist and enabled him to turn, instead, to the other members of the group, with whom he was able to develop intense emotional relationships, with resultant emotional interaction that quickly and clearly brought out the significant underlying emotional attitudes and conflicts. He was able to see his characteristic provocative and childlike attitudes, and he was clearly able to see some of the transference manifestations that occurred as a result of the interaction in the group. Finally, he was able to apply his new awareness and understanding to his current situation at work and, especially, to the difficulties with his wife. He was then able to see the kind of acting-out pattern occurring in his marriage—his childlike, angry attitude toward his wife, the subsequent emotional tensions, and the drinking and sexual acting out. As a result of his new awareness and understanding of his attitudes and tensions, he was able to stop drinking almost completely, develop more realistic and more constructive attitudes in his marriage and toward his wife, and begin to work out his sexual problems.

An Unsuccessful Use of Group Therapy

Irwin was placed in a group where the other patients did not have problems with alcoholism, but their emotional difficulties and underlying psychopathology were similar to his. The therapist hoped that the identifications and interactions necessary for therapy would occur in the group discussions.

Background. Irwin, a 35-year-old writer, worked as an editor, critic, and writer on periodicals in a field related to art. He was a college graduate and a very intelligent, almost brilliant man in terms of his knowledge and creative ability.

He was the only child of parents who had had a difficult marriage, partially because of the mother's depressive, anxious attitudes and her tendency to dominate both her husband and her son. The father died when Irwin was about 12, and Irwin began a close but extremely difficult relationship with his mother. She was probably a basically psychotic person who was so anxious and overprotective toward her son that every aspect of his life was controlled by her. Her concern about matters connected with his health was so extreme that he was forced to eat only certain foods and he had to exercise the utmost precaution to avoid infections and colds. The mother needed to know about and would attempt to control every relationship and every activity from the time of the father's death on.

Irwin went on to college and did well; his mother frequently visited him. While attending college, he began to drink. Toward the end of his college days, his drinking was aggravated when he became seriously involved with a girl, over his mother's objections. The girl had a nervous breakdown and was hospitalized, which made Irwin feel extemely guilty. He then began a series of intense and unhappy relationships with girls, although he continued to maintain a close relationship with his mother.

He began his writing career immediately after college and did well. During this time, he lived in New York with his mother. A few years after graduating from college, he married his present wife, despite the mother's not-too-veiled objections. In the meantime, he had become a heavy but periodic drinker. In times of stress, whether in relation to his work or in relation to his mother or his wife, he would drink heavily for several months at a time. Despite his drinking, he was able to function and was successful in his work as a writer. After his marriage, his relationship to his mother continued to be extremely close.

Irwin's wife was a bright, outgoing person who made every effort to give her husband the attention and support that he needed, even submitting to some extent to the mother's close relationship to the patient and to her domineering attitude. He and his wife had two children, both girls, but there were sexual problems from the outset. The wife had difficulty in achieving orgasm, and Irwin had difficulties with impotence and premature ejaculation. He preferred oral sex and masturbatory activities to intercourse, which made him feel anxious and tense. He had constant quarrels with his wife.

Irwin was a self-absorbed, narcissistic person who had little to do with his wife and children. At home he spent most of his time in his study, writing, reading, listening to music, and sometimes drinking heavily.

The births of the children increased difficulties between the husband and wife, and his withdrawal from his wife became more marked. His resentment and frustration because of his wife's attention to the children was obvious—but not to him. A change in his job and some difficulties because of his children's illness further increased his drinking. Finally, his wife, who had tried to help Irwin by keeping an eye on him and stopping him from drinking, consulted her internist, who suggested that her husband enter psychiatric treatment.

When a psychiatrist saw him, Irwin had been drinking heavily for several months. He was tremulous and complained of an upset stomach and weakness and pains in his arms and legs. He talked incessantly, but his affect and his speech were intellectual; beyond extreme tension and obvious depression, he showed little affect in his communications.

Individual Therapy. In individual treatment Irwin's close relationship with his mother and his resultant difficulties with sex and marriage quickly became clear. His pathological relationship with his mother was a symbiotic one. His tremendous involvement with his mother existed on the basis of an identification that was seen as harmful and destructive. There was a paranoid quality to the fearful aspects of the relationship.

Although Irwin talked freely in individual therapy, he was quite skeptical about it. After a few months, he continued to be intellectual and guarded in his attitude, and he resisted every attempt to help him see the underlying nature of his emotional reactions. For example, although he had clearly been upset by the births of his children and went through periods of prolonged heavy drinking, he strongly resisted any attempt to talk about his reactions. Similarly, he denied any connection between his mother's accusations and interference and his anxiety and depression, drinking bouts, and quarrels with his wife. And he could not see the relationship between his difficulties in sex and his drinking to relieve the tension involved.

The psychiatrist thought that a group might help Irwin see how other people react to similar situations and that other members of the group might point out matters in a way that was more acceptable than individual therapy had been. The therapist also felt that in a relationship with peers the patient might be able to interact in a freer and more emotional fashion. Irwin expressed doubts about the usefulness of group psychotherapy but agreed to try it.

Group Therapy. Irwin was placed in a group with two other men and four women. Two of the women were the same age as he, were married, and had children. The other two women were older; one was single, and the other was married and had two children. One of the men was older than Irwin, owned his own business, had been married twice, and had two children. The other man was just a few years older than Irwin, was married, and also had two children. All the patients had moderately severe psychiatric problems. One of them had fairly severe character problems and was subject to periods of tension, anxiety, and depression in relation to interpersonal relationships. One of the women, like Irwin had many psychosomatic symptoms. All the married people had sexual and marital difficulties similar to Irwin's.

The group had been together for about a year when Irwin joined them. They were functioning reasonably well but were still in the initial phase of group therapy. The interaction between members was quite limited, and they continued to press their claims for special attention from the therapist and from one another. The discussions in the group tended to be intellectual and analytical. Although interactions did occur, their emotional quality was subdued and not really free or intense enough. The discussions were long and rambling, dominated by one or two patients, with the other patients asking questions but not discussing any of their own difficulties. The therapist's efforts to point out the resistance involved in this kind of interaction had not, at the time Irwin entered the group, succeeded in overcoming this type of resistance.

Difficulties before Entering Group. Several weeks prior to his being put into the group, Irwin became increasingly resentful and angry at a change in his wife's attitude toward him in relation to his drinking. With his consent, she had come to see his therapist to discuss how to correct her own attitude toward her husband's drinking. The therapist saw her alone, which in retrospect he realized was an error, in view of Irwin's distrustfulness and paranoid tendencies. The therapist pointed out to the wife that the most helpful thing would be to leave the patient alone about his drinking, beyond acknowledging briefly the realistic difficulties resulting from it, and to leave it to the patient to work out the problem of his drinking in his therapy. With considerable relief, the wife agreed to do so, and she did. But the change in their relationship was quite frustrating and anxiety-provoking to Irwin.

At about this same time, he began to blame his wife a great deal for his sexual difficulties. Frequent quarreling resulted. Finally, several weeks before he entered the group, Irwin called up an old girlfriend of his and began to see her. He discussed his marital problems and his other difficulties at great length with her instead of bringing them into the individual treatment. When his therapist pointed out that this behavior was a form of resistance Irwin was unable to understand it.

When group therapy was recommended, his girlfriend was enthusiastic about it and supported the patient in going along with the therapist's recommendation. But at this time, the patient began to feel disgruntled and resentful of his relationship with this girlfriend. In retrospect, the therapist realized that this was not a good time to have introduced the patient to the group.

Difficulties in Group. From the first, Irwin was resistive and defensive in the group. At first, he sat quietly and said he wanted to listen to try to understand how it worked and what the other people were saying. In the individual sessions, which continued along with the group sessions, he protested that he could not see how the group would help him. He was troubled about other people's difficulties and could not see how they related to him. He was anxious about exposing himself and his difficulties and was extremely troubled if any of the other members were critical toward him.

During the first several weeks, he attended regularly. Then he became interested in some of the group discussions and from time to time would venture a comment or question about some of the other members' difficulties. But he did so in an intellectual and somewhat philosophical fashion, displaying rigid emotional attitudes. The group members became resentful of his somewhat superior attitude, and they began to point out that he was not discussing any of his own difficulties and had not even indicated what the nature of his difficulties were. At this point, Irwin became quite defensive and told the group he did not feel he was ready to talk about his own difficulties and did not see how any of the others could in any way understand or be helpful with his difficulties.

As time went on, some of the more aggressive women began to question him and challenge some of his silences and resistive attitudes. On several occasions he became quite angry and said that he did not see how they had the right to question him or challenge any of his statements or attitudes. Finally, after the group had pressed him sufficiently, he began to indicate something of his marital and drinking difficulties.

When he began to speak critically of his wife—saying that she did not seem to understand his needs in relation to the tension and strains of his work and that she did not help and comfort him—the more aggressive women in the group immediately attacked him as being a dependent, childish person who was clinging to his wife as though she were his mother. The patient became anxious, angry, and resentful about these comments. He could not see that they had any value at all. He resented the attitude of the women who criticized him and put the blame on him. As he put it:

You're a bunch of castrating dames who just want to take the woman's side and aren't really interested in trying to understand my point of view.

After a particularly angry interchange with one of the women, he did not attend the next group session. The therapist persuaded him to come to the session after that, but Irwin declared that he did not want to continue with the group, and he said so in the next group session. When the group tried to point out that this decision was part of his resistance, he again became quite irritated, said he saw no use in continuing the discussion, and lapsed into a silence that lasted the rest of the session.

Irwin did not attend any more group sessions and shortly afterward he began to miss individual sessions. When he did appear, he showed increasingly clear-cut signs of being intoxicated, something he had previously avoided. He gave up the girlfriend who had urged him to join the group and called up another old girlfriend, someone who drank a great deal. He began to see her frequently and began to drink more heavily. Finally, at her instigation, he stopped his individual treatment.

Reasons for Failure. Irwin was not helped in the slightest degree by individual or group treatment. The reasons are related to his serious psychiatric illness of psychotic proportion. His paranoid, narcissistic psychosis stemmed from tremendous underlying oral, aggressive conflicts that led to periods of agitation and aggressive behavior alternating with depressive episodes. He tried to handle his problems by perverse sexual behavior and bouts of drinking. He had a rigid personality with extreme resistance and defense against any awareness of his underlying emotional tensions and conflicts. He had a mother who was also psychotic, and he had remained fixated in a narcissistic, symbiotic identification with her. His psychotic illness was manifested by alcoholism and he probably fell into the category of the essential or primary alcoholic.

A Homogeneous Group

The group, composed entirely of alcoholics, was formed from two older groups because of scheduling changes.

The Group Members. In the beginning, the group consisted of 11 members, five of whom later dropped out for various reasons. They were, for the most part, well-educated, and several had achieved considerable success in their fields. Some had been or were in individual psychoanalytic treatment or psychotherapy, either prior to or during their participation in the group. They verbalized readily and interacted quite actively.

Most of the group were A.A. members. They all had a mixture of positive and negative feelings about A.A. such as:

It has helped me to stop drinking, but it hasn't helped me with my emotional problems.

I can't take the spiritual aspects of the program.

Everybody in A.A. gives you advice.

I follow the A.A. program, and I've stayed sober.

Frieda. Frieda was a 27-year-old, attractive graduate student who was referred to the clinic by a psychiatrist who had been treating her individually for some time. At first she was in a group led by a woman psychiatrist. When this psychiatrist left the clinic, Frieda was transferred. At the time of the transfer, she was an extremely inhibited, shy, tense, scared "little girl," and, she reported, she had just come off a long drunk, during which she was promiscuous, picking up men and having one-night stands. She was unable to say whether this behavior was related to her previous therapist's leaving. Frieda had a history of homosexual relationships and other perversions.

Her parents were both college teachers, although her mother had given up her career. Frieda was the oldest in a family of three daughters, and she saw herself as having a special relationship with her father, a relationship her mother was continually sabotaging.

Frieda participated actively in A.A., which was her main source of friends and social life.

After joining the group, Frieda interrupted her studies to go to work, left her parents, and established herself in her own apartment. She obtained a number of positions with increasing responsibility. She abstained from alcohol after the time she came to the group drunk, carrying a can of beer, and loudly "told off" a number of group members.

She also stopped being promiscuous. Instead she had relationships with one man at a time. Her last relationship was with a widower considerably older than her. He worked in the college where she was employed and, like her father, had a Ph.D. She became pregnant and was married but then underwent a therapeutic abortion. She felt that she was getting a great deal out of their relationship, despite her disappointment at not having borne the child. But she was seriously thinking of ending the marriage because of her inability to have children and an active social life with her husband, who refused to have anything to with her A.A. friends. Also, her husband was unable to satisfy her sexual needs.

Richard. Richard was in his late forties and worked in the field of business administration. He had been separated from his wife and two children for six years. He maintained only the most tangential contact with his family, such as sending gifts for the children's birthdays. Although he recognized that he had obligations to his family, he refused to send money to his wife because he felt his in-laws might benefit. His wife and children were living in his former home with his in-laws who, he felt, were instrumental in breaking up his marriage.

Richard had been in group therapy for five years, with a number of interruptions because of drinking bouts or because he wanted to be out on his own. When he was sober, he completely eschewed women; but while drinking, he became promiscuous, picked up streetwalkers, got "rolled," and then berated himself for getting into such compromising situations.

He dated the origins of his difficulties to the time of his father's death. His father was the owner of a modest bar and grill that was heavily in debt. Richard had to liquidate it to pay off the estate's creditors, and he experienced this liquidation as a tremendous failure. One of the two dreams he reported in the five years of his treatment was as follows: His father has been away; no one knows where he is, and Richard is taking care of his mother and the business. He has just gotten the business out of the red when his father returns and tells him that he is taking the business back.

While in treatment, Richard improved his economic status, moving from office-temporary positions to a junior executive position. He still felt that he was working below his capacity and resented not being in a better position, but he never sought other opportunities. He expressed resentment toward his immediate superior, seeing him as a threat.

After being in treatment several years, Richard stopped drinking and abstained for a year. He moved to better quarters and was progressing at a slow but even pace. He appeared to have substituted gambling on horses for his drinking. Then he started drinking again. The group members commented that the only time he could have sex was when he was drinking, since at times he had to drink when he took up with a woman who was not a prostitute.

As a result of his drinking, his absenteeism at work increased. When one of his superiors offered him a genuine promotion in his field, he felt he was being kicked upstairs, continued drinking, and had to be let go.

Richard had been active in A.A. off and on, since coming to the group, but he did not regard himself as a member in good standing, even when sober, since he was not following the program.

His difficulties stemmed from a passive-aggressive character disturbance and a pathological clinging to old fantasies, leading to such self-destructive actions as drinking.

Drinking for him appeared to help him overcome severe superego injunctions against strong oedipal and promiscuous sexual urges.

Ronald. Ronald was a Negro homosexual in his thirties who was so fair that he easily passed for white. He was employed in a minor managerial position and was apparently doing well at his work, since he had been given regular raises. He was maintaining a stable relationship with another homosexual.

Ronald dated his drinking from the time he was in the Army and was overcome with guilt about his homosexual impulses, which he was finding difficult to contain. Drinking allowed him to express and gratify these impulses. He had had ups and downs, with long periods of unemployment, living in cheap flats, and leading a lonely and isolated existence. After taking up with his current lover, he felt obliged to go to work or to school, since he didn't want to feel kept, nor did he feel his lover would tolerate keeping him. But his drinking still remained a problem. He was unable to abstain and was fearful that he would lose control and would require hospitalization, even though he had at no time given evidence of acute psychiatric disturbance due to his drinking.

Although he was alert and active in the group, he revealed little about himself to the other members other than that he was a homosexual. But he appeared to be able to cut through other people's defenses and rationalizations, and in that sense he made a good group member.

Frances. Frances was in her fifties and was an unmarried professional worker in the field of social welfare. During the course of her analysis, she was admitted to a hospital for treatment of acute alcoholism. Her analyst decided, after consultation, to place her on Elavil and referred her for group therapy.

A poised and well-informed woman, Frances was able to converse intelligently about her illness and treatment and, in a deceptive fashion, seemed to have achieved some insight into her emotional difficulties. But her drinking appeared, in some ways, to have been exacerbated by her analytic treatment, although she admitted to pathological drinking even before seeking analytic help.

She felt that the pain from her osteoarthritis was the major factor in her drinking, since the drinking relieved her of the severe pain. She reported that she was relatively free of pain at the time the homogeneous group was formed but was fearful that, should the pain return, she would return to drinking.

Frances was continually ingratiating in the group so as not to offend others, for fear they might attack her. This ingratiating behavior was explored with her in individual sessions and by the group. She was quite aware of it and related it to the fact that her mother was a continually angry woman who focused much of her anger on her. Frances felt that much of her lack of progress in analysis was due to her fear of an angry attack from her analyst.

Frances had remained sober since joining the group and had used the group mainly as a source of support. She was perceptive, quick, and insightful with problems of others but fearful of personal involvement.

Evelyn. Evelyn was a secretary in her late thirties who had never married and was fearful of becoming an old maid who couldn't break away from her mother. At the time she came to the group, she had been in individual treatment for some time but felt her therapist did not understand the problems of alcoholism. At first she was seen on a regular individual basis, but she persisted in drinking rather heavily both at home and at work. She was surprised that the quality of her work did not appear to have suffered as a result of her excessive drinking. She was referred to A.A. by a former patient and promptly stopped drinking. She remained in individual therapy for another year and then was transferred to the group, to which she went reluctantly. She was a regular if not overly active participant in the group.

She was a passive-dependent woman who had an extremely limited social life. She rarely had a date, although she was quite attractive. She appeared to have little interest in sex, although she had had crushes on men from afar. She claimed to be interested in writing and painting but had not done anything active along these lines.

Evelyn still lived with her mother. While in treatment with her previous therapist, she moved away from her mother into her own apartment, hoping that her then-supervisor, one of her secret crushes, would take an interest in her. While living alone, her drinking became much worse, and she was unable to care for herself. She then moved back with her mother, experiencing the move as a defeat. She was attempting to please her therapist by becoming independent but was unable to do so.

Her mother's parents had been divorced. Her father became ill early in her life and required numerous hospitalizations for general paresis; she remembered him as weak and helpless, a person nobody respected very much. Her maternal grandmother lived with them and was a chronic alcoholic. Her grandfather, a rather successful artist, also had a history of excessive drinking.

Evelyn developed bronchial asthma at an early age, and it persisted in a mild form. Later she developed a school phobia. After treatment and consultation, she was placed in a residential school, where she completed her education. She returned home after completion of high school and chose to become a secretary rather than go on to college. She began drinking with her co-workers after work. Drinking seemed to help her anxiety about her lack of social life and helped her tolerate her humdrum existence.

Her experience with A.A. was highly dramatic in terms of symptom relief. With regard to helping her to stop drinking, A.A. seemed much more beneficial than therapy.

Mary. Mary was an attractive, married office worker in her mid-fifties who came to the clinic for help with her drinking. Consciously, she felt that her drinking did not give her any gratification. She reported feeling much better when not drinking and usually remained abstinent for about three-week intervals, only to return to drinking. Drinking made her feel tired, weak, and sluggish. Her family was perplexed and concerned about her behavior, and she was sometimes an embarrassment to them at family functions when she got drunk.

Mary had had previous treatment, once because of phobias and later because she felt she needed help in deciding whether to marry. Finally, she did marry her suitor. She described her husband as a quiet, withdrawn, undemanding person. She said he was just like her father, and she felt she could be married only to someone like him.

She appeared to be a very efficient worker and reported that her drinking did not interfere with her work. Since she started working at a new and responsible position, she no longer drank in the morning but did drink when out with friends at a local bar before going home.

Her mother died when she was around eight. Her father developed tuberculosis and was hospitalized. The family was held together by an older brother and sister. Mary developed a profound attachment for her younger brother, although prior to her mother's death she was resentful toward her mother for expecting her to take care of her little brother.

In the group she participated fairly well but was not overly revealing about herself. She was reluctant to talk about intimate aspects of her life. Instead, she talked mostly about her drinking and how it affected her marriage.

Tony. Tony was a 51-year-old professed homosexual; however, his isolation from others was profound in terms of both ordinary social relationships and sexual relationships. He had been in treatment, both individual and group, on and off for many years at a number of places. He represented himself as having a severe drinking problem. He became a member of A.A. but did not attempt to abstain from drinking for many months. Whenever he was under pressure from a member of the group or when he was touched by what anyone said, he characteristically reversed what was said. For example, when a member of the group suggested that Tony's feelings of isolation may have been the result of his being rejected because he was a homosexual, Tony attacked him as being a latent homosexual and being prejudiced against homosexuals. After that Tony tended to dominate group sessions by hostile barrages aimed at the members, with indiscriminate accusations of homosexuality and attempts to provoke the members when the group was discussing sex. One could characterize his behavior as a continuous infan-

tile temper tantrum. The group was patient with him, and the therapist took an active role in his case, making direct interventions and structured interpretations.

Rita. Rita was a tall, attractive young college graduate who worked in the advertising business. She was first seen because of a severe phobia and anxiety. At that time, she had been abstinent for 18 months with the help of A.A. She was fearful of jumping out of a window and of returning to alcohol. An increase in her anxieties, related to conflicts over sex and masturbation, led her to seek treatment. Because of her extreme anxiety, she was referred to a day-night hospital. She was admitted and obtained some relief. After her discharge she was placed on chlordiazepoxide, apparently became dependent on it, and resumed drinking. Since then, she had had a series of bouts with alcohol but required hospitalization only once. The other times she was able to stop her drinking on an ambulatory basis.

Rita established a steady relationship with a young man who was getting a divorce but later terminated the relationship and went on a drinking bout. Her contact with A.A. had been minimal for about two years, but after this drinking bout, she became active once again.

Rita had a generally upward course in treatment. When she entered group psychotherapy, she was extremely anxious and panic-ridden. She became an active go-getter and moderately successful in a creative aspect of the advertising business. She was aware of many deep difficulties and was trying to work on them. She was an active, helpful participant in the group, shifting from a supportive role to a more aggressive role as the occasion warranted.

Robert. Robert was in his early fifties, had worked for many years in advertising, but had been unemployed for two years, except for one brief period. He was trying to make his livelihood by free-lancing and was fairly successful but not as much as he could be. He was dependent on his wife's earnings, which contributed to his own negative self-evaluation.

He had been in treatment eight years—longer than any other patient in the group.

During that period he had always been able to hold jobs for long periods of time—until recently. He had dropped out of treatment on two occasions, once to try making it on his own and another time to try disulfiram. When the homogeneous group started he had been abstinent for more than a year and was continuing the disulfiram.

Robert was married to a woman somewhat his senior, and she had two children by a previous marriage. His relationship with his stepson was somewhat stormy, but he appeared to be able to maintain an adequate relationship with his stepdaughter and her husband. He described his relationship with his wife as being good, particularly after he stopped drinking.

His parents had separated when he was 12 years old. He described his father as an alcoholic. When his father was drunk, Robert was frightened and tried to avoid him. Shortly after his parents' separation, his mother became ill and required hospitalization. Robert was placed in a home for boys for a brief period of time. His mother recovered about a year later, and he returned home.

He was an abrupt, abrasive kind of man, yet mild and easily intimidated. He continually complained of getting nowhere in treatment. Occasionally he had rather marked phobic reactions, with strong obsessive overtones. For instance, he was afraid to drive home because he was fearful he might step on the gas and hit somebody while he was waiting at a traffic light, and he was fearful of pushing someone, at times a fellow patient, off a subway platform. He never acted out any of these fears, but he became preoccupied with them at times.

He described himself as a periodic drinker. He discussed his fear of possible homosexuality and had marked curiosity about the sex life of others in the group. He related many of his drinking episodes to attempts to get up the courage to pick up women in bars, particularly barmaids. In the group he discussed, for the first time, his past peeping-Tom activity and an adolescent homosexual experience.

Tim. Tim was a young executive, married, with three children. He had been in a state hospital on two occasions because of his alcoholic difficulties. His marriage was less than satisfactory. He and his wife had developed a pattern of her withholding sex, his getting angry and drunk, her withholding some more, and so on.

Because of his drinking, he had lost two jobs, the first of which he had held for many years. The loss of his first job precipitated his entering a state hospital for rehabilitation.

He was an intelligent, articulate man who had completed about three years of college at night. He had been able to establish a generally good work record and find suitable employment in his industry.

His father was a union official who had political ambitions. Tim described his father as a severe alcoholic who, one day, abruptly stopped drinking. His father was not usually a violent man, but one time he beat Tim severely for some school infraction.

Tim had been quite active in A.A., which appeared to serve an important function for him because he found help by being in the company of fellow sufferers. He attended group sessions regularly; although not an active group member, he listened intently and was not reluctant to discuss rather intimate areas of his life when asked about them. He was quite aware that he saw things in others much more readily than in himself.

Len. Len, a 36-year-old Negro, had come to New York from the South to pursue his studies. He was intellectual in a self-conscious way, spoke in a very low voice, and was always very correct and proper. He revealed as little as possible about himself, although, when questioned about any area, he tended to give some information. On a number of occasions, he stated that there were things he would never be able to talk about and that no one could ever fathom how deeply he had been hurt.

His father had died when Len was 10 years old. His father was 36 at the time, and Tim fully expected to die at the same age as his father. When he first came for treatment, he had just stopped drinking. He asked for vocational assistance in choosing a new career.

He indicated that he was sexually impotent. When queried about it, he said he was not upset by his impotence since he had always had a low level of libido, and he was rather glad he no longer had to contend with his sexual impulses. Later, when asked directly in the group whether he was married, he reported that he was. He was married to a white girl back home and he had a child.

He attended the group regularly, usually sitting formally and stiffly and rarely participating spontaneously. He could easily be brought into the discussion, and he appeared to welcome the opportunity to talk. Much of what he talked about were problems at work. He rarely discussed his personal life or even his drinking difficulties.

Sample Group Sessions. Generally, two or three of the 11 members were absent each week for one reason or another. Rita did not attend any of the three sessions described here because she was working out of town.

Session One. This session began with seven members present. Two other members arrived later on: Ronald, who came ten minutes late, was detained at his job, and Frances arrived 25 minutes late, explaining that she had had a meeting to attend.

The session prior to his one was taken up with discussions about different kinds of addicitions and their relationship to alcoholism. At that meeting Len said he had been suffering severe pain and had refused treatment with Demerol for fear of another addiction. Mary spoke about her fear of not being able to hold onto her new job because of her drinking, even though this was a job she had always wanted. She discussed the futility of going to A.A., although she had remained sober for a year as a result of her participation in that program. The discussion then shifted to careers, with a focus on Len's difficulties in pursuing a musical career. At this point, one of the group members asked Len whether he was married. He said he was married to a white girl back home. He also announced he had a child.

This session began with Tony discussing an event that occurred to him in A.A. the previous summer. He picked up a young man, Charlie, at a meeting and brought him home. He felt that the young man was homosexual, and it turned out that Charlie really

did want to have sex with him. Tony concurred but couldn't consummate it. One of the group members questioned him about offering an alcoholic a drink; Tony agreed this was wrong. Mary began to ask a question, but, before she could complete it, Tony told her to "shut up." He continued protesting that he didn't want to seduce Charlie, insisting that he felt only paternal and affectionate toward him. He ended up by protesting that he was in a state of total confusion, did not know how to deal with new men he met, and felt isolated and lonely. Frieda wondered why he worried about sick people and why he had to suffer so much. Tony angrily stated that Charlie appealed to his paternal needs and that he wanted to protect him.

Len wondered why he let things of this sort bother him so and asked, "Why do you give so much of a damn?" Tony, getting louder and angrier, said, "Who are you to comment about me that way?" Tony reported that he worked hard all week and was tired. Mary commented that Tony was probably feeling on the defensive in a throwback to his childhood, when he felt dominated by all the women in his family, his mother and sisters.

Mary then shifted to an event that had happened some time ago in her office. A safe was robbed, and she was the first to be accused. She said she had no reaction, nor was she perturbed. But, this event had caused her to remember stealing from her mother's pocketbook as a child and to recall how she felt about it then. She then suggested that Tony explore his past. Tony explained that he could not remember his childhood, that he just felt guilty about everything.

Len commented that he been in bed all week and had gotten out of bed to come to this session. Frieda asked him why he had been in bed all week. Len replied that he had been depressed, had no energy at all, and had been getting out of bed at 2:00 in order to get to the group meeting by 5:30 and that he didn't want to miss a session. When queried, he insisted that his depression was not related to what had transpired in last week's session, when he spoke of being married and having a child.

Tony made a statement about emotional isolation and that he didn't care if he missed a session from time to time. Len replied that it was important for him to get to the meeting but that he was anxious to get home after the meeting to get back into bed. Tony advised him to go to two or three meetings a day in A.A. because "it would help you."

The focus then shifted to Frieda, who talked about getting involved in her music again. Len suggested that she practice at home for a while before taking lessons. Frances, who had just come in 25 minutes late, commented about her working with someone who had succeeded in the musical world but now had to compromise by doing something else and was finding life worthwhile. The session continued with a discussion about careers.

At this point, the therapist intervened, commenting about how polite everybody was and wondering whether they were being polite to avoid something. The group then refocused on Len, who felt he had been given the third degree the previous week, and he began to feel angry. The group then shifted to what had transpired between Tony and Mary when he had told her to shut up. Tony said, "You all want to put on a hairshirt," and complained about being attacked by Mary, describing her as a castrating woman. The group confronted him for always turning things around. Frances then asked whether Tony somehow didn't see his mother in Mary and, as a result, attacked her.

Tony ignored the remark and went on to pontificate about his A.A. experiences and his drinking and then began to focus on masturbation. Tim wondered whether he wasn't being too personal, to which Tony said, "Kiss my ass in front of Macy's window." Then he left the room to get a drink of water, and for a few minutes the group talked about his being terribly provocative and angry.

Frieda asked Mary whether or not she was upset, to which Mary said that she was upset about all this sort of talk about sex. Tony returned and began doing a survey of everybody's sex life. He started with Mary and asked her specifically about an inventory of perversions, demanding to know if she "went down on guys." To this she replied that she didn't and that she considered her sex life with her husband adequate. Tony then turned to Tim and asked him about his sex life. Tim freely discussed his feelings of deprivation in his marriage, his wife's lack of availability, and his own constant state of frustration. These things had caused difficulties in his marriage prior to his becoming an alcoholic; later, he would try to dampen his rage and his sexual impulses by drinking. Often his drinking was accompanied by the feeling toward his wife, "See what you are doing to me." He admitted that drinking hadn't solved the problem he had with his wife and said that, by coming to the group meetings, he hoped to be able to come to better grips with the situation.

Tony commented that women have faults. He turned to Frances and suggested her as a good example, knitting like Madame De-Farge. He went on in this vein, commenting that he didn't like the people in the group, that they wouldn't admit who they are—all homosexuals—and that he would be better off in A.A. with a sponsor.

Frieda turned to Tim after Tony's comments and asked what he did to handle his sexual needs when his wife refused him because she had the same problem with her husband. Tim humorously suggested that perhaps they ought to get together.

The therapist pointed out that the group had used Tony's provocations and questions about sex to avoid discussing the interaction in the group and their reluctance to talk about their past lives with their families.

Session Two. At the next session, Frieda, Tony, Robert, Rita, and Len were absent. Indeed, Len never returned to the group. Ronald came in 15 minutes late. Frieda did not attend the next few sessions because of a change in her schedule.

Richard asked Frances whether Christmas was the only time she drank. In the past, Frieda had confessed to taking a drink at an office party, and she said she felt almost obligated to, under the circumstances.

Richard pointed out that she shouldn't have called that drink an obligation.

After a period of silence, Mary commented that Tony wasn't present and said it was a golden opportunity. He was so provocative that she did not feel free to talk about things when he was around. She then commented that; in coming to the meetings, one was supposed to work on personality problems, and one of the things she had to be careful about at work was being too critical.

After another brief silence, Mary wanted to known whether anyone in the group felt that he had improved since coming to the meeting. Evelyn commented that, since starting group therapy, she had less concern or worry about what others might say. Mary said that she was not so fearful about being on time. Then she added:

But coming here hasn't helped my compulsive drinking. All the determination in the world doesn't help it.

She said that recently she had been happy until she and her husband went shopping together. Doing so pleased her, but it seemed to start her drinking again. She turned to Frances and commented that she had been successful.

Frances said that she was angry at Tony, was fearful of his anger, and wanted to talk about her fears. She was fearful of starting to drink again, and thinking about it lent itself to making excuses to start drinking. But she did not fear that about her own drinking now. She remarked that something happened when she was hospitalized in a special metabolism project. As a result, she hadn't had a drink since last Christmas. She said that she had a life style of making people dependent on her because she didn't want to be dependent herself. This need, she felt, contributed somewhat to her drinking behavior. She then talked about her father's illness and death when she was a child and how her mother burdened her with the care of the younger siblings. Mary said that her father had been a quiet, passive man who had been hospitalized for tuberculosis when she was young and that she had had to fend for herself.

The group then focused on Tony, who was not present, and wondered whether he really had a drinking problem. Ronald felt that perhaps he only thought he had, and Richard commented that Tony didn't seem to be an alcoholic since he drank and didn't seem to suffer any negative consequences.

Mary commented that she didn't get into trouble with her drinking, to which Richard commented, "The hell it doesn't; it bothers you with your husband." She snapped, "He'll take me the way I am." She went on to complain of not feeling well, having been drinking for a week and a half. The group discussed her course of treatment and her difficulties with her drinking and her marriage. Tim asked whether Ronald had had any feelings about himself and whether he'd changed. Ronald said that he felt he hadn't changed much but that he had better control of himself.

Richard started to talk about his gambling, saying that he was never a gambler but that he had been going to the track with some friends. He commented that it's pretty hard to change your personality:

I was sick when I came around here, but now I don't externalize my problems. I'm starting to be aware of internal conflicts, anger, frustration, and anxiety, but I haven't been able to resolve what I call my basic problems. The drinking is a piece of me; I don't want to let go. It's a defeat for me to say I can't handle it.

Tim said:

I felt as you do now. Now I'm not as nervous as I used to be, and I realized one day I didn't have the tremendous anger I used to have. I've never been able to look at things intellectually before, and then I realized what was going on. It helped, even though I know I haven't gotten to the basis of it.

Frances suggested that perhaps Richard was repeatedly testing and setting up situations in order to defeat himself. It was almost like gambling and hoping that this time you are going to win. Richard agreed, commenting, "Maybe it's a bigger gamble, like gambling with my life." Tim and Richard continued to discuss the difficulty of stopping drinking and how they had come to see that drinking had some connection with their anger at their families—Tim's anger at his father, Richard's at his wife and in-laws. Richard said that he used to love the unknown and delighted in

not knowing what would happen and where I would end up, but right now I'm not drinking because I want to get something done.

He talked about having to write and get some resumes made up—something he'd been saying for four years. Tim then said to Richard:

Suppose you get the job you want. You haven't seen your kids for the past four years. Would you renew contact?

And Richard said:

I've attempted to stop smoking, and it's the same problem as alcohol. What do I want to break it off for, if I enjoy it? It relieves tension and pressure, but it's a test of will. Have I strength enough to do it, to will something?

The therapist underlined the possible relationship between the need to control drinking and the struggle to control anger.

Session Three. Frieda and Rita were absent again, and Evelyn, Frances, and Mary were also absent. All who attended were on time.

Tony sat down close to the door, moving away from Ronald, who sat next next to him, and Tony commented that he was sitting there so that no homosexual would upset him. He then reported that the reason he had been absent the previous week was that he had an A.A. anniversary party at his house. He said he had bought a considerable amount of food and had never treated himself that well before.

Tim said that it sounded as if he was treating himself well, commenting that A.A. anniversary parties are usually celebrated after a year of sobriety. Tony had not reported any abstinence to the group.

Robert talked about his feeling of alienation in the group, which he thought was some kind of resistance. He then turned to Tony and said:

I resent you tremendously, but it's nothing personal. I'm trying to articulate it. Your presence in the group bothers me; I'm trying to understand it. I've seen a lot of people, and I usually don't give a damn. Yet I don't want to drop it because it could be some subconscious reason.

Robert went on that the group seemed to be a sheer waste of time, that he had been in a number of groups, and that on only a couple of occasions had he touched on meaningful things. This comment led to an altercation between Robert and Tony. Robert said that he was thinking of quitting, but he knew that leaving therapy might be a resistance against something important. Ronald commented that, even though Robert was symptom-free with the help of disulfiram, he hadn't gotten down to the basis for his drinking. Ronald believed drinking was a symptom. Robert continued to state that he was not getting enough out of group therapy, but recognized that leaving might be resistance and perhaps it would be wise to stay on. The group seemed to be a waste of time, but he felt that something meaningful did happen from time to time.

Tony, still smarting from Robert's attack, suggested that Robert was angry at him because he was a homosexual himself, and maybe Robert ought to find out whether he wasn't avoiding his own homosexual problems. Tim said that Tony was always trying to turn things around and could never deal with anything anybody said. Richard said that Tony had to get something straight—that he was the one who had the homosexual problem. But Richard said he could appreciate part of Tony's dilemma because at one time he also felt he couldn't turn to anybody, not even his parents, for help.

Richard then shifted the discussion to his feelings of rejection, particularly when on a bender. This comment led into a discussion about what alcohol does for different kinds of problems. Richard commented that alcohol left him without any sense of confidence but that, since he had been sober for a while, his confidence was returning. However, he still had to become high in order to have sex.

The group shifted into talking about sex, with Tim mentioning that, in his instance, a lack of sex with his wife appeared to incite his drinking behavior. Richard then started talking about a dream he had had about a girl he was once in love with. Ronald said that the group always seemed to be talking about what they didn't want, not what they did want, and that perhaps they were searching for love.

This theme of what they were searching for led to discussion about whether they were expecting too much out of group therapy. Richard said that he had been trying to listen more. Ronald remarked that he had been trying to talk about his emotional problems but that he seemed to drift around and find such talk upsetting.

The therapist suggested that, in view of Tony's terrible feelings of loneliness and isolation, perhaps his behavior in the group might help him understand why people tended to reject him. Tony responded that he didn't know how to deal with feelings of rejection, and he started talking about his feelings of loneliness.

The therapist commented at this point that Ronald's feelings of aimlessness and purposelessness in the group might be the same as his feelings of aimlessness outside of the group, and perhaps they all had been talking about something similar to what happened with Tony: they set things up to defeat themselves in their search for the love and closeness they wanted.

There was a moment of silence. Then Richard began to talk about his feelings of frustration. At this point the session ended.

Developments in the Group. The group was formed mostly from two earlier groups. Six members were from the older of these two groups: Robert and Richard had been original members; Rita, Evelyn, Tim, and Frances joined it later, in the order mentioned. Three members came from the other group: Mary had been an original member; Frieda and Ronald joined later. The new group was brought together after a four-week break occasioned by the therapist's vacation. Tony and Len were introduced into the group after a few months because attendance by the other members had become sporadic.

The group tended to focus on their current vocational difficulties. Richard complained about his job and the need to make a resume —a task he'd been attempting for four years. Tim expressed dissatisfaction with what he was doing. Frances was beginning a new job. Frieda was planning to change jobs.

As the group members became more comfortable with one another, they talked more about themselves. Frieda, Rita, Robert, and Richard were the most active. They attempted to draw the others out, but, generally, these four dominated the group. Frances was fearful of offending. Ronald and Tim sat on the sidelines, waiting for something to happen. Evelyn felt her life was so dull that no one would be interested in her. And Mary tended to complain about her husband.

In later sessions the discussion shifted to the themes of Frieda's and Rita's relationships with their boyfriends. Frieda was very pleased with her situation, since this was the first relationship she had had with a man that did not result in a sadomasochistic, self-damaging experience. Rita had an on-again-off-again relationship with her boyfriend. Since both women were quite attractive, their presence and their frank discussion about their sexual experiences proved to be provoking to the men in the group and resulted in occasional angry outbursts directed toward the women.

The attendance of some of the group members tended to be sporadic for a variety of reasons—resumption of drinking, job commitments out of town, and so on. Because this is a common attendance pattern among patients in alcoholic groups, ten to 12 patients are usually selected, with attendance by six to eight members being usual. The failure to attend regularly is dealt with as a resistance in both individual sessions and group sessions. After the group had been meeting for eight weeks, a pattern was set of five to six members attending each week, so the therapist introduced Tony and Len into the group. They had been in an orientation group together for a short time and, as a result, knew each other when they joined the new group.

Tony said that he suffered from severe loneliness, isolation, rejection, and a homosexual problem. Richard, in an attempt to reach out, asked whether Tony's feelings of rejection weren't due to society's general tendency to reject homosexuals. This comment led to an outburst of rage by Tony. He accused Richard of being a latent homosexual and accused all the other men in the group of suffering from homosexual difficulties of one form or another. From this point on, Tony tended to dominate the group sessions with angry outbursts and hostile provocations, to the point where group members said nothing and were relieved when he failed to show up. Tony tended to reverse whatever was said to him, misinterpreting attempts at friendliness as attacks. He provoked rejection from the group, which was continually interpreted to him by the therapist and by the group members.

For the next two months, attendance was suprisingly regular, with all 11 members showing up on two occasions. During this time a new crisis occurred when Frieda became pregnant She insisted on getting married and carrying the child to term. She stated that, if she underwent an abortion, it would destroy her relationship with her husband. Much of the activity in the group at this time was focused on Frieda's predicament, with some of the group members discussing similar experiences. Mary reported that she had undergone an abortion and now regretted never having had any children. Richard had gotten a girl pregnant during the war, and she had obtained an abortion; he felt that it was something he never got over.

During the Christmas holidays, Richard began drinking heavily and came to the group in the next two months in a semi-intoxicated condition, looking for support in tapering off. He came on one occasion with a supply of chloral hydrate and sipped on his prescription to keep him from the shakes. During that period he went to drying-out farms, returned to work, started drinking again, came to the group intermittently, was fired, and then disappeared from the group for a number of weeks.

When the therapist changed the night of the meeting from Wednesday to Monday, attendance dropped almost 50 per cent. Frieda couldn't come on Monday because it interfered with an individual therapy session. Rita resumed symptomatic drinking and went to an A.A.-sponsored drying-out farm. Len's aunt died, and he went home for her funeral. And Richard, as mentioned above, disappeared.

Frances withdrew from the group after about a year of group therapy, feeling that she had had about as much therapy as a person could stand and that she would like

to give living-without-therapy a try. She felt she had made an important gain in coming to the group because she had learned to face up to and deal with other people's anger.

Tony left the group, reporting that he wasn't getting anything out of it. He left after attacking each member in turn.

Len returned to his hometown in the South for his aunt's funeral. After returning to New York, he called the therapist while obviously drunk to inform him that he was discontinuing treatment and was going to live in Europe.

Two group members had lengthy absences because of their drinking, and they could be considered drop-outs. Both Richard and Rita were absent for more than two months; they had to be admitted to hospitals and drying-out farms before they succeeded in establishing some equilibrium without alcohol.

Thus, of the five members who withdrew from the group, three discontinued because of alcohol abuse, one because of incompatibility with the group, and one because she felt she had achieved maximal benefits.

The therapist encouraged expression and interaction by the group members. They tended to complain that he was insufficiently active, did not give new information or advice, and never told them what to do. The therapist was an active listener, one who attempted to point out the way they used discussion of alcoholism and A.A. and other topics in much the same way they used alcohol itself, as a means of avoiding painful feelings or areas of conflict. After a while, the group became trained to this approach and, when these topics arose, some would say, "What's going on here?" or "Are we avoiding something?" or "There's something we were trying to get away from."

For example when a group member brought up a painful topic, such as the loss of a parent or a very humiliating experience, someone would find a way to bring in the subject of alcohol. Then the therapist would point out what had occurred and why the need had arisen to talk about alcohol or bars or A.A. at that point.

A relatively new member of the group began talking about the kind of women he became interested in: He wondered about women who can take and take and take and not give anything in return, saying that he couldn't understand them. He mentioned how he tried to please his mother, but somehow nothing would satisfy her. None of the group members attempted to deal with this question, which was asked in an abstract way. One of the group members began teasing him about picking up girls in bars. The therapist intervened, asking the group, most of whom had been together for about ten months, why they were avoiding the question, and whether their avoidance of the question was not related to the fact that what was being stirred up was too painful to go into.

An argument occurred between a man and a woman in the group. The man, who tended to attack others but was unable to keep a job or support his family, began upbraiding the woman for her passivity. She was complaining about how difficult life was for her because of her limited education and training, which restricted the kind of work she could obtain. He said that nothing was stopping her from going to school for some training. The two began yelling at each other. The therapist interrupted and asked whether they didn't relate to their respective spouses in the same manner. The woman agreed and then said that she was reminded of her father, who always made demands upon her. The only way she could please and mollify him was to bring him a bottle. Perhaps she resented the demands he made on her, and maybe she selected impossible men because of her history. She began to realize that the man she chose to become involved with and marry resembled her father.

Evaluation. During the ten-month period that the 11-member group met, they moved from superficial discussions of vocational and job problems and toward discussions of interpersonal relationships and individual feelings. Because of the introduction of Tony into the group, Robert was able to discuss—but only when Tony was absent—adolescent homosexual experiences he had never been able to talk about in individual or group sessions. Exposing himself enabled others in the group to offer him

support and to share equally painful aspects of their own difficulties, such as Frieda's sexual perversions and Mary's extramarital affairs.

For those who were concerned about measuring up and who feared exposure, the group process appeared to provide an opportunity to present unacceptable shortcomings, become aware of their shame and fear concerning these shortcomings, and understand that they resorted to alcohol when they were under stress because of the painful feelings connected with these conflicts.

The group did not appear to be able to help either Tony, whose constant angry tirades were probably used to ward off a schizophrenic disorganization, or Len, who went into a profound depression when he had to deal with the questions of his personal background and of his being black.

Great difficulties were involved in treating these patients. First and most important, they were very sick, much sicker than the patients in the nonalcoholic groups previously described. Their narcissistic and infantile personalities, inability to withstand separation from or loss of important objects, fixation and regression to conflicts, ambivalence over sexual and aggressive drives, paranoid-depressive projections, and extreme self-directed and self-destructive guilt stemming from a cruel and harsh superego—all were evidence of the severe psychopathology that is characteristic of the alcoholic. Two or three members of this group were the primary type of alcoholic—either actual or borderline psychotics with severe personality and ego disturbances.

Second, the great amount of acting out of various kinds in the group and outside of it made psychotherapy very difficult. Marked and frequent absences and lateness, instances of coming to the group while drinking, and nontherapeutic quarreling were manifestations of acting out that were disruptive to treatment. The acting out outside of the group—involving sex, drinking, being fired—was both marked and characteristic for this kind of severely ill alcoholic.

Finally, the usual type of resistance encountered in group psychotherapy was much more marked—even massive—with this group of patients. Denial, isolation, avoidance, persistent discussion of drinking and A.A., and other forms of resistance kept them away from significant material.

Despite all this, the group psychotherapy was helpful to several members. Seeing that others had the same difficulties and hearing others talk about their feelings connected with these difficulties helped them overcome their denial and become aware, to some extent at least, of feelings they had not known existed within them. The interactions in the group helped them see their own personality and character difficulties. The support of the group and the identifications with one another and with the therapist helped them overcome the punitive strictures of their primitive superegos. They found new outlets for the tensions connected with their aggressive-sexual impulses. They found that they could verbalize and control these impulses instead of acting them out. The identifications in the group and the support of the group increased awareness, improved reality-testing, and strengthened mature ego defenses.

With all the difficulties involved and despite the severe illness of the group members, this group functioned in an effective fashion for almost a year. Group psychotherapy is clearly useful for the patient with alcoholism, and for many it is unquestionably the treatment of choice.

Special Problems

Drunken Member at Session. In a group composed entirely of alcoholics, how does the therapist handle the issues involved when a patient comes to the session while drinking or drunk?

Alcoholic patients in group therapy usually have a tacit agreement that one of their treatment goals is abstinence. Occasionally, a patient states that his goal is not abstinence or sobriety but a return to normal drinking. But almost all alcoholics who enter treatment have been in Alcoholics Anonymous, so their attitudes about drinking, the control of drinking, alcoholism, sobriety, and abstinence tend to be derived from exposure to A.A.

Since a person is unable to cope competently or adequately with the usual demands of existence while intoxicated or semi-intoxicated, there is a common-sense basis for insisting on total abstinence. But many alcoholics in treatment rationalize a failure to remain abstinent by claiming that they lack sufficient insight, and they put off the time of stopping their drinking until they have achieved insight. Of course, a continuation of drinking can be viewed as a defense and a resistance. Probably one of the reasons why certain segments of A.A. are so adamantly against psychotherapy is that many patients use this wait-for-insight rationalization.

Alcoholic patients may have many different attitudes and feelings about sobriety, drinking, and coming to group therapy while drinking. But the group members' attitudes toward a drunken member closely parallel the usual "civilian" attitude toward drunks in general. If a group member arrives silly drunk—that is, if he makes a fool of himself —they smirk at each other, often appear disgusted, and chastise the group leader for permitting a member to attend while drunk. These attitudes often follow on the heels of similar drunken behavior by the person expressing them. If a member is disruptive, talks loudly, and otherwise indicates by his behavior that he has been drinking, another member may say:

You've been in therapy long enough to know that you can't get anything out of it while you're drinking, so why did you come here tonight?

Frieda came in high, flaunting a can of beer, and gave each group member a hostile analysis of his personality. The therapist intervened by wondering whether she needed to come to the group drunk in order to say these things. Some of the group members stepped in to defend her from what they anticipated would be rejection and the therapist's criticism. Said one:

You're not going to kick her out now, just because she's drunk, are you?

Two years later, Frieda said that she felt that session was the turning point in her treatment. For the first time she had been able to express criticism, and she felt free to do so later, without fear of disapproval from others.

Some patients come to sessions drunk and demand help in getting hospitalized, thus interfering with the group session. Others, feeling contrite and mortified as did Richard, appear at the end of a bender—tapering off, ruminating over events that precipitated the bout, and reviewing all later events in minute detail. The group members are often torn between a need to support the sufferer, who is in obvious distress, and a need to express anger and resentment at the person who is interfering with their therapy by doing something forbidden to them–drinking. They express the wish to be free to drink but feel the other group member has failed them. They are also angry at being reminded of how they must appear in similar circumstances. Often, these negative feelings are never expressed in the group.

A group member, Richard, resumed drinking after a year's abstinence. He alternated between periods of drinking heavily and brief periods of sobering up. He finally ended up in a severe alcoholic debauch, was mugged in the street and rolled by a prostitute, and was fired from a job he had carefully nurtured for a number of years.

His fellow group members were angry and upset because they felt let down by what he had done. This feeling was associated with the fear that the same thing might happen to them. They were also concerned that he might lose all his savings while drunk and be dispossessed. They urged him to seek hospitalization immediately, while he still had financial resources. They even offered to help him pack and accompanied him to the hospital.

In general, the problem of the member who arrives drunk is handled by helping him to become aware of his feelings, by pointing out the reality factors involved, and by pointing out to him that coming to a group session while drunk is a major form of resistance.

Hospitalization. Many of the difficulties encountered by a patient who accepts hospitalization for drinking involve loss of control and fear of loss of autonomy. When he realizes that hospitalization is necessary, the patient has to acknowledge that his drinking is out of control, and he has to surrender his autonomy to the physician and the hospital. The patient becomes fearful that they will find other things wrong—even that he is really crazy. This fear, coupled with a profound sense of shame and inadequacy, often makes patients unwilling to enter a hospital and leads to their signing themselves out soon after they are admitted.

In one instance, a patient manipulated the therapist into hospitalizing him by threatening suicide in front of the entire group. A few male group members assisted the therapist in placing the patient in the local acute psychiatric hospital. Upon admission, the patient demanded representation by his attorney—his brother, with whom he was not on good terms. The next day he got his mother to sign him out. The patient, who had been hospitalized for detoxification on two previous occasions, left the group.

The important point is to help the group see the reality factors involved and to help them overcome the denial and become aware of the great fear and guilt connected with the need to be hospitalized as a result of drinking.

CONCLUSION

With individual psychotherapy, most writers agree, 20 to 40 per cent of alcoholics improve. The figures rise to 50 or 60 per cent when alcoholics receive individual psychotherapy while they are hospitalized. With group psychotherapy the figures reported in the literature are considerably higher. Pfeffer reports that 90 per cent of his patients improved, with 30 per cent of them considered much improved. Figures from various clinics using group psychotherapy, as cited by Hill and Blane, range from 45 to 90 per cent improved. The most frequently cited figures for improvement are 60 to 70 per cent. But Hill and Blane stress the many difficulties involved in correctly evaluating these figures.

The authors found, in a subjective clinical estimate of the percentage of alcoholics who improved when treated with analytic and modified group psychotherapy, that 50 to 60 per cent improved. But improvement was seen only in patients who remained in the group for six months or more. Still, when one considers the character disorders and psychopathological difficulties of alcoholics, group psychotherapy definitely seemed to be the treatment of choice and to be far more effective than any other form of psychotherapy.

The nature of the group member's transference to the therapist, the deflection of the transference onto the other group members, and the resultant interaction are especially useful in bringing out and helping the alcoholic deal with his characteristic psychopathological difficulties. For these reasons, group psychotherapy has proved to be a specifically useful and effective form of treatment for the patient with alcoholism. For many such patients, it is definitely the treatment of choice.

REFERENCES

Agrin, A. The Georgian clinic: a therapeutic community for alcoholics. Quart. J. Stud. Alcohol, *21:* 113, 1960.

Allison, S. G. Nondirective group therapy of alcoholics in a state hospital. Quart. J. Stud. Alcohol, *13:* 596, 1952.

Bahn, A. K., Anderson, C. L., and Norman V. B. Outpatient psychiatric clinic services to alcoholics, 1959. Quart. J. Stud. Alcohol, *24:* 213, 1963.

Blum, E. M. Psychoanalytic views of alcoholism: a review. Quart J. Stud. Alcohol, *27:* 259, 1966.

Blum, E. M., and Blum, R. H. *Alcoholism: Modern Psychological Approaches to Treatment.* Jossey-Bass, San Francisco, 1967.

Brung, K. Outcome of different types of treatment of alcoholics. Quart J. Stud. Alcohol, *24:* 280, 1963.

Brunner-Orne, M. The utilization of group psychotherapy in enforced treatment programs for alcoholics and addicts. Int. J. Group Psychother., *6:* 272, 1956.

Brunner-Orne, M. Ward group sessions with hospitalized alcoholics as motivation for psychotherapy. Int. J. Group Psychother., *9:* 219, 1959.

Brunner-Orne, M., and Orne, M. T. Directive group-therapy in the treatment of alcoholics: technique and rationale. Int. J. Group Psychother., *4:* 293, 1954.

Brunner-Orne, M., and Orne, M. T. Alcoholics. In *The Fields of Group Psychotherapy*, S. R. Slavson, editor. International Universities Press, New York, 1956.

Burdick, J. A. Field independent alcoholic population. J. Psychol., *73:* 163, 1969.

Cabrera, F. J. Group psychotherapy and psychodrama for alcoholic patients in a state hospital rehabilitation program. Group Psychother., *14:* 154, 1961.

Chafetz, M. E. Practical and theoretical considerations in the psychotherapy of alcoholism. Quart. J. Stud. Alcohol, *20:* 281, 1959.

Chafetz, M. E. The alcoholic symptom and its therapeutic relevance. Quart. J. Stud. Alcohol, *31:* 444, 1970.

Chafetz, M. E., and Blane, H. T. Alcohol-crisis treatment approach and establishment of treatment relations with alcoholics. Psychol. Rep., *12:* 862, 1963.

Chafetz, M. E., Blane, H. T., Abram, H. S., Golner, J., Lacy, E., McCourt, W. F., Clark, E., and Meyers, W. Establishing treatment relations with alcoholics. J. Nerv. Ment. Dis., *134:* 395, 1962.

Chafetz, M. E., and Demone, H. W., Jr. *Alcoholism and Society.* Oxford University Press, New York, 1962.

Cork, R. M. Case work in a group setting with wives of alcoholics. Soc. Worker, *24:* 73, 1956.

Ends, E. J., and Page, C. W. A study of three types of group psychotherapy with hospitalized male inebriates. Quart. J. Stud. Alcohol, *18:* 263, 1957.

Esser, P. H. Group psychotherapy with alcoholics. Brit. J. Addict., *57:* 105, 1961.

Esser, P. H. Group psychotherapy with alcoholics. Quart. J. Stud. Alcohol, *22:* 646, 1961.

Evseeff, G. S. Group psychotherapy in the state hospital. Dis. Nerv. Syst., *9:* 214, 1948.

Ewing, J., Long, V., and Wenzel, G. G. Concurrent group psychotherapy of alcoholic patients and their wives. Int. J. Group Psychother., *11:* 329, 1961.

Feibel, C. The archaic personality structure of alcoholics the its indications for group therapy. Int. J. Group Psychother., *10:* 39, 1960.

Fogarty, P. J. The use of group therapy with selected alcoholics. Alcohol. Rev., *2:* 3, 1957.

Forizs, L. Brief intensive group-psychotherapy for the treatment of alcoholics. Psychiat. Quart., *29(Suppl.):* 43, 1955.

Foulkes, S. H., and Anthony, E. S. *Group Psychotherapy: The Psychoanalytic Approach*, ed. 2. Penguin Books, Baltimore, 1965.

Fox, R. Group psychotherapy with alcoholics. Int. J. Group Psychother., *12:* 56, 1962.

Gallant, D. M. Group staffing on an alcoholism treatment service. Int. J. Group Psychother., *14:* 218, 1962.

Gallant, D. M. A comparative evaluation of compulsory (group therapy and/or Antabuse) and voluntary treatment of the chronic alcoholic municipal court offender. Psychosomatics, *9:* 306, 1968.

Gallant, D. M., Bishop, M. P., and Stoy, B. The value of a "first contact" group intake session in an alcoholism outpatient clinic: statistical confirmation. Psychosomatics, *7:* 349, 1966.

Glasscote, R. M., *The Treatment of Alcoholism: A Study of Programs and Problems.* Joint Information Service, American Psychiatric Association and National Association for Mental Health, Washington, D. C., 1967.

Glatt, M. M. A treatment centre for alcoholics in a public mental hospital: its establishment and its working. Brit. J. Addict., *52:* 55, 1955.

Glatt, M. M. Treatment centre for alcoholics in a mental hospital. Lancet, *268:* 1318, 1955.

Glatt, M. M. Group therapy in alcoholism. Brit. J. Addict., *54:* 133, 1958.

Gliedman, L. H., Rosenthal, D., Frank, J. D., and Nash, H. T. Group therapy of alcoholics with concurrent group meetings of their wives. Quart. J. Stud. Alcohol, *17:* 655, 1956.

Greenbaum, H. Group psychotherapy with alcoholics in conjunction with Antabuse treatment. Int. J. Group Psychother., *4:* 30, 1954.

Harber, S. Treatment of problem drinkers at Winter Veterans Administration Hospital. Bull. Menninger Clin., *13:* 24, 1949.

Heath, R. G. Group psychotherapy of alcohol addiction. Quart. J. Stud. Alcohol, *5:* 555, 1945.

Hill, M. J., and Blane, H. T. Evaluation of psychotherapy with alcoholics: a critical review. Quart. J. Stud. Alcohol, *28:* 76, 1967.

Ingersheimer, W. Group psychotherapy for non-alcoholic wives of alcoholics. Quart. J. Stud. Alcohol, *20:* 77, 1959.

Karp, S. A., Kiss-in, B., and Hustmyer, F. E., Jr. Field dependence as a predictor of alcoholic therapy dropouts. J. Nerv. Ment. Dis., *150:* 77, 1970.

Knight, R. P. The psychodynamics of chronic alcoholism. J. Nerv. Ment. Dis., *86:* 538, 1937.

Koljonen, H. Alkoholistien vaimojen rhymätoiminta (The group work of the wives of alcoholics). Alkoholikysmys, *26:* 69, 1958.

Lerner, A. An exploratory approach in group counseling with male alcoholic inmates in a city jail. Quart. J. Stud. Alcohol, *14:* 427, 1953.

Lindt, H. The "rescue fantasy" in group treatment of alcoholics. Int. J. Group Psychother., *9:* 43, 1959.

Macdonald, D. Group psychotherapy with wives of alcoholics. Quart. J. Stud. Alcohol, *19:* 125, 1958.

Martensen-Larsen, O. Group psychotherapy with alcoholics in private practice. Int. J. Group Psychother., *6:* 28, 1956.

McCarthy, R. G. Group therapy in an outpatient clinic for the treatment of alcoholism. Quart. J. Stud. Alcohol, *7:* 98, 1946.

Mullan, H., and Sangiuliano, I. Alcoholism. In *Group Psychotherapy and Rehabilitation.* Charles C Thomas, Springfield, Ill., 1966.

Olsen, R. An experimental program for alcoholic patients. Ment. Hosp., *13:* 28, 1962.

Paley, A. Hypnotherapy in the treatment of alcoholism. Bull. Menninger Clin., *16:* 14, 1952.

Pfeffer, A. J. *Alchoholism.* Modern Monographs in Industrial Medicine, vol. 25, A. J. Lanza, editor. Grune & Stratton, New York, 1958.

Pfeffer, A. J., Friedland, P., and Wortis, S. B. Group psychotherapy with alcoholics. Preliminary report. Quart. J. Stud. Alcohol, *10:* 198, 1949.

Plaut, T. F., editor. *Alcohol Problems: A Report to the Nation by the Cooperative Commission on the Study of Alcoholism.* Oxford University Press, New York, 1967.

Pope, B. Attitudes toward group therapy in a psychiatric clinic for alcoholics. Quart. J. Stud. Alcohol, *17:* 233, 1956.

Preston, F. B. Combined individual, joint and group therapy in the treatment of alcoholism. Ment. Hyg., *44:* 522, 1960.

Schneidemuhl, A. M. Group psychotherapy program at the Spring Grove State Hospital. Group Psychother., *4:* 41, 1951.

Scott, E. M. A special type of group therapy and its application to alcoholics. Quart. J. Stud. Alcohol, *17:* 288, 1956.

Scott, E. M. Joint and group treatment for married alcoholics and their spouses. Psychol. Rep., *5:* 725, 1959.

Scott, E. M. A suggested treatment plan for the hostile alcoholic. Int. J. Group Psychother., *13:* 93, 1963.

Shearer, R. J., editor. *Manual on Alcoholism.* American Medical Association, Chicago, 1968.

Shulman, A. J. Group psychotherapy in the treatment of alcoholic addiction. Bull. Vancouver Med. Assoc., *26:* 274, 1950.

Shulman, B. H. Group psychotherapy in a post stockade. J. Soc. Ther., *3:* 14, 1957.

Soden, E. W. Constructive coercion and group counseling in the rehabilitation of alcoholics. Fed. Probation, *30:* 56, 1966.

Stein, A. The nature and significance of interaction in group psychotherapy. Int. J. Group Psychother., *20:* 153, 1970.

Stewart, D. A. Empathy in the group therapy of alcoholics. Quart. J. Stud. Alcohol, *15:* 74, 1954.

Stewart, D. A. Ethical aspects of the group therapy of alcoholics. Quart J. Stud. Alcohol, *15:* 288, 1954.

Strayer, R. Social intergration of alcoholics through prolonged group therapy. Quart. J. Stud. Alcohol, *22:* 471, 1961.

Thomas, G. W. Group psychotherapy: a review of the literature. Psychosom. Med., *15:* 166, 1943.

Thomas, R. E., Gliedman, L. H., Imber, S. D., Stone, A. R., and Freund, J. Evaluation of the

Maryland alcoholic rehabilitation clinics. Quart. J. Stud. Alcohol, *20:* 65, 1959.

Thomas, R. E., Gliedman, L. H., Imber, S. D., Stone, A. R., and Freund, J. Favorable response in the clinical treatment of chronic alcoholism. J. A. M. A., *169:* 1994, 1959.

Usdin, G. L., Rond, P. C., Hinchliffe, J. A., and Ross, W. D. Meaning of disulfiram to alcoholics in group psychotherapy. Quart. J. Stud. Alcohol, *13:* 590, 1952.

Vogel, S. Some aspects of group psychotherapy with alcoholics. Int. J. Group Psychother., *7:* 30, 1957.

Voth, A. C. Group therapy with hospitalized alcoholics: a twelve-year study. Quart. J. Stud. Alcohol, *24:* 289, 1963.

Wallerstein, R. S. Comparative study of treatment methods for chronic alcoholism: the alcoholism research project at Winter Veterans Administration Hospital. Amer. J. Psychiat., *113:* 228, 1956.

Wallerstein, R. S. *Hospital Treatment of Alcoholism.* Basic Books, New York, 1957.

Walton, H. Group methods in hospital organization and patient treatment as applied in the psychiatric treatment of alcoholism. Amer. J. Psychiat., *118:* 410, 1961.

Weiner, H. B. An overview of the use of psychodrama and group psychotherapy in the treatment of alcoholism in the United States and abroad. Group Psychother., *19:* 159, 1966.

Williams, L. An experiment in group therapy Brit. J. Addict., *54:* 109, 1958.

Witkin, H. Psychological differentiation and forms of pathology. J. Abnorm. Psychol., *70:* 317, 1965.

4

Group Psychotherapy and Psychopharmacology

Nathan S. Kline, M.D. and John M. Davis, M.D.

INTRODUCTION

The psychotropic drugs can be broadly classified as (1) antipsychotic agents (phenothiazines, thioxanthenes, butyrophenones), (2) antidepressants (tricyclic antidepressants and monoamine oxidase inhibitors), (3) antimanic agents (lithium salts), (4) antianxiety agents (minor tranquilizers), and (5) sedatives and stimulants. This classification is useful as a heuristic model; however, drugs that are considered to be primarily useful in one type of psychiatric illness occasionally show clinical efficacy in other types of mental disease as well. For example, under certain circumstances some of the phenothiazines have been shown to be effective both as antianxiety agents and as antidepressants, even though their major clinical use is in the therapy of schizophrenia. Similarly, some investigators are convinced that lithium salts, which are effective in mania, are prophylactically effective in the prevention of recurrent depressive attacks, and antidepressants have been claimed to be of use in treatment of phobias with severe anxiety.

A core of knowledge is available concerning each class of psychotropic drugs, and, although there are minor overlaps, the basic information remains quite reliable. Although the available knowledge often fails to explain adequately *how* these drugs act, it does provide an empirical or factual basis for therapy. Much of the data have resulted from double-blind investigations and constitute quite solid information. This section presents this basic core of information on therapeutic efficacy and side effects, discusses studies on drugs and their interactions with group therapy, gives practical hints on drug therapy, discusses particular problems that arise in group therapy when some of the patients are on drugs, and deals with the importance of having an accurate knowledge of psychopharmacology in order to provide for reality-testing in the therapeutic situation. One is best equipped to deal with fantasies, preconceptions, and indirect communications about drugs if one can clearly delineate what is actually known about these medications. To prescribe drugs effectively, one must, of course, know how to make the best medical use of their therapeutic properties; but the therapist also needs to possess basic information about their psychological actions, so that he may effectively deal with transference problems that may hide behind drug-related issues. Table 1 summarizes the pharmacological classification of most psychotropic drug structures.

DRUGS FOR TREATMENT OF PSYCHOSIS

Phenothiazines

The phenothiazines are best described as antipsychotic or antischizophrenic in action, since they reduce the intensity of the fundamental and accessory symptoms of schizophrenia. These symptoms include thought disorder, withdrawal, blunted affect, apathy, hallucinations, and delusions. The phenothiazines have made possible the more successful management of the schizophrenic patient and have been largely responsible for a dramatic decline in the population of the public mental hospitals, as shown in Figure 1. This decline is even more impressive when one considers the rate of increase in hospitalized mental patients in the previous ten years. In many patients, there is a rapid and almost complete remission of schizophrenic symptoms, and other patients, although still showing residual symptoms, are able to function outside the hospital. Some patients may still require continuous hospitalization, but they are often able to function on an open ward, without restraints.

The following phenothiazines are currently marketed in the United States: *promazine* (Sparine®, Wyeth), *chlorpromazine* (Thorazine®, Smith, Kline & French), *triflupromazine* (Vesprin®, Squibb), *prochlorperazine* (Compazine®, Smith, Kline & French), *trifluoperazine* (Stelazine®, Smith, Kline & French), *perphenazine* (Trilafon®, Schering), *fluphenazine* (Prolixin®, Squibb; Permitil®, White), *acetophenazine* (Tindal®, Schering), *carphenazine* (Proketazine®, Wyeth), *butaperazine* (Repoise®, Robins), and *thioridazine* (Mellaril®, Sandoz). Phenothiazines not currently marketed include *mepazine* (Pacatal®, Warner-Chilcott) and *thiopropazate* (Dartal®, Searle), and those under investigation or on foreign markets include *mesoridazine* (Serentil®, Sandoz), *thioproperazine* (Majeptil®, Vontil®, Rhone-Poulenc), *methophenazine* (Frenolon®, Medimex), *propericiazine* (Neuleptil®, Rhone-Poulenc), *levomepromazine* (Nozinan®, Levoprome®, Lederle; Veractil®, May & Baker), *piperacetazine* (Quide®, Pitman-Moore), *prothipendyl* (Timovan®, Ayerst), and *dixyrazine* (Esucos®, Union Chemique Belge).

Efficacy.

Phenothiazines vs. Placebo. More than 150 double-blind studies of the efficacy of phenothiazine derivatives have been reported in the literature and are summarized here

(Davis, 1965). Although in a double-blind study neither the patient nor the investigator is supposed to know which medication is being administered, sometimes side effects are revealing. This is more often true if a placebo is being compared with an active medication than if two active medications are being compared. Other important criteria in a well-designed study are: random assignments of subjects to drug groups, an adequate dose for an adequate period of time, careful qualitative and quantitative assessment of patient change, and a group sufficiently large to permit adequate statistical analysis of the data collected. This is not necessarily to downgrade the thousands of open studies where the control element is the prior response of the patient or the investigator's expectation based on the natural history of similar patients. However, since double-blind and open studies tend to confirm each other, the authors have limited this report to scientifically demonstrated studies. Criteria for inclusion here are thus more rigid than for most demonstrations of psychotherapeutic activity.

Table 2 summarizes those double-blind studies in which phenothiazines were compared with a placebo. All the phenothiazine derivatives, except possibly mepazine and promazine, are clearly more effective than placebo (Casey, Bennett, Lindley, and Hollister, 1960; Cole et al., 1966; National Institute of Mental Health, 1964; Overall et al., 1963; Schiele et al., 1961). The studies showing a placebo to be as effective as chlorpromazine, for the most part, used low doses of the drug (less than 500 mg. a day), with many instances of a dosage of 300 mg. a day or less. It is immediately evident that in addition to the criteria already listed for a scientific study, one must add that an adequate dose of the drug has to be administered for an adequate period of time. The lower limit is thus shown to be 500 mg. a day of chlorpromazine or an equivalent dose of some other phenothiazine.

Phenothiazines vs. Other Phenothiazines. Having established that most phenothiazines are better than a placebo, one may now determine whether any phenothiazine is better than the others. In Table 3, an analysis is made of the double-blind studies that have

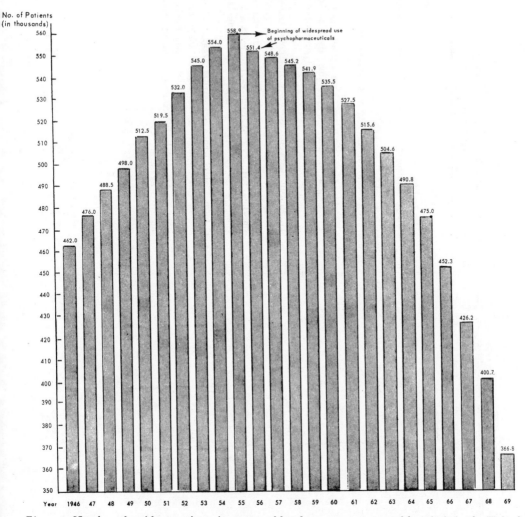

Figure 1. Number of resident patients in state and local government mental hospitals in the United States. (Based on United States Public Health Service figures, 1946 to 1968.)

compared chlorpromazine with the other phenothiazines. By the use of an efficacious standard drug, one may obtain data concerning the relative efficacy of the phenothiazine derivatives. As can be seen in Table 3, all the phenothiazines are about equally effective, with the exception of promazine and mepazine (Cole and Davis, 1969). No study has shown any phenothiazine to be more effective over-all than chlorpromazine.

Clinical experience shows that some patients who fail to respond to one phenothiazine may respond to another. This type of information is not of much use in predicting which drug to use and only tells us that it is

probably worth trying the patient on more than one medication. But are there methods to use in selecting the most effective medication? For instance, is one phenothiazine better than another for a particular subtype of schizophrenia? The assumptions that a withdrawn patient may respond better to the more activating phenothiazines such as trifluoperazine, perphenazine, and fluphenazine and that a patient characterized by excitement may respond better to the more sedating phenothiazines such as chlorpromazine have not been substantiated in controlled studies. Indeed, extremely apathetic and retarded patients did particularly well

Table 1. *Psychotropic Drugs*

Generic and Trade Names	Drug Structure	Drug Actions
Antipsychotic Agents Phenothiazine Derivatives Promazine (Sparine)	(phenothiazine structure; $(CH_2)_3$–N with two CH_3)	A. Action and indications: 1. Antipsychotic in almost in all forms of psychosis. 2. Antipsychotic in schizophrenia. 3. Tranquilizing in anxiety and depression. B. Side effects: 1. Central nervous system. Extrapyramidal effects (parkinsonism, dystonia, dyskinesia, akathisia, tardive oral dyskinesia), drowsiness, convulsions. 2. Autonomic nervous system. Dizziness, faintness, weakness, dry mouth and throat, nasal congestion, nausea, vomiting, constipation, diarrhea, urinary disturbances, blurred vision, orthostatic hypotension, inhibition of ejaculation. 3. Others. Galactorrhea, menstrual irregularities, moniliasis, dermatitis, skin pigmentation, corneal and lenticular opacities, pigmentary retinopathy (with thioridazine), obstructive jaundice, agranulocytosis. C. Contraindication: Previous sensitivity to the drug.
Chlorpromazine (Thorazine)	(phenothiazine structure with Cl; $(CH_2)_3$–N with two CH_3)	
Triflupromazine (Vesprin)	(phenothiazine structure with CF_3; $(CH_2)_3$–N with two CH_3)	
Prochlorperazine (Compazine)	(phenothiazine structure with Cl; $(CH_2)_3$–N piperazine N–CH_3)	
Trifluoperazine (Stelazine)	(phenothiazine structure with CF_3; $(CH_2)_3$–N piperazine N–CH_3)	

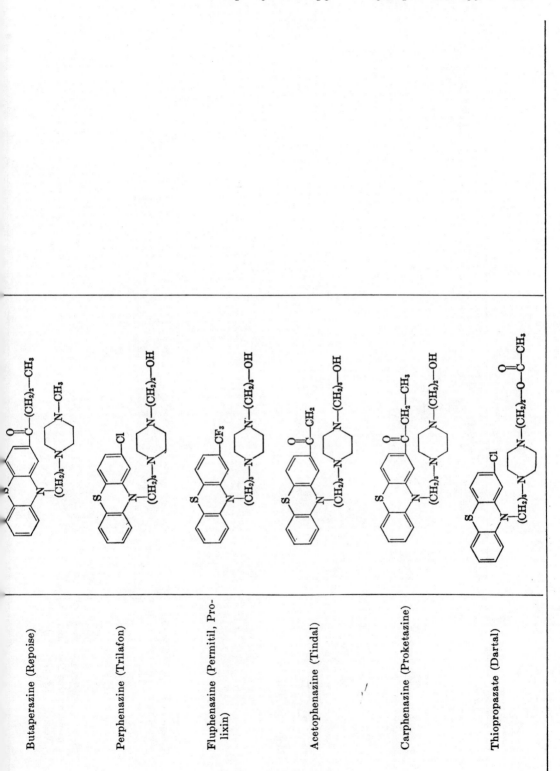

Butaperazine (Repoise)

Perphenazine (Trilafon)

Fluphenazine (Permitil, Pro-
lixin)

Acetophenazine (Tindal)

Carphenazine (Proketazine)

Thiopropazate (Dartal)

Table 1—Continued

Generic and Trade Names	Drug Structure	Drug Actions
Thioridazine (Mellaril)	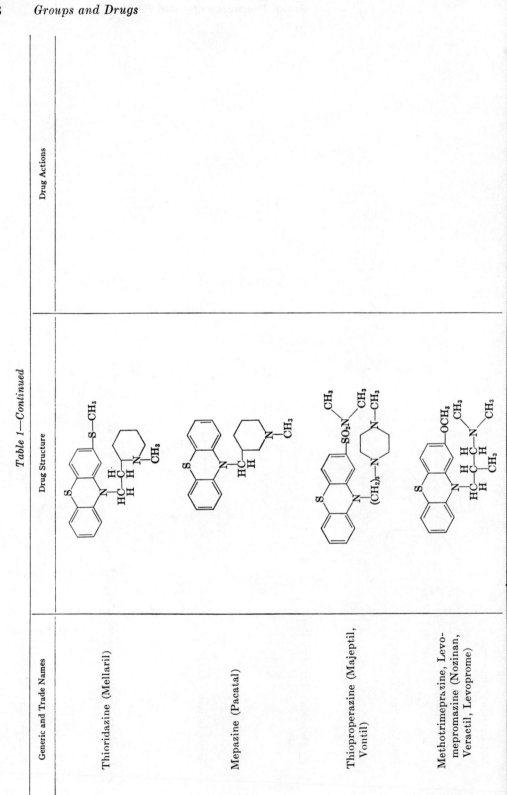	
Mepazine (Pacatal)		
Thioproperazine (Majeptil, Vontil)		
Methotrimeprazine, Levo-mepromazine (Nozinan, Veractil, Levoprome)		

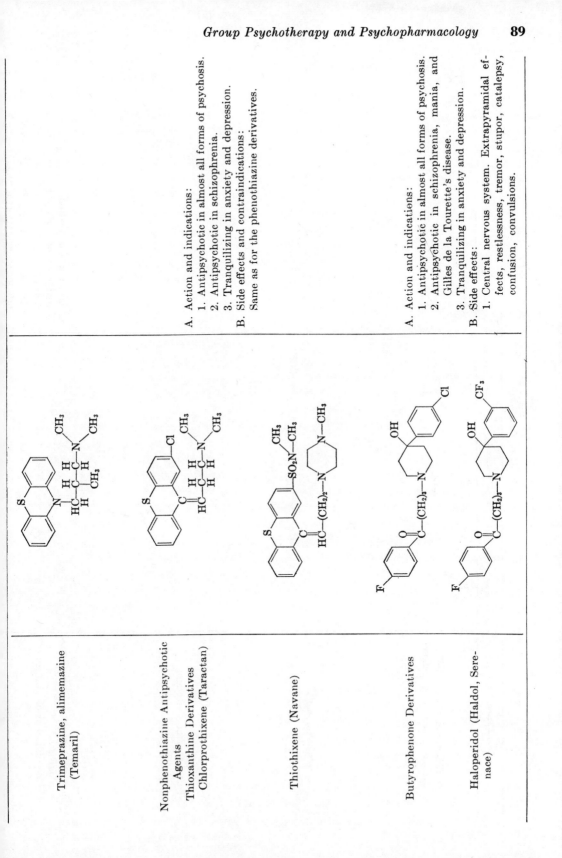

Trimeprazine, alimemazine (Temaril)

Nonphenothiazine Antipsychotic Agents
Thioxanthine Derivatives
Chlorprothixene (Taractan)

Thiothixene (Navane)

A. Action and indications:
1. Antipsychotic in almost all forms of psychosis.
2. Antipsychotic in schizophrenia.
3. Tranquilizing in anxiety and depression.
B. Side effects and contraindications:
Same as for the phenothiazine derivatives.

Butyrophenone Derivatives

Haloperidol (Haldol, Serenace)

A. Action and indications:
1. Antipsychotic in almost all forms of psychosis.
2. Antipsychotic in schizophrenia, mania, and Gilles de la Tourette's disease.
3. Tranquilizing in anxiety and depression.
B. Side effects:
1. Central nervous system. Extrapyramidal effects, restlessness, tremor, stupor, catalepsy, confusion, convulsions.

Table 1—Continued

Generic and Trade Names	Drug Structure	Drug Actions
Trifluperidol (Triperidol) Haloanisone (no trade name)		2. Autonomic nervous system. Tachycardia, fever, vomiting, genitourinary disorders, hypotension. 3. Others. Liver impairment, jaundice, agranulocytosis.
Reserpine (Serpasil)		
Tetrabenazine (Nitoman)		
Antianxiety Agents (Minor Tranquilizers) Chlordiazepoxide (Librium)		A. Action and indications: Reduction of anxiety, tension, etc. B. Side effects: Drowsiness, ataxia, lethargy, skin rashes, increased sensitivity to alcohol.

C. Precaution:
Warn patients of possible potentiating effects with ethyl alcohol and with sedatives and hypnotics.

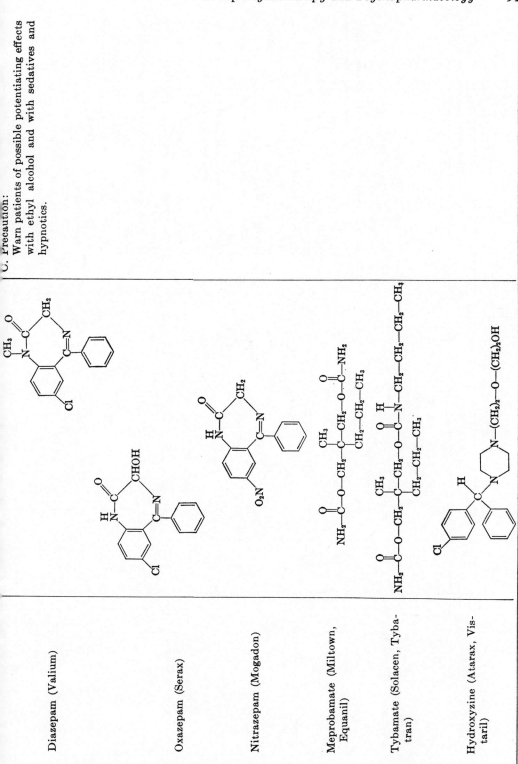

Diazepam (Valium)

Oxazepam (Serax)

Nitrazepam (Mogadon)

Meprobamate (Miltown, Equanil)

Tybamate (Solacen, Tybatran)

Hydroxyzine (Atarax, Vistaril)

Table 1—Continued

Generic and Trade Names	Drug Structure	Drug Actions
Antidepressant Agents Tricyclic Antidepressants Imipramine (Tofranil)		A. Action and indications: Mood elevation in endogenous depressions. B. Side effects: 1. Central nervous system. Drowsiness, weakness, fatigue, dizziness, headache, parkinsonism, muscle tremor, seizures, peripheral neuropathy, confusion, muscle incoordination, hypomania, mania, activation of schizophrenic psychosis, hallucinations, delusions, insomnia, dysarthria, paresthesia, ataxia, tinnitus. 2. Autonomic nervous system. Dry mouth, blurred vision, perspiration, aggravation of glaucoma, urinary impotence or frequency impotence. 3. Cardiovascular. Tachycardia, palpitations, arrhythmias, orthostatic hypotension, ankle edema. 4. Gastrointestinal. Constipation, epigastric distress, nausea, cramps, jaundice (obstructive type). 5. Hematological. Agranulocytosis, eosinophilia, purpura. 6. Skin. Rash, itching, flushing, photosensitivity. 7. Miscellaneous. Galactorrhea, bad taste, weight gain or loss, orbital edema. C. Contraindications: Benign prostatic hypertrophy, glaucoma, quiescent schizophrenia, recent myocardial infarction, chronic brain syndrome.
Desipramine, desmethylimipramine (Norpramin, Pertofrane)		
Amitriptyline (Elavil)		
Nortriptyline (Aventyl)		

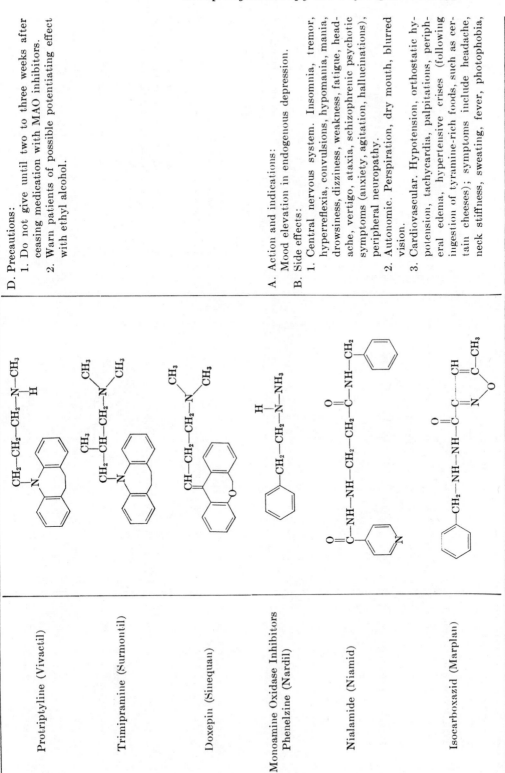

D. Precautions:
1. Do not give until two to three weeks after ceasing medication with MAO inhibitors.
2. Warn patients of possible potentiating effect with ethyl alcohol.

A. Action and indications:
Mood elevation in endogenous depression.

B. Side effects:
1. Central nervous system. Insomnia, tremor, hyperreflexia, convulsions, hypomania, mania, drowsiness, dizziness, weakness, fatigue, headache, vertigo, ataxia, schizophrenic psychotic symptoms (anxiety, agitation, hallucinations); peripheral neuropathy.
2. Autonomic. Perspiration, dry mouth, blurred vision.
3. Cardiovascular. Hypotension, orthostatic hypotension, tachycardia, palpitations, peripheral edema, hypertensive crises (following ingestion of tyramine-rich foods, such as certain cheeses); symptoms include headache, neck stiffness, sweating, fever, photophobia,

Protriptyline (Vivactil)

Trimipramine (Surmontil)

Doxepin (Sinequan)

Monoamine Oxidase Inhibitors
Phenelzine (Nardil)

Nialamide (Niamid)

Isocarboxazid (Marplan)

Table 1—Continued

Generic and Trade Names	Drug Structure	Drug Actions
Tranylcypromine (Parnate)	(cyclopropane ring bearing phenyl and NH_2 groups)	dilated pupils (may lead to intracranial bleeding and death).
Pargyline (Eutonyl)	$\text{C}_6\text{H}_5\text{—CH}_2\text{—N(CH}_3)\text{—CH}_2\text{—C}\equiv\text{CH}$	4. Gastrointestinal. Hepatocellular damage, constipation, nausea, diarrhea, abdominal pain, anorexia.
		5. Miscellaneous. Leukopenia, inhibition of ejaculation, impotence, rashes, edema of glottis, hyperpyrexia, urinary difficulties, photosensitivity.
		C. Contraindications and precautions:
		1. Wait two to three days after medicating with imipramine-like drugs; use of both drugs simultaneously or without an interval may result in a syndrome characterized by headache, dizziness, sweating, nausea and vomiting, agitation, tremulousness, muscle twitching, convulsions, coma, uncontrollable hyperpyrexia, and death.
		2. Cerebrovascular defects.
		3. Cardiovascular disease.
		4. Liver disease.
		5. Pheochromocytoma.
		6. Sympathomimetic amines, central nervous system depressants, anti-parkinsonian agents, diuretics, foods with high amine content.
		7. Quiescent schizophrenia.
Psychomotor Stimulants Amphetamine (Benzedrine)	$\text{C}_6\text{H}_5\text{—CH}_2\text{—CH(CH}_3)\text{—NH}_2$	A. Action and indications:
		1. Mood elevation, appetite suppression, combat effects of sedatives and fatigue.
		2. Indicated in *mild* psychodepression, hyperactivity syndrome in children, obesity, narcolepsy.
Dextroamphetamine (Dexedrine)	$\text{C}_6\text{H}_5\text{—CH}_2\text{CH(CH}_3)\text{—NH}_2$	B. Side effects:
		Agitation, cardiovascular effects, insomnia, may aggravate or even produce psychotic states in large doses.

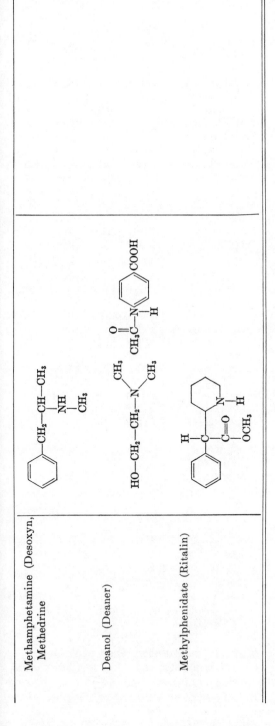

Methamphetamine (Desoxyn, Methedrine)

Deanol (Deaner)

Methylphenidate (Ritalin)

on chlorpromazine, a sedating drug, in a National Institute of Mental Health study (Goldberg, 1968). One author found that acetophenazine was more effective in treating paranoid patients, while perphenazine was more effective in treating "core" schizophrenics, but an attempt to replicate this finding was not successful. In a National Institute of Mental Health Psychopharmacology Service Center Collaborative Study using chlorpromazine and fluphenazine, patients assigned to the drug on which they were predicted to improve least still did better than those patients receiving a placebo (Goldberg, 1968). Thus, any active phenothiazine is better than no drug at all in the treatment of schizophrenia.

Dosage. The mean dose levels used in 11 well-done studies (all finding the phenothiazines to be more effective than placebos) were calculated and averaged. The range of the means and their averages are presented in Table 4 (Cole and Davis, 1969).

As already indicated, it is important to think of dosages as well as of the drug in evaluating patient improvement. A patient not improving on a drug could be receiving

Table 2. Drug-Placebo Comparisons in Double-Blind Controlled Studies of Schizophrenia

Drug	No. of Studies	Percentage of Studies in Which Drug Was:	
		More Effective than Placebo	Equal to Placebo
Phenothiazines			
Chlorpromazine	66	78.8	21.2
Trifluoperazine	16	81.2	18.8
Triflupromazine	10	90.0	10.0
Thioridazine	7	85.7	14.3
Perphenazine	5	100.0	0.0
Prochlorperazine	8	75.0	25.0
Fluphenazine	12	91.7	8.3
Mepazine	6	33.3	66.7
Promazine	7	28.6	71.4
Total for all phenothiazine	137	77.4	22.6
Others			
Reserpine	29	69.0	31.0
Oxypertine	4	75.0	25.0
Phenobarbital	5	0.0	100.0

Table 3. Comparisons of Chlorpromazine with Other Phenothiazines in Double-Blind Controlled Studies of Schizophrenia

Drug	No. of Studies	Percentage of Studies in Which Drug Was:		
		More Effective than Chlorpromazine	Equal to Chlorpromazine	Less Effective than Chlorpromazine
Trifluoperazine	11	0.0	100.0	0.0
Triflupromazine	10	0.0	100.0	0.0
Thioridazine	12	0.0	100.0	0.0
Perphenazine	6	0.0	100.0	0.0
Prochlorperazine	9	0.0	100.0	0.0
Fluphenazine	8	0.0	100.0	0.0
Mepazine	5	0.0	0.0	100.0
Promazine	5	0.0	40.0	60.0

Table 4. Dose Levels of Phenothiazines Used in Controlled Studies of Drug Effects

Drug	Controlled Studies*		Author's Experience*, †	
	Range	Mean	Range	Mean
Chlorpromazine (Thorazine)	300–1,800	692	300–1,500	800
Triflupromazine (Vesprin)	96–621	224	75–250	200
Trifluoperazine (Stelazine)	12–35	21	15–40	32
Promazine (Sparine)	400–439	420	—	—
Prochlorperazine (Compazine)	45–338	131	50–150	120
Perphenazine (Trilafon)	31–181	75	16–80	64
Fluphenazine (Permitil, Prolixin)	6–10	8	6–20	10
Acetophenazine (Tindal)	152	152	80–160	160
Thioridazine (Mellaril)	193–958	674	200–800	800
Mepazine (Pacatal)	135–190	163	—	—

* All doses are given in milligrams per day.
† J. M. D.

an inadequate dosage, even while he manifests sedation. On the other hand, a patient not responding to a high dose of one phenothiazine may respond to another phenothiazine, to a phenothiazine used in combination with another psychotropic drug, or to a different type of antipsychotic drug. There are wide variations in drug response, and dosage must be individualized for each patient; hence, no exact recommendation can be made. However, a typical dose schedule may be helpful (Klein and Davis, 1969). The usual starting dose of chlorpromazine or thioridazine is 200 mg. daily with a dosage increase of 100 to 200 mg. daily until a level of 600 to 800 mg. is reached. Often there is a satisfactory clinical response at this dosage, but if not, chlorpromazine dosage may be pushed as high as 2,000 to 3,000 mg. a day. It is doubtful, however, that greater improvement with chlorpromazine will occur beyond 1,500 mg. a day. Thioridazine dosage should not be increased beyond 800 to 1,000 mg. a day because of the possibility of pigmentary retinopathy. Although these doses may seem high, particularly for outpatients, underdosage is much more prevalent than overdosage. Failure of a patient to respond to chlorpromazine in doses such as 25 mg., 50 mg., or even 100 mg. three times a day cannot be considered adequate for a drug trial in patients (Kline and Davis, 1969).

Equivalent doses of other phenothiazines are obviously necessary. For instance, an initial dose of 5 mg. a day of trifluoperazine is recommended, building over a period of a week to 15 to 25 mg. a day. With perphenazine, an initial dose of 4 mg. a day, building to a plateau of 25 to 75 mg. a day, is recommended. With fluphenazine, the recommended initial and plateau doses are 2.5 mg. a day and 7.5 mg. a day, respectively. Many patients should also receive prophylactic antiparkinsonian agents.

Time-Course of Action. Rapidity of response to phenothiazine treatment varies considerably from one patient to the next, but there are average responses. Figure 2 illustrates the time-course of improvement in response to each of three phenothiazines. Improvement is most evident during the first six to nine weeks, but further recovery may continue slowly for months. Clearly, one cannot judge the efficacy of a phenothiazine unless one administers it for an adequate time period, which is on the order of three to four months. In many cases, satisfactory results are obtained much more rapidly, but a minimal trial of three months would not appear to be unreasonably long. An initial tranquilizer effect can, of course, be seen a few minutes after an intramuscular injection, but the full therapeutic effect takes longer.

Maintenance Therapy. Unequivocal evidence is available from double-blind studies that patients on phenothiazines who are shifted to placebo medication tend to

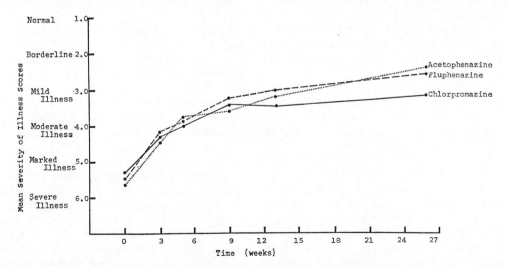

Figure 2. Severity of illness over time in patients treated with phenothiazines for schizophrenia. (Based on data from the National Institute of Mental Health-Psychopharmacology Service Center Collaborative Study II (1967).)

relapse more often than do comparable patients maintained on phenothiazines. In one group of chronic schizophrenics, 45 per cent of the patients who were transferred to a placebo relapsed, as compared with 5 per cent of those who were maintained on antipsychotic drugs (Caffey et al., 1964). At present, it is not possible to predict which patients will relapse after medication is discontinued. If phenothiazines are discontinued, they should not be withdrawn abruptly but should be withdrawn slowly over several days (Simpson et al., 1965).

Side Effects.

Central Nervous System Effects. The frequency and severity of effects vary with both the drug and the individual patient's central nervous system (Caffey and Klett, 1961; Hollister et al., 1960). It is extremely important to recognize them as side effects since they may easily be mistaken for manifestations of the disease. The acute extrapyramidal effects produced by phenothiazines can be classified as: (1) parkinsonism-like effects (akinesia, alterations of posture, masklike facies, tremor, shuffling gait, muscular rigidity, loss of associated movements, hypersalivation); (2) dystonia (uncoordinated spasmodic movements of the body and limbs, arching of the back, twisting posture of neck and body, oculogyric crises, salivation) and dyskinesia (involuntary, stereotyped rhythmic movements); or (3) akathisia (involuntary motor restlessness, constant pacing, inability to sit still, fidgeting, finger and leg movements, and a subjective feeling of "wanting to get out of my skin").

Akathisia is, on occasion, confused with agitation, parkinsonism with apathy, and dystonias with catatonic symptoms; however, the extrapyramidal side effects can be differentiated by rapid response to antiparkinsonism agents, whereas agitation is unaffected by these drugs. Dystonias and dyskinesias often develop in an hour to ten days following the onset of phenothiazine therapy, whereas parkinsonism and akathisia often develop over the first few weeks of treatment. These effects, if they occur, usually develop in the first 100 days of phenothiazine therapy, unless, of course, dosage is subsequently increased. There is

no correlation between the effectiveness of a given phenothiazine and the prevalence of extrapyramidal effects caused by that drug, despite early claims by some investigators. Thioridazine, which produces the fewest extrapyramidal side effects, and fluphenazine, which produces the most, are equally effective.

Since the appearance of extrapyramidal effects is not necessary for antipsychotic activity to occur, one should not necessarily wait for the development of manifest extrapyramidal disorder; in fact, antiparkinsonism drugs can be prescribed prophylactically. A dose of 5 mg. of *procyclidine* (Kemadrin®, Burroughs Wellcome) for every 400 mg. of chlorpromazine, or its equivalent, with a daily maximum of 15 mg. is recommended in some instances. Other antiparkinsonism agents and their recommended doses are: *benztropine methanesulfonate* (Cogentin®, Merck, Sharp & Dohme), 2 to 4 mg. a day; *trihexyphenidyl* (Artane®, Lederle), 4 to 8 mg. a day; and *biperiden* (Akineton®, Knoll), 2 to 6 mg. a day (Klein and Davis, 1969).

Crane and others have described a type of extrapyramidal side effect called "tardive oral dyskinesia," which can occur after long-term, high-dose phenothiazine therapy. This condition is characterized by bucco-facial-mandibular movements and is relatively unresponsive to antiparkinsonian drugs.

Drowsiness often occurs in the first few days of treatment. Since in most patients this effect rapidly disappears, the dosage should be maintained. The use of stimulants should be avoided.

Convulsions may infrequently occur with high doses or rapid increases in dosage. The convulsions are most simply dealt with by temporarily reducing the dosage or by adding anticonvulsive medication.

Autonomic Effects. Orthostatic hypotension may occur, particularly during the first few days of phenothiazine therapy. The patient should be instructed not to rise rapidly and to sit or lie down if in danger of fainting. Orthostatic hypotension is probably the most common cause of dizziness and weakness, but sometimes these symptoms develop with normal blood pressure. Tolerance develops rapidly to this side effect, and it is seldom a significant problem.

Some patients develop nasal congestion during phenothiazine treatment. The use of nasal decongestants affords temporary relief, but they should not be used continuously because of the danger of chemical rhinitis. Use of a vaporizer in the room may help, or a different phenothiazine may be tried.

Both the phenothiazines and the antiparkinsonism agents may cause dry mouth. The patient may control this condition by frequently rinsing his mouth with water or by chewing sugarless candy or gum. Candy or gum containing too much sucrose may, in the presence of damaged oral mucous membranes, form a good culture medium for *Monilia albicans*, and the prevalence of dental caries may be increased.

The phenothiazines and antiparkinsonism drugs often cause blurring of near vision by inducing mydriasis and cycloplegia. A tolerance to this side effect usually develops after a time. Patients should be warned that, whereas distance vision remains unaltered, they may for a time have difficulty focusing well enough to read. This side effect is more common in middle-aged or elderly patients whose muscles of accommodation do not always accommodate obligingly, even in the undrugged state.

Electrocardiogram changes have been observed with many phenothiazine derivatives, most often with thioridazine, and consist of lengthened Q-T intervals and flattened T-waves. This abnormality is a benign disturbance. Most pre-existing heart conditions are not contraindications, but the examining internist should know that the patient is on such a drug to avoid making a misdiagnosis of the cause of such a change.

Inhibition of ejaculation may also occur with phenothiazines, most commonly with thioridazine. Other autonomic effects of the phenothiazines are nausea and vomiting, diarrhea, constipation, and urinary disturbances. Nausea can usually be prevented by giving the medication with milk after meals. The gastrointestinal effects can be troublesome on rare occasions, particularly when the anticholinergic side effects of antidepressants and antiparkinsonism agents

are added to those of the phenothiazine. Paralytic ileus and urinary retention have rarely occurred, but constipation is quite common.

Metabolic and Endocrine Effects. These effects include weight gain, menstrual irregularities, and galactorrhea. It is particularly important to be aware of this triad so as to avoid a misdiagnosis of pregnancy.

Skin and Eye Effects. Minor skin rashes caused by the phenothiazines often respond to treatment with antihistamines. Corticosteroids may be used if antihistamines are ineffective. Generally, most skin rashes are transient and disappear with time. A persistent rash may be alleviated by switching to another phenothiazine.

Many phenothiazines produce phototoxicity, and patients can develop painful sunburns with only a few minutes' exposure to sunlight. Patients should be warned of this hazard. Prior application of lotions containing para-aminobenzoic acid is usually effective prophylactically, although caution is still urged.

Long-term, high-dose chlorpromazine therapy has been associated in some patients with a blue-gray metallic discoloration over areas exposed to sunlight. The skin changes often begin with a tan or golden brown color and progress to slate gray, metallic blue or purple, or a marked purple color. Skin biopsies show golden brown pigment granules similar to, but not identical with, melanin. Treatment for this side effect includes giving the patient *d*-penicillamine or confining him to relative darkness or both.

With long-term, high-dose chlorpromazine therapy, bilateral whitish-brown granular deposits appear usually in the anterior lens and posterior cornea. These lens changes are generally visible only by slit lamp examination. They progress to opaque white or yellow-brown granules, often stellate in shape. The lens changes almost never affect visual acuity and are found during routine examinations or research surveys. Although not of great clinical significance, the eye changes can be prevented or controlled by adjusting the dosage level, using phenothiazines other than chlorpromazine, having the patient wear dark glasses, protecting him from sunlight, and using special window glasses to screen out ultraviolet light.

A completely different side effect, a pigmentary retinopathy, has been observed with thioridazine. This can be avoided by not exceeding a daily dose of 800 to 1,000 mg. of thioridazine.

Jaundice. Chlorpromazine-induced allergic jaundice, if it appears, will usually do so in the first month of therapy. It has a reported incidence of about 0.1 per cent, but this incidence seems to be decreasing. The jaundice is essentially an obstructive one, histologically consisting of bile plugs in the canaliculi. Generally, the offending agent is discontinued and the condition improves. Cross sensitivity to other phenothiazines rarely occurs, so a change to another phenothiazine or a nonphenothiazine antipsychotic drug can be made.

Agranulocytosis. Agranulocytosis is rare, but, when it does appear, it occurs most commonly during the first six weeks of drug therapy. It develops relatively abruptly and in the early stages presents no special symptoms. In theory, it can be picked up by routine white blood cell counts; however, such detection occurs rarely because of its relatively rapid onset. It usually presents with symptoms of fever and sore throat, which are noticed before any alteration in the white cell count is detected. The patient should be instructed to notify his psychiatrist immediately if he develops a sore throat and fever. Agranulocytosis should be treated by an internist. Treatment consists of immediate discontinuation of all medication, isolation from possible sources of secondary infection, and the rational use of antibiotics if infection develops.

Differential Incidence of Side Effects. Although chlorpromazine, triflupromazine, prochlorperazine, trifluoperazine, perphenazine, fluphenazine, acetophenazine, and thioridazine are similar in their therapeutic properties, they differ in the relative incidence of side effects. Promazine, mepazine, and chlorpromazine show a differentially high incidence of agranulocytosis, jaundice, autonomic side effects, and excessive sedation; trifluoperazine and fluphenazine show a high incidence of extrapyramidal effects; thio-

ridazine is associated with a high differential incidence of retinopathy and inhibition of ejaculation.

Overdose. A total of 419 cases of drug overdose involving phenothiazines was reviewed by Davis et al. Only six adult fatalities, three with chlorpromazine and three with thioridazine, were found, and in these cases, idosyncratic factors may have played a role. Patients have been reported to have ingested as much as 17,000 mg. of chlorpromazine and survived. The authors know of no deaths from overdoses of the high-potency phenothiazines. Indeed, 1,000 mg. of fluphenazine and 700 mg. of perphenazine have been used clinically with safety (Davis, Bartlett, and Termini, 1968).

Drug Metabolism. Some patients fail to show any clinical response to phenothiazine drugs. This may be explained by differences in drug metabolism between patients. For example, it may be that patients who do not respond to chlorpromazine metabolize the drug very rapidly, so that few chlorpromazine molecules reach the brain, the presumed site of action of the drug. Research by Curry, Davis, Janowsky, and Marshall has shown this to be the case in a few patients. One patient had a plasma chlorpromazine level near zero, in spite of having been given enormous oral doses for long periods of time. Another interesting problem is whether a different phenothiazine or an antipsychotic agent of a different class, such as haloperidol or thiothixene, would help these patients. A rational approach would be to try such patients on different drugs. Other patients were found to have abnormally high blood levels of chlorpromazine, substantially above those usually seen in the average patient. In one such patient, it was found that, if the dose was reduced below the oral dose needed for the average patient, the blood levels fell to within the normal range, and the patient improved. Even at normal oral dose levels, some patients may be getting a toxic dose.

The marked variation among individual patients in their metabolic response pattern to chlorpromazine was quite striking: Plasma chlorpromazine levels varied from 0 to 770 mg. per ml., the rise in plasma levels after dosage showed a 15-fold variation, and the half-life of the drug in plasma varied from two to 31 hours.

The effects of phenobarbital on chlorpromazine metabolism were also investigated, since chlorpromazine is in part destroyed by enzymes in the liver. By treatment with phenobarbital, one can induce the production of this enzyme system. Phenobarbital enhances the destruction of chlorpromazine, resulting in a lower plasma level of the drug and a worsening of the patient's clinical condition.

After intravenous injection of chlorpromazine, the curve of disappearance of chlorpromazine from the plasma seemed biphasic, with a very rapid half-life for the first phase (about one hour) and a slower half-life for the second phase (about $4\frac{1}{2}$ hours). Furthermore, a much higher blood level of chlorpromazine was found after intramuscular injection of the drug than after administration of the same dose orally.

There are significant differences among different patients in the amount of drug that reaches the brain. Of three patients receiving the same dose, it is conceivable that one patient may be overtreated, with resultant psychotoxic manifestations; the second may be undertreated as a result of too rapid a rate of metabolism of the drug; and the third patient may be receiving an optimal dose. This research emphasizes the danger of attempting to use the same dosage schedules for all patients and supports the clinical dictum that the dose must be individualized.

Other Antipsychotic Agents

Reserpine. Reserpine is derived from the Rauwolfia plant, which has been used in India for thousands of years in the treatment of a variety of mental ills. In 1954, Kline tried it in the treatment of schizophrenia at Rockland State Hospital, Orangeburg, New York, and found it to have definite antipsychotic properties.

In controlled studies, reserpine is an effective antipsychotic drug (see Table 1); however, for most patients, it is a less effective drug than the phenothiazines. For example, a Veterans Administration study compared reserpine with chlorpromazine, thioridazine,

triflupromazine, and fluphenazine and found reserpine to be less effective than the four phenothiazines (Lasky et al., 1962). The side effects of reserpine may include severe depression, gastric ulcers, nasal congestion, and sedation. Today, the principal use of reserpine is in the treatment of hypertension.

Thioxanthenes. The thioxanthenes differ structurally from the phenothiazines in that the aromatic nitrogen atom is replaced by a carbon atom. Two thioxanthene derivatives are currently marketed in the United States, *chlorprothixene* (Taractan®, Roche) and *thiothixene* (Navane®, Roerig).

Table 5 summarizes double-blind studies in which thioxanthenes were compared with a placebo. Chlorprothixene and thiothixene as well as the experimental thioxanthene derivatives are effective antipsychotic agents. Furthermore, chlorprothixene and thiothixene are about as efficacious as the phenothiazines.

The dosage range is approximately 300 to 600 mg. a day for chlorprothixene and 3 to 60 mg. a day for thiothixene.

Both chlorprothixene and thiothixene may cause extrapyramidal side effects, and other side effects associated with the phenothiazines have occasionally been noted with the thioxanthenes.

Butyrophenones. The butyrophenones seem to be chemically unrelated to the other antipsychotic drug groups. The only butyrophenone currently on the United States market is *haloperidol* (Haldol®, McNeil). In addition to its use in the treatment of schizophrenia, haloperidol is effective in the treatment of mania and of Gilles de la Tourette's disease, a rare disorder marked by involuntary tics and coprolalia (Crane, 1967).

Haloperidol has been found superior to placebo in nine controlled studies. No study has found haloperidol merely equal to placebo. Considered over-all, haloperidol is about as effective as the phenothiazine and thioxanthene derivatives. Trifluperidol has also been found to be approximately as effective as the phenothiazines. The newer butyrophenone derivatives, haloanisone and spiroperidol, are currently under investigation and may also prove to be effective antipsychotic agents.

Table 5. *Summary of Double-Blind Controlled Studies of Nonphenothiazine Antipsychotic Agents in the Treatment of Schizophrenia, Showing Comparisons with Chlorpromazine, Trifluoperazine, and Placebo*

Drug	No. of Studies in Which Drug Was:							
	Better than Placebo	Equal to Placebo	Better than Chlorpromazine	Equal to Chlorpromazine	Worse than Chlorpromazine	Better than Trifluoperazine	Equal to Trifluoperazine	Worse than Trifluoperazine
Thioxanthenes								
Chlorprothixene	4	0	0	6	0	0	0	0
Thiothixene	0	0	0	0	0	0	2	0
Butyrophenones								
Haloperidol	9	0	0	2	0	0	3	0
Triperidol*	2	0	2	2	0	0	4	0
Haloanisone*	0	0	0	0	0	0	1	0
Methylperidol*	1	0	0	0	0	0	0	0

* Not presently available on the United States market.

The recommended dosage of haloperidol is 2 to 15 mg. a day. Side effects include extrapyramidal effects as well as other effects characteristic of the phenothiazines. The frequency of extrapyramidal effects is relatively high, so that haloperidol has a side effect profile similar to that of trifluoperazine or fluphenazine. Similarly, haloperidol has a lower incidence of autonomic effects than does chlorpromazine. Cases of jaundice or agranulocytosis have been so rare that it has not been established that those observed were etiologically related to haloperidol instead of coincidental.

Drug Combinations

Clinically, combinations of psychotropic drugs are frequently used in the treatment of all types of patients. An important question is whether there is an advantage to any of the commonly used combinations when compared to single-drug therapy, since not only are drug combinations more expensive but they may produce a greater range of side effects.

Several studies done at the Spring Grove State Hospital, Catonsville, Maryland, compared the effect of adding either *imipramine* (Tofranil®, Geigy) or *chlordiazepoxide* (Librium®, Roche) to either thioridazine or chlorpromazine (Michaux et al., 1966). There was no large statistical advantage to the addition of these drugs to either of the phenothiazines used. However, several small but consistent trends were observed with regard to certain symptom variables. The groups receiving a phenothiazine combined with chlordiazepoxide did less well than the other groups, perhaps because the sedating effect of chlordiazepoxide caused them to receive lower doses of the phenothiazine. There was a suggestion that thioridazine-imipramine was of differential benefit to patients with motor disturbances. Depressed schizophrenics—particularly, depressed nonretarded schizophrenics—did especially well with this combination. The combination of chlorpromazine with imipramine was more effective in the highly retarded (catatonic) group and in schizophrenics with depression.

These results suggest that some benefit may be obtained from adding imipramine to phenothiazines in depressed and possible catatonic schizophrenics. The addition of chlordiazepoxide was not particularly advantageous, although it was clinically shown to be helpful in a few carefully chosen cases.

A clinically important question is whether the addition of an antidepressant drug will benefit chronic, burned-out, anergic schizophrenics. One study compared perphenazine, amitriptyline, a perphenazine-amitriptyline combination, and a placebo in such a group of patients. The patients receiving either a placebo or amitriptyline alone did poorly, but groups receiving perphenazine alone or the perphenazine-

Table 6. *Drug Therapy vs. Social Therapies in Chronic Schizophrenia—Results of Four Treatment Regimes**

Treatment Regime†	Percentage Showing High Improvement at 6 Mo.	Percentage Discharged after 6 Mo.	Percentage Showing High Improvement at 36 Mo.
High Social Therapies			
Drug Therapy	33	27	35
No Drug Therapy‡	0	7	26
Low Social Therapies			
Drug Therapy	23	9	19
No Drug Therapy‡	10	5	6

* Data from Greenblatt et al.

† High social therapies were administered at Massachusetts Mental Health Center; low social therapies were administered at a state hospital (see text).

‡ All patients received drug therapy after six months.

amitriptyline combination improved. Each of these groups showed about the same degree of improvement, with a slight trend in favor of the combination in improvement of social contacts. Several other studies have failed to find any significant advantage in the addition of an antidepressant drug to a phenothiazine in the treatment of schizophrenia, although subtypes of schizophrenia that might differentially respond to such a combination remain a possibility (Casey et al., 1961). Much additional research is needed in this area.

Antipsychotic Drugs and Social Therapies

Relative Efficacy. In studies in which phenothiazines have been used in comparison with psychotherapy or social therapy, the drugs have proved to be an important and often necessary condition for maximal improvement. In one critical study (see Table 6), four different treatment methods were studied in 115 chronic schizophrenic patients who had been patients in one of two state hospitals for five to ten years (Greenblatt et al., 1965). All patients were under 50 years of age and showed no clinical evidence of mental deterioration or retardation.

The patients were divided into four matched groups: Group A was transferred to the Massachusetts Mental Health Center (M.M.H.C.) and treated with social therapy and antipsychotic drugs. Group B was transferred to M.M.H.C. and received social therapies only. Group C remained at the state hospital and received the same drug treatment as Group A. Group D remained at the state hospital and received no special drugs. The male patients in the drug groups received 100 mg. of chlorpromazine three times a day, 1 mg. of reserpine three times a day, and 5 mg. of trihexyphenidyl three times a day. The female patients received the same drugs in one-half the dosage. Treatment was assessed at the end of six months, and subsequently all patients could receive drugs.

The group receiving drugs at the mental health center showed an improvement rate of 33 per cent, as compared with an improvement rate of 23 per cent shown by the patients receiving drugs in the state hospitals, thus suggesting that drugs may be slightly more effective (but not significantly so) when administered in a superior social setting. No patients at M.M.H.C. improved if they received only high social therapy without drugs, suggesting that, without drugs, social therapies were of limited efficacy. Only 10 per cent of the state hospital patients not receiving drugs improved. In terms of ultimate outcome, the discharge rate was higher in the group receiving both high social therapy and drugs (27 per cent) than in the other three groups (5 to 9 per cent). At the end of 36 months, those patients receiving high social therapy and drugs from the beginning showed an improvement of 35 per cent, but those patients receiving no drugs for the first six months and no social therapy showed an improvement of only 6 per cent. The M.M.H.C. group receiving no drugs for the first six months had an improvement rate of 26 per cent, never catching up with the drug group, and the state hospital group receiving drugs from the beginning had an improvement rate of 19 per cent. The results demonstrate that social therapies and drug therapies potentiate each other in terms of ultimate social prognosis.

Evangelakis (1961) compared the effects of group therapy, adjunctive social therapies, and drug therapy in chronic patients. Those receiving both group and social therapy but no drugs did poorly; those receiving various combinations of drug treatment with group, nongroup, adjunctive, and nonadjunctive therapy did consistently better. The discharge, trial visit, and boarding home visit rates of the group receiving adjunctive and drug therapies were slightly higher than the rates of the other groups.

King (1963) investigated 20 matched pairs of hospitalized schizophrenics. Both groups received 100 mg. of chlorpromazine three times a day, and one group also received group psychotherapy once a week. There was no significant difference in outcome between the two groups.

May and Tuma (1965) compared the effects of trifluoperazine therapy alone, drug therapy combined with individual psychotherapy, individual psychotherapy alone, and milieu therapy in state hospital patients. Drug treatment, whether given alone or in combination with psychotherapy, increased the release rate, shortened the length of the hospital stay, decreased the necessity for use of sedatives or hydrotherapy, and produced more beneficial changes in clinical status (see Table 7).

Grinspoon et al. (1968) studied 20 chronic schizophrenics treated at least twice a week for two years by experienced psychotherapists. In addition, half of the patients received 300 to 1,000 mg. a day of thioridazine, and the other half received a placebo. Psychotherapy alone was ineffective in treating these patients. Phenothiazine therapy was effective in reducing florid symptoms and in making the patient more receptive to communication with the therapist and others. These patients showed greater improvement than the placebo group and greater involvement with events such as the therapist's vacations, the ward administrator's departure, and President Kennedy's death. The findings did not bear out the claim of some psychotherapists that pharmacotherapy interferes with progress in psychotherapy; indeed, the reverse seemed to be true.

In a cooperative study done at nine Veter-

Table 7. *Drug Therapy vs. Social Therapies in Acute Schizophrenia—Comparison of Four Methods of Therapy**

Treatment	Percentage of Patients Released in Study Period
Control	65
Psychotherapy Only	70
Drug Therapy Only	90
Drug Therapy and Psychotherapy	95

* Data from May and Tuma.

ans Administration hospitals (Gorham and Pokorny, 1964), 150 patients were treated for 12 weeks with (1) 300 to 350 mg. a day of thioridazine, (2) group psychotherapy for three one-hour sessions a week, or (3) both drug and group therapy. Drug therapy alone or in combination with group therapy was superior to group therapy alone in reducing symptoms commonly associated with schizophrenia. Psychotherapy was superior in relieving tension and reducing somatization. The two treatments had potentiating effects in reducing motor retardation and anxiety.

In another large Veterans Administration study (Honigfeld et al., 1965), 276 chronic schizophrenic men over 54 years of age were given either acetophenazine (20 to 240 mg. a day), imipramine (25 to 300 mg. a day), trifluoperazine (2 to 24 mg. a day), or a placebo. In addition, half of the patients in each drug group attended social group sessions. The two phenothiazines were clearly effective in reducing motor disturbances, conceptual disorganization, and manifest psychosis and in increasing personal neatness; however, acetophenazine was superior to trifluoperazine in reducing irritability and excitement and increasing social competence. Imipramine was relatively ineffective. Social therapy was a worthwhile addition to drug treatment, since it reduced motor disturbances and irritability and increased cooperation and personal neatness.

Results of social therapy and psychotherapy are subject to the limitations of the skills of the therapist, and it can always be claimed that, had the therapist been more skillful, the results would have shown social therapy to be more effective than drugs. However, one cannot base national health policies on a competence level that few are alleged to achieve. Generalizations concerning the relative efficacy of drugs and social therapies should take cognizance of the level of skill of the average practitioner. Although more work is needed on the interaction of drugs and social therapies, the evidence here consistently demonstrates the antipsychotic effects of the drugs. Social therapies have little, if any, antipsychotic effect and are relatively ineffective alone. On the other hand, drugs do not substitute for social therapies. There is evidence from some but not all of these studies that social therapies may produce an added benefit above drug therapy alone in social adjustment and utilization of drug-induced gains.

Effects of Drugs on Group Psychotherapy Patients

A number of psychological issues frequently arise when patients on drugs enter individual or group psychotherapy. Patients frequently worry about the effects that drugs may produce, and this worry is often an elaboration of generalized anxiety about their underlying mental disorder. For example, very frequently patients will complain of various nonspecific side effects, such as "fullness in the head." To the physician, such a complaint may seem minor and insignificant, but, if the concern is not dealt with, the patient may stop taking his medication, thereby foregoing the benefits the drug can only provide when given in adequate doses. It is, therefore, very important to deal with worries of this type either in the therapy session or through phone calls. In group therapy, the discussion of medication problems is often quite beneficial, providing both informational and emotional support for the patients.

Patients receiving drugs often seize on their medication as a focal issue over which many concerns can be expressed. Therapists are familiar with the use of procedural details for this purpose and are often prepared to deal with the matters in terms of transference and related problems. Surprisingly, however, therapists are somewhat

less willing to deal with underlying problems when confronted with concerns about medication. For example, a patient in individual psychotherapy may question the use of the couch as opposed to an armchair; in group therapy, certain procedural aspects may be discussed. It is generally understood that many of these concerns may be associated with more basic issues. But physicians who feel defensive about using drugs often accept at face value the patient's complaints about the drug and do not deal effectively with the underlying problems.

An important finding relevant to this matter was presented at the 1970 meeting of the American Psychiatric Association by O'Brien and Hamm. Their study indicated that group therapy was superior to individual psychotherapy in treating schizophrenic patients. The study population consisted of 100 consecutive aftercare patients admitted to a large community mental health center and rated independently by two raters. All patients were schizophrenics, and all were maintained on phenothiazine-derivative drugs, with the dose adjusted as necessary. After one year, rehospitalization rates were 13 per cent for group therapy patients and 24 per cent for patients receiving individual therapy. After two years, the rehospitalization rates were 22 per cent and 40 per cent, respectively; drop-out rates were 5 per cent for group therapy and 24 per cent for individual therapy. These differences are of considerable magnitude and suggest that group plus drug therapy may be a particularly useful way of managing schizophrenic aftercare.

One possible explanation for this finding is that group therapy reduces the likelihood that the patient will stop taking his medication, since the group seems to deal with drug issues more adequately than does individual therapy. Phenothiazines, it must be remembered, are of particular importance in preventing rehospitalization of schizophrenics, since a good number tend to relapse if medication is withdrawn.

DRUGS FOR TREATMENT OF DEPRESSION

The antidepressants may be divided into three classes: psychomotor stimulants, monoamine oxidase (MAO) inhibitors, and tricyclic drugs. Iproniazid, the first of the MAO inhibitors, was initially used in the treatment of tuberculosis and was unexpectedly found to cause euphoria in some of these patients. Kline and Crane, working independently with their respective colleagues, administered the drug to depressed patients with favorable antidepressant results. Imipramine was next synthesized during a search for an antipsychotic agent. It was found to be *not* an effective antipsychotic agent in schizophrenia; but, since it made depressed schizophrenics less depressed, Kuhn tried it as an antidepressant and found that it worked.

Psychomotor Stimulants

The drugs in this group include *amphetamine* (Benzedrine®, Smith, Kline & French) *d-amphetamine* (Dexedrine®, Smith, Kline & French), *methamphetamine* (Methedrine®, Burroughs Wellcome; Desoxyn®, Abbott), and *methylphenidate* (Ritalin®, Ciba). These drugs have little value in the treatment of severe depression. In all efficacy studies, amphetamine has been found no more effective than a placebo; and in some studies, depressed patients treated with amphetamines became worse. Methylphenidate was found to be of only slightly more value than a placebo in one study of mildly to moderately depressed patients. These drugs have never been demonstrated to be effective as antidepressants in any adult population. Uncontrolled clinical experience suggests that some patients benefit from them. It may be that the controlled studies done so far have not included the type of patient who is helped by psychomotor stimulants. They may be useful when given in the first few days of tricyclic drug treatment in order to provide an initial mood elevation.

Side effects of amphetamine and other psychomotor stimulants include jitteriness, irritability, palpitations, postamphetamine fatigue, dejection, and, at high doses, a paranoia-like psychosis. These drugs have a definite liability in their potential for abuse. Interestingly, amphetamines are often dramatically effective in the treatment of hyperkinetic behavior in children.

Monoamine Oxidase Inhibitors

The MAO inhibitors may be divided into two classes: hydrazines and nonhydrazines. *Iproniazid* (Marsilid) was the first hydrazine MAO inhibitor introduced; subsequent hydrazines include *isocarboxazid* (Marplan®, Roche), *nialamide* (Niamid®, Pfizer), *phenelzine* (Nardil®, Warner-Chilcott), *pheniprazine* (Catron®, Lakeside), *etryptamine* (Monase®, Upjohn), and *mebanazine* (Actomol®, Imperial Chemical Industry). Of these, mebanazine has never been available commercially on the United States market, and iproniazid, pheniprazine, and etryptamine were withdrawn because of toxicity. The nonhydrazine derivatives are *tranylcypromine* (Parnate®, Smith, Kline & French) and *pargyline* (Eutonyl®, Abbott). The latter, although an effective antidepressant, is currently marketed only as an antihypertensive.

Mechanism of Action. The MAO inhibitors act by inhibiting the enzyme monoamine oxidase, an enzyme that intracellularly breaks down catecholamines and serotonin. This inhibition increases the amount of amines in the brain.

Efficacy.

MAO Inhibitors vs. Placebo. Table 8 summarizes those double-blind studies comparing MAO inhibitors with a placebo. It will be seen that about half of the studies found the drugs superior to the placebo.

MAO Inhibitors vs. Other MAO Inhibitors. Few studies of adequate research design have compared MAO inhibitors with each other. In the opinion of the authors, tranylcypromine, pargyline, and phenelzine are the most effective of the MAO inhibitors, in that order, and isocarboxazid and nialamide show the least antidepressant activity.

MAO Inhibitors vs. Tricyclic Drugs. Table 9 summarizes studies comparing MAO inhibitors with imipramine. In general, the MAO inhibitors are slightly less effective than imipramine, although tranylcypromine approaches imipramine in efficacy. The possibility cannot be ignored, however, that certain distinct types of depression may be uniquely sensitive to the MAO inhibitors. Indeed, clinical evidence suggests that this may be so and may run in families. Definite evidence is not yet available on this point.

Table 8. *Antidepressant Drugs vs. Placebo in Controlled, Double-Blind Studies of Drugs in the Treatment of Depression*

Drug	No. of Studies	Percentage of Studies in Which Drug Was:	
		Better than Placebo	Equal to Placebo
Tricyclic Antidepressants			
Imipramine (Tofranil)	38	68.4	31.6
Amitriptyline (Elavil)	11	81.8	18.2
Nortriptyline (Aventyl)	4	100.0	0.0
Desipramine (Pertofrane)	5	60.0	40.0
Trimipramine (Surmontil)*	3	66.7	33.3
Protriptyline (Vivactyl)	2	100.0	0.0
Opipramol (Ensidon)*	6	100.0	0.0
Iprindole (Pramindole)	3	100.0	0.0
All Tricyclic Drugs	72	76.4	23.6
MAO Inhibitors			
Iproniazid (Marsilid)*	7	57.1	42.9
Nialamide (Niamid)	4	0.0	100.0
Phenelzine (Nardil)	7	57.1	42.9
Isocarboxazid (Marplan)	6	33.3	66.7
Tranylcypromine (Parnate)	3	66.7	33.3
Pargyline (Eutonyl)	2	100.0	0.0
Pheniprazine (Catron)*	2	50.0	50.0
Etryptamine (Monase)*	1	100.0	0.0
All MAO Inhibitors	32	50.0	50.0
Other Therapies			
Amphetamines	3	0.0	100.0
Chlorpromazine (Thorazine)	3	100.0	0.0
Electroconvulsive Therapy	8	87.5	12.5

* Not currently available on the United States market.

Dosage. The daily doses for the MAO inhibitors are: phenelzine, 30 to 90 mg.; tranylcypromine, 10 to 60 mg.; isocarboxazid, 10 to 30 mg.; and nialamide, 25 to 300 mg. Phenelzine may be preferable to tranylcypromine, since the former is not associated with so high an incidence of hypertensive crisis.

Time-Course of Action. MAO inhibitors show a latency of action of about three weeks. Thus, it is unreasonable to give a MAO inhibitor for a few days or a couple of weeks and then conclude that it is ineffective. If no improvement occurs after four weeks, then another drug should be

Table 9. *Antidepressant Drugs vs. Imipramine in Controlled, Double-Blind Studies of Drugs in the Treatment of Depression*

Drug	No. of Studies	Percentage of Studies in Which Drug Was:		
		Better than Imipramine	Equal to Imipramine	Worse than Imipramine
Tricyclic Antidepressants				
Amitriptyline (Elavil)	8	25.0	75.0	0.0
Desipramine (Pertofrane)	7	0.0	85.7	14.3
Trimipramine (Surmontil)*	2	100.0	0.0	0.0
Protriptyline (Vivactyl)	3	0.0	100.0	0.0
Monochlorimipramine*	1	0.0	100.0	0.0
Opipramol (Ensidon)*	1	0.0	100.0	0.0
All Tricyclic Drugs	22	18.2	77.3	4.5
MAO Inhibitors				
Phenelzine (Nardil)	7	0.0	57.1	42.9
Isocarboxazid (Marplan)	5	0.0	60.0	40.0
Tranylcypromine (Parnate)	3	0.0	100.0	0.0
Iproniazid (Marsilid)*	2	0.0	50.0	50.0
Nialamide (Niamid)	2	0.0	50.0	50.0
Pheniprazine (Catron)*	2	0.0	50.0	50.0
All MAO Inhibitors	21	0.0	61.9	38.1
Other Therapies				
Electroconvulsive Therapy	7	42.9	57.1	0.0
Thioridazine (Mellaril)	1	0.0	100.0	0.0
Chlorpromazine (Thorazine)	3	0.0	100.0	0.0
Chlorprothixene (Taractan)	1	0.0	100.0	0.0
Dibenzepin	1	0.0	100.0	0.0

* Not currently available on the United States market.

tried. When changing from an MAO inhibitor to a tricyclic drug, one should wait a week or two after discontinuation of the MAO inhibitor before instituting tricyclic therapy. In changing from a tricyclic drug to a MAO inhibitor, four days is an adequate time period.

Contraindications. Headaches and hypertensive crises may occur when patients on MAO inhibitors ingest cheese, particularly cheeses, such as cheddar, containing large amounts of tyramine (tyramine is a pressor amine normally destroyed by MAO). Other foods containing appreciable amounts of tyramine include beer, Chianti wine, yeast products (Bovril, Marmite), chicken livers, and pickled herring. These foods should be avoided by patients on MAO inhibitors.

MAO inhibitors potentiate a wide variety of drugs, such as tricyclic antidepressants, sympathomimetic amines (such as amphetamine, ephedrine, and phenylephrine), analgesics (such as opiates and meperidine), barbiturates, dopa (including that found in fava beans), alpha-methyldopa, ganglionic blocking agents, reserpine, and ether and other anesthetic agents. These drugs are relatively contraindicated in patients receiving MAO inhibitors. Patients should be warned against over-the-counter preparations such as nose drops and decongestants that contain sympathomimetic agents. There have been few problems as a result of local anesthetics used in dental work, but some patients have increased jitteriness in response to the epinephrine present in such injections. MAO inhibitors should be discontinued one to two weeks prior to surgery. There may be an interaction between *meperidine* (Demerol®, Winthrop) and some MAO inhibitors through a different mechanism, suggesting that meperidine is relatively contraindicated in patients on MAO inhibitors.

Side Effects.

Liver Effects. Iproniazid was removed from the market because it was said to cause severe hepatic necrosis, although this has never been proved. The incidence of this side effect ranged from 1 in 3,000 patients to 1 in 10,000, and the fatality rate from this condition was about 25 per cent.

There have been reports of jaundice occurring with other hydrazine MAO inhibitors, but it occurs less frequently with these drugs than with iproniazid. Cross sensitivity has been observed: Patients given a second trial of a different hydrazine MAO inhibitor may have a recurrence of jaundice. Therefore, the free hydrazine is suspected as the causative agent rather than the MAO-inhibiting property of these drugs. Jaundice has not been reported with nonhydrazine MAO inhibitors.

If jaundice occurs, the drug should be stopped immediately until the cause of the jaundice can be determined. This is a very rare side effect, so rare, in fact, that the role of the MAO inhibitor as a causative agent in the jaundice has never been proved.

Central Nervous System Effects. MAO inhibitors can convert a retarded depression into an agitated depression and occasionally can precipitate hypomania or an acute schizophrenic psychosis. These drugs may also produce an acute confusion reaction, with disorientation, mental clouding, hallucinations, and illusions. The MAO inhibitors have been associated with altered erotic desires, edema, and muscle tremor and can cause dizziness, generalized weakness, drowsiness, fatigue, slurred speech, insomnia, overactivity, overstimulation, jitteriness, increased muscle tone, hyperreflexia, clonus, and an occasional peripheral neuropathy.

In most cases, reducing the dosage or switching to another medication is the best course of action in treating these side effects. More typically, there is reduced need for sleep, but this does not require treatment. Induced mania or schizophrenia should be treated as any other case of mania or schizophrenia.

Autonomic Effects. Hypertensive crisis is a particularly serious side effect. This syndrome is also accompanied by headache and occasionally by intracranial hemorrhage. The headaches have a sudden onset and are usually occipital, but they may radiate frontally and become generalized. Other symptoms are sweating, pallor, chills, painful stiff neck, nausea, vomiting, fright, restlessness, muscle twitching, chest pains, and palpitations. There is now ample evidence that hypertensive crisis is associated with incompatible foods and drugs.

The best treatment for hypertensive crisis is prophylactic. The patient should be given a detailed list of those foods and drugs to be avoided. If hypertensive crisis does occur, it can be treated by 5 mg of phentolamine intravenously or 50 to 100 mg. of chlorpromazine intramuscularly.

Most autonomic side effects of the MAO inhibitors are anticholinergic and may include orthostatic hypotension, dizziness, blurred vision, dry mouth, epigastric distress, constipation, delayed micturition, delayed ejaculation, and impotence. Patients often adjust to the hypotension, and no medication should be given unless the patient complains of symptoms. Dry mouth may be treated with glycerine-based lozenges.

Patients should be cautioned that reduction of bowel frequency may occur without loss of health. In fact, one bowel movement a week is often sufficient. If a laxative is necessary, a bulk laxative, mineral oil, or the addition of laxative foods to the diet is to be preferred. The next step would be the addition of a stool-softening agent or a saline cathartic such as milk of magnesia. Peristaltic agents should be avoided.

Increase in appetite and weight is common. If there is an improvement in weight without an increase in appetite, the physician should be suspicious, since such patients are occasionally suicide risks.

Overdose. Davis, Bartlett, and Termini (1968) surveyed the literature on overdoses of MAO inhibitors and found 12 deaths attributable to these drugs. Symptoms of overdosage typically do not appear until several hours or more after ingestion of the drug, so the patient should be kept under observation for at least 24 hours. Chlorpromazine, presumably because of its adrenergic-blocking activity, may be useful drug in the treatment of such overdoses

Tricyclic Drugs

The tricyclic drugs currently available on the United States market are *imipramine* (Tofranil®, Geigy), *desipramine* (Norpramin®, Lakeside; Pertofrane®, Geigy), *amitriptyline* (Elavil®, Merck Sharp & Dohme), *nortriptyline* (Aventyl®, Lilly), *protriptyline* (Vivactil®, Merck Sharp & Dohme), and *doxepin* (Sinequan®, Pfizer). Tricyclics not on the American market include *trimipramine* (Surmontil®, Rhone-Poulenc), and *opipramol* (Ensidon®, Geigy).

Mechanism of Action. The tricyclic drugs inhibit the re-uptake of catecholamines by the neurons, but it has not been established that this is the mechanism of the antidepressant effect in man.

Efficacy. Table 8 summarizes those double-blind studies in which tricyclic drugs were compared with a placebo. The tricyclic drugs are clearly more effective than a placebo. When the data from the individual studies were pooled, it was found that 70 per cent of the patients on imipramine improved, compared with 39 per cent of the patients on a placebo.

Those studies comparing tricyclic drugs with imipramine as a standard drug are summarized in Table 9. Most of the tricyclic drugs are approximately equal to imipramine in efficacy.

The imipramine-type drugs show a consistent superiority to MAO inhibitors. More patients improve on tricyclic drugs than on MAO inhibitors. Thus, the tricyclic drugs should be considered the drugs of first choice in treating depressed patients.

Imipramine and MAO inhibitors have been found to be effective in patients who are not depressed but show phobic symptoms associated with recurrent severe anxiety attacks. These patients do not respond to any of the existing tranquilizers. In general, paranoid patients and patients with a self-critical premorbid personality tend not to do well on imipramine.

Dosage. Tricyclic drugs are effective in a wide range of doses, since patients metabolize these drugs at different rates. The dosage regimen for imipramine, amitriptyline, and desipramine is 75 to 150 mg. a day for the first week, and 150 to 225 mg. a day for the second week, with the dose of nortriptyline being slightly less. The effective dose range for protriptyline is between 10 and 60 mg. a day.

Time-Course of Action. The tricyclic antidepressants should be tried for a period of at least four weeks before concluding that the patient is not being helped by these drugs. If no effect is noted after four weeks of treatment with a particular tricyclic drug, it is unlikely that further improvement will occur. There is little evidence that the desmethyl derivatives, desipramine and nortriptyline, are substantially more rapid in action than their parent compounds (imipramine and amitriptyline), although this was a theoretical possibility, since the parent drugs are metabolized to their desmethyl derivatives.

Recent reports have suggested that administration of thyroid hormone may shorten the latency of action of the tricyclic drugs. Dexamethasone has also been reported to shorten the lag period before clinical improvement is seen with these drugs.

Contraindications. Tricyclic drugs should not routinely be given simultaneously with MAO inhibitors. If a patient on an MAO inhibitor is switched to a tricyclic drug, a washout period of two weeks should be allowed.

Tricyclic drugs should be used with caution in patients with glaucoma or urinary retention. Since tricyclic drugs lower the seizure threshold, anticonvulsant drug dosage may need to be increased in patients with epilepsy. Tricyclic drugs should also be used with caution in patients with hyperthyroidism and cardiovascular disease. Sympathomimetic drugs should be used with caution in patients receiving tricyclic drugs.

Side Effects.

Central Nervous System Effects. The tricyclic drugs may cause a persistent, fine, rapid tremor in the upper extremities and in the tongue. Twitching, convulsions, dysarthria, paresthesia, peroneal palsies, and ataxia may occur in very rare instances. Disturbances of motor function are rare but may occur in elderly patients. These effects are best handled by decreasing the dosage or by switching to other drugs. Insomnia occurs occasionally, but for most patients the drugs have a sleep-regularizing action. When insomnia does occur, giving the medication at the beginning of the day effectively combats it. Occasionally, these drugs may precipitate schizophrenic, manic, or hypomanic excitement. Simply terminat-

ing the drug is usually not sufficient in such patients, and they should be treated as any acute schizophrenic or manic patient would be.

Autonomic Effects. The autonomic effects are primarily anticholinergic and include dry mouth, palpitations, tachycardia, loss of visual accommodation, postural hypotension, fainting, dizziness, vomiting, profuse sweating, urinary bladder atonia, constipation, and aggravation of glaucoma. On the whole, these side effects are very mild and become even less troublesome after the first few weeks. They can usually be controlled by adjusting the dosage of the drug. The management of dry mouth and constipation has been discussed under side effects of MAO inhibitors. Mild withdrawal symptoms (such as malaise, nausea, and headache) may occur on rare occasions after abrupt termination of the tricyclic drugs. Such symptoms are best treated by reinstituting treatment and then gradually withdrawing the drug over a period of a few days.

Urinary retention and paralytic ileus can occur with the tricyclic drugs, particularly when they are given with other anticholinergic drugs. In controlled studies, several of the tricyclic drugs have been found to be effective in treating enuresis.

Other Side Effects. Both imipramine and amitryptyline may cause flattened T-waves, prolonged Q-T intervals, and depressed S-T segments on the electrocardiogram. Skin reactions, photosensitivity, jaundice of the chlorpromazine type, and agranulocytosis occur in rare instances. The jaundice results from a mild degree of obstruction, with a mechanism similar to that of phenothiazine-induced jaundice.

Overdose. In their literature review of overdose of psychotropic drugs, Davis, Bartlett, and Termini (1968) found 203 adult cases of poisoning from tricyclic antidepressant drugs, 20 of which were fatalities. Of 47 cases of overdosage in children, 15 were fatal. Suitable caution must thus be observed in the prescription of large amounts of these drugs, particularly since patients for whom these drugs are prescribed are often high suicide risks. Problems in management consist of seizures and abnormal cardiac rhythms. Dilantin can be helpful in the prevention of both of these toxic manifestations.

Other Antidepressants

A number of phenothiazines have been found to be effective as antidepressants. Chlorpromazine and imipramine were found to be comparably effective and much superior to placebo in agitated depressions. A National Institute of Mental Health study found chlorpromazine to be superior to a placebo in depressed inpatients. In a Veterans Administration study, thioridazine and perphenazine were found to be effective antidepressants (Overall et al., 1964). One group found that retarded depressions responded better to tricyclic drugs, anxious depressions responded better to phenothiazines, and hostile depressions responded equally well to both types of drugs. The role of tricyclics in endogenous and retarded depression is well established. More research needs to be done to define the role of phenothiazines in anxious and hostile depressions.

Doxepin (Sinequan®, Pfizer) is a new drug that has been claimed to have both antidepressant and antianxiety properties. It has been shown to be equivalent to amitriptyline in the treatment of depression in several double-blind studies and has also been shown to be the equivalent of chlordiazepoxide in the treatment of anxiety. No study has shown this drug to be less effective than either amitriptyline or chlordiazepoxide. Although it is possible that the initial reports of the efficacy of this drug in both anxiety and depression represent a certain overenthusiasm for a new drug, these reports are nevertheless impressive. This drug may prove particularly useful in the treatment of mixed depression-anxiety states. It is discussed at greater length below.

Lithium carbonate may be effective as a prophylactic in patients with recurrent depression (see following 3 pages).

Drug Combinations

A Veterans Administration study found amitriptyline superior to the combination of amitriptyline and perphenazine in retarded depressives, but the combination was superior in anxious and hostile depressives (Hollister et al., 1966). The General Practitioner Research Group found the perphenazine-amitriptyline combination no more efficacious than either drug alone, and another study found the combination equal to amitriptyline alone. Other studies have found the combination superior to placebo and to chlordiazepoxide.

Parstelin is a combination of tranylcypromine (Parnate®, Smith, Kline & French) and trifluoperazine (Stelazine®, Smith, Kline & French). It was shown to be effective in three groups of psychotically depressed patients.

Antidepressants and Social Therapies

Only a few controlled studies have tested the relative efficacy of drug therapy with social or psychotherapy in the treatment of depression. In one study, Daneman (1961) treated 195 depressed patients, of whom 159 had psychoneurotic depressions, 32 had psychotic depressions, and four had organic brain syndromes with depression. All patients were seen in psychotherapy once or twice a week and were treated with either 100 to 200 mg. a day of imipramine or 0.7 to 1.4 mg. a day of an atropine placebo. Drug administration was double-blind, and all patients were assessed after two months. In the imipramine group, complete remission occurred in only 10 per cent of the patients, and there was a failure rate of 52 per cent. This study shows that imipramine is a useful adjunct to psychotherapy in depressed patients.

In the experience of the authors, exploratory psychotherapy with extremely depressed patients is not likely to be rewarding. The patient's life should be structured to discourage withdrawal, brooding, and ruminating. Social support and interaction are of marked value. Once the depression has lifted, insight psychotherapy is likely to be more productive. Indeed, the timing of insight psychotherapeutic intervention can be important. In many cases it is best to intensify efforts just as the depression lifts.

DRUGS FOR TREATMENT OF MANIA

Lithium

Lithium is a chemical element belonging to the same family as sodium and potassium. As a free metal, it is highly toxic, but in the form of a salt, such as lithium carbonate, it becomes a highly specific agent for the therapy of manic excitement when properly administered. In the 1940's, lithium chloride was used as a salt substitute in patients on low-salt diets. This was a most unfortunate usage, since the two major contraindications to the use of lithium salts are cardiac and renal decompensation, and these were precisely the conditions present in the patients to whom large amounts of lithium chloride were given, and the consequences were disastrous; several patients died. The subsequent toxic reputation of lithium served to hinder its widespread acceptance in psychiatry for many years.

In 1949, Cade, an Australian psychiatrist, first noted the beneficial effects of the lithium ion in mania. This experimenter was studying the question of whether urates enhanced the toxicity of urea in guinea pigs, and he was using lithium urate, simply because it was the most soluble urate. After administering lithium to experimental animals, he noted that it made the animals lethargic and unresponsive to stimuli. This and later observations led him to use lithium salts in manic patients, and all ten of his original group of patients with mania showed improvement.

Lithium salts attracted little attention in psychiatry for the next 15 years because (1) the geographic isolation of Australia hindered communication; (2) psychiatrists were not oriented to the use of drugs in psychiatry in 1949; (3) the toxic hazards of lithium salts discouraged their use; (4) manics are rarely seen in psychiatric practice, so an antimanic drug did not attract much attention; and (5) the drug was not commercially profitable, so drug companies did not investigate or promote it. In recent years, however, this drug has been studied quite intensely, and it is now available on the United States drug market in several preparations (Eskolith®, Smith, Kline & French;

Lithenate®, Rowell; Lithane®, Roerig).

Indications for Use. Lithium salts are the drug of choice for hypomanic states and have been considered to be very useful in acute mania (often combined with haloperidol or a phenothiazine) and in the prophylaxis of recurrent mania, cyclic manic-depressive reactions, and recurrent depression. They may be useful in some types of schizo-affective disorders as well as in some cases of obsessive-compulsive conditions, premenstrual tension, excitement states, and personality disorders. The use of lithium is not recommended in schizophrenia, neuroses, organic brain disease, and toxic psychoses.

Mechanism of Action. The action of lithium is clearly antimanic, without the production of sedation. The lithium-treated patient is able to feel appropriate happiness, joy, or excitement without manic elation or loss of control. On a biochemical level, it has been postulated, with much supportive evidence, that the lithium ion acts in a manner opposite to that of the antidepressant drugs. That is, by increasing the reuptake or norepinephrine at the synaptic junction, it reduces the amount of norepinephrine present at the receptor sites in the brain.

Dosage. Lithium is a drug with a narrow therapeutic index. That is, the ratio between the toxic level in the serum and the effective dose level is very low. This is a drug that is to be used with care, and its use should be restricted to the specialist who is familiar with the drug and is able to take appropriate precautions against the possibility of overdose toxicity. It has been recommended that serum lithium levels be drawn on a weekly basis during dosage adjustment, or twice weekly if the dose is being adjusted rapidly, and on a monthly basis for the first year of maintenance therapy. Of course, serum lithium levels should be tested immediately if signs of early toxicity appear or if the patient begins to relapse into either a manic or depressed state. In addition, serum should be drawn one week after any change in maintenance dosage, after any significant change in the patient's salt intake, or after the initiation of treatment with diuretics.

Lithium is most commonly administered

in the form of 300-mg. (5-grain) lithium carbonate tablets, which correspond to a lithium ion content of 56 mg. or 8 mEq. The initial dosage is four to six tablets daily, but the therapeutic dose is variable and relates to the patient's age, body weight, clinical condition, and the amount needed to bring blood levels of lithium ions up to a minimal level of 1.5 mEq. per liter in acute mania and 0.6 to 1.0 mEq. per liter maintenance. A concentration higher than 2 to 2.5 mEq. per liter is unwise.

Time-Course of Action. The effect of therapy usually becomes apparent in a few days to a week and reaches a reasonable degree of antimanic action in six to 20 days. After two or three weeks, the dosage can usually be decreased to about three to five tablets daily. Dosage individualization is essential, and monitoring of serum lithium ion levels is required. The usual maintenance dose of 900 mg. of lithium carbonate daily gives serum Li^+ levels of 0.6 to 1.0 mEq. per liter.

In acute manic states, lithium is often given in combination with a phenothiazine or haloperidol. This combination results in a faster reduction of mania, and the phenothiazine or haloperidol may be gradually reduced after control of the acute episode is achieved. In depressive states, lithium may be given in combination with an antidepressant drug. The antidepressant may be continued for two to six weeks after the depression has lifted and then reduced gradually. In states of remission, lithium alone is usually sufficient.

Side Effects. Lithium salts are relatively contraindicated in patients with cardiac or renal failure and should be used with care in patients who are hypertensive or are being treated with thyroid extract. They are not contraindicated in children but must be given in lower doses in the elderly patient due to reduced renal clearance and possibly greater sensitivity.

Diarrhea, nausea, and vomiting are common during the first few days of lithium therapy and can be controlled by reducing the dose for a few days. Many lithium-treated patients show a fine tremor of the hand. It is often impossible to keep the dose low enough to avoid the tremor and still obtain therapeutic benefit. If the tremor becomes severe enough to interfere with body activity or the use of the hand or if it is accompanied by a tremor of the jaw, lithium carbonate dosage should be reduced. These symptoms will disappear within a few days and lithium therapy can then be restarted.

Signs of impending severe lithium toxicity are drowsiness, tinnitus, blurred vision, fatigue, thirst, vertigo, uncertain gait, dry mouth, slight confusion, slurred speech, coarse tremor, muscle twitching, and dysarthria. Other nondangerous side effects that may occur are weight gain, a subjective feeling of motor weakness, headache, mild cramps, insomnia, minimal edema, acne, skin rashes, alopecia areata, and angioneurotic edema. Lithium intoxication is also marked by excessive thirst, with increase in water intake and urine output, ataxia, giddiness, tremor, confusion, fasciculation, hyperreflexia or hyporeflexia, persistent diarrhea and vomiting, nystagmus, seizures, focal neurological signs, and, occasionally, visual and tactile hallucinations. These symptoms can progress to coma and death.

The treatment of lithium intoxication is generally supportive in nature. Lithium is excreted primarily through the kidney with four-fifths of the filtered lithium being reabsorbed via the proximal tubule. Lithium has a plasma half-life of about 24 hours. The half-life may be increased in patients with renal disease or in the elderly. In the treatment of lithium intoxication, electrolytes, respiration, blood pressure, caloric requirements, pH, and water intake should be monitored at regular intervals and maintained at normal levels. The drug should be discontinued and its rate of disappearance followed by monitoring serum lithium levels. Lithium excretion may be promoted with urea (20 mg. intravenously two to five times a day) or mannitol (50 to 100 gm. intravenously a day), and clearance may be increased with aminophylline (0.5 gm. by slow intravenous administration). Alkalinization of urine has also been recommended, and dialysis may be used in especially severe cases.

A few patients, less than 1 per cent in one study, have developed goiter during lithium therapy. The euthyroid patient being treated with lithium undergoes a transient mild hypothyroidism with a rapid return to a euthyroid state after physiological compensatory mechanisms have had an opportunity to exert their effects. The patient who initially has underlying thyroid pathology may be unable to respond to the antithyroid effect of lithium and may develop a goiter. This condition, however, is not an indication for discontinuing lithium therapy, since the goiter can be controlled by the administration of thyroid hormone or desiccated thyroid. The clinician should be aware of the possibility of obtaining abnormal laboratory values for thyroid function tests while a patient is being treated with lithium.

About a fifth of patients on lithium therapy show reversible electrocardiographic changes similar to those occurring during treatment with imipramine. These changes are not accompanied by other abnormalities.

Several women who were undergoing treatment with lithium gave birth to babies with birth defects, although this result has not been shown to occur more frequently than in the general population, and most lithium mothers have had normal babies. However, it is recommended that lithium be avoided in the first trimester of pregnancy unless it is strongly indicated.

Side effects of lithium therapy can appear during intercurrent disease or hot weather. The physician should warn the patient of possible side effects and be prepared to reduce the dose if necessary. In addition, low-salt diets should be avoided during lithium therapy.

Other Antimanic Drugs

Haloperidol has been reported to be particularly effective in treating mania (Crane, 1967). Large doses of parenteral chlorpromazine have also been used. Of particular interest are two reports on the use of methysergide, an antiserotonin agent, which appears to have a marked, rapid-acting effect in mania. Unfortunately, these findings have not been replicated by other investigators.

DRUGS FOR TREATMENT OF ANXIETY

The term "minor tranquilizer," which is often applied to this group of drugs, is most unfortunate, since it implies that these agents act as major tranquilizers, but to a lesser degree, and that large doses of the minor tranquilizers have the same clinical effects as small doses of the major tranquilizers. Such is not the case. The minor tranquilizers resemble the sedative-hypnotic drugs more closely than they do the antipsychotic drugs.

The principal antianxiety drugs on the United States market are the propanediol derivatives *meprobamate* (Miltown®, Wallace; Equanil®, Wyeth) and *tybamate* (Solacen®, Wallace; Tybatran®, Robins) and the benzodiazepine derivatives *chlordiazepoxide* (Librium®, Roche), *diazepam* (Valium®, Roche), and *oxazepam* (Serax®, Wyeth). *Nitrazepam* (Mogadon®), a benzodiazepine, is available on the European market. *Doxepin* (Sinequan®, Pfizer) is a new drug, related to the tricyclic drugs, that has both antidepressant and antianxiety properties. *Dixyrazine* (Esucos®, Union Chemique Belge) is a phenothiazine derivative with a benzodiazepine side chain; it has both antipsychotic and antianxiety effects and is available on the European market. Other anxiety drugs currently marketed in America include *hydroxyzine* (Atarax®, Roerig; Vistaril®, Pfizer), *emylcamate* (Striatran®, Merck Sharp & Dohme), *buclizine* (Softran®, Stuart), *phenaglycodol* (Ultran®, Lilly), and *benactyzine* (Suavitil®, Merck Sharp & Dohme).

Meprobamate and Tybamate

Meprobamate was first synthesized in 1950, and several derivatives of this drug are now on the market. These include tybamate, another antianxiety agent, and *carisoprodol* (Soma®, Wallace; Rela®, Schering), which has selective properties as a skeletal

Table 10. *Summary of the Controlled, Double-Blind Evaluations of the Minor Tranquilizers*

Drug	No. of Studies in Which Drug Was Compared to:*										
	Placebo		Barbiturates			Meprobate			Chlordiazepoxide		
	+	−	+	=	−	+	=	−	+	=	−
Barbiturates	12	4	—	—	—	—	—	—	—	—	—
Meprobamate (Miltown, Equanil)	16	6	4	3	1	—	—	—	—	—	—
Chlordiazepoxide (Librium)	25	2	4	3	0	2	3	1	—	—	—
Diazepam (Valium)	15	2	5	1	0	—	—	—	4	2	0
Oxazepam (Serax)	9	1	—	—	—	—	—	—	2	2	0
Tybamate (Solacen)	15	0	—	—	—	2	1	0	2	2	0
Doxepin (Sinequan)	5	0	—	—	—	—	—	—	1	1	0

* +, Drug was significantly better; =, there was no significant difference between drug and comparison agent; −, drug was equivalent to placebo or significantly less effective than its comparison agent.

muscle relaxant but negligible antianxiety effects.

Table 10 compares meprobamate and tybamate with a placebo. Meprobamate is significantly more effective than a placebo in some of the double-blind studies that have been done, and tybamate is significantly more effective than a placebo in all the double-blind studies that have made this comparison. Most of the studies found meprobamate to be equal to the barbiturates in efficacy, and in some studies there was a trend for meprobamate to be superior.

Dosage and Time-Course of Action. The usual dosage of meprobamate is 400 mg. three or four times a day, although dosages as high as 3,200 mg. a day may be given. The onset of action is rapid. When large doses of meprobamate have been given, sudden discontinuation of the drug may cause convulsions. The usual dosage of tybamate is two 250-mg. capsules three or four times a day. Tybamate appears to be particularly effective in the somatically oriented hypochrondriacal patient.

Side Effects. About half the patients on meprobamate develop drowsiness as a side effect. It is, therefore, wise to start with a small dose and build up to a therapeutic dose within three or four days. While on these drugs, patients should be warned against driving and undertaking other hazardous tasks that require alertness. The sedative effect of meprobamate is potentiated by alcohol and other central nervous system depressants, and patients should be warned against even mild use of these agents. As little as one alcoholic drink can cause confusion or fainting or both.

Large doses of meprobamate are very rarely addicting; however, physiological dependence on tybamate is to the authors' knowledge unknown. Sudden withdrawal after high doses of meprobamate may cause anxiety, restlessness, weakness, convulsions, and delirium. This condition is best treated by reinstitution of the medication and slow withdrawal in a supervised setting.

Such paradoxical reactions as stimulation, hyperactivity, angry outbursts, depersonalization, difficulty in concentrating, and thought blocking can occur, as can abnormalities in any of the physiological systems. These reactions, fortunately, are rare.

In their review of overdosage, Davis, Bartlett, and Termini (1968) found 120 cases of poisoning in which meprobamate was the only drug taken. Of these, 16 were fatalities, with the lowest fatal dose being 12 gm. (or 30 400-mg. tablets).

Benzodiazepine Derivatives

The first of the benzodiazepine derivatives, synthesized in 1957, was chlordiazepoxide. Two additional derivatives of this class are now available in the United States, diazepam and oxazepam (Daneman, 1964; Gardos et al., 1968; Lipman et al., 1965). Other benzodiazepines are available on foreign markets and/or are under study in the United States and elsewhere. These drugs include *nitrazepam* (Mogadon) and *prazepam.*

Table 10 shows comparisons of chlordiazepoxide, diazepam, and oxazepam with a placebo, meprobamate, and barbiturates. All three of the benzodiazepine drugs are better than a placebo in almost all the studies that have been done. About three-fourths of double-blind studies find the benzodiazepines to be more effective than the barbiturates; the remainder of these studies found no significant difference.

Dosage and Time-Course of Action. Typical daily dose schedules for the benzodiazepine minor tranquilizers are: chlordiazepoxide, 10 to 20 mg. three or four times a day; diazepam, 2 to 6 mg. three or four times a day; and oxazepam, 15 to 30 mg. three times a day. The drug effect usually manifests itself in a few days.

Side Effects. The benzodiazepines, like other antianxiety agents, cause sedation. Because of this, it is wise to start with a small dose and build up to the full therapeutic dose in three or four days. Patients should be warned against the concurrent use of alcohol and other sedative agents and should also be cautioned about driving and undertaking other tasks that require alertness.

Other central nervous system effects include blurred vision, diplopia, slurred speech, tremor, and hypotension. In doses far exceeding the therapeutic range, chlordiazepoxide can cause physiological dependence, but its use as an intoxicant is relatively uncommon. As with meprobamate, paradoxical reactions can occur, as can abnormalities of any of the physiological systems.

Davis, Bartlett, and Termini (1968) located 27 cases of benzodiazepine overdose, of which only three cases were severe. No fatal cases were found in the literature. Thus, from the standpoint of overdose lethality, these drugs are relatively nontoxic.

Antianxiety Drugs and Psychotherapy

Lorr et al. (1963) studied 150 male Veterans Administration outpatients who were divided into six groups according to their therapy: chlordiazepoxide and psychotherapy, chlordiazepoxide without psychotherapy, placebo and psychotherapy, placebo without psychotherapy, psychotherapy alone, and no treatment. Patients receiving psychotherapy were treated by psychotherapists at a frequency of one 50-minute session a week. Chlordiazepoxide was given in a dosage range of 20 to 80 mg. a day. According to the patients' reports, at the end of one week the drug was more effective than the placebo, and either the drug or the placebo was more effective than no capsule at all. After four weeks, either the drug or the placebo was still more effective than no capsule, but there was no longer a difference between the drug and the placebo, nor was there a difference between psychotherapy and no psychotherapy. According to the therapists' reports, at the end of four weeks, chlordiazepoxide was more effective than a placebo, and capsules were more effective than no capsules. Patients receiving chlordiazepoxide showed more rapport in interviews. The medication did not impede the interview relationship with any patient; indeed, it facilitated psychotherapy for about a third of the patients. Interestingly, the drop-out rate was higher for patients receiving psychotherapy than for patients not receiving psychotherapy.

Rickels et al. (1966) studied the effect of meprobamate compared with placebo under double-blind conditions, combined with psychotherapy by five private psychiatrists. The study involved a total of 114 patients, some of whom received meprobamate at a dose of 1,600 mg. a day. Psychotherapy was conducted once a week. Ratings at the end of four and six weeks showed that meprobamate was more effective than placebo. In other words, meprobamate appeared to produce an added benefit in patients undergoing psychotherapy.

Jacobs et al. (1966) found that diazepam, also, helped patients in psychotherapy more than did placebo. In fact, in all such studies drugs were found to be helpful to patients undergoing psychotherapy. We know of no instance when drug treatment has been detrimental to psychotherapy.

Barbiturates

The first barbiturate to be used in medicine was *barbital* (Veronal®), introduced in 1903. *Phenobarbital* (Luminal®, Winthrop) was introduced in 1912, *amobarbital* (Amytal®, Lilly) in 1923, *pentobarbital* (Nembutal®, Abbott) and *secobarbital* (Seconal®, Lilly) in 1930, *thiopental* (Pentothal®, Abbott) in 1935, and *hexobarbital* (Evipal®, Winthrop) in 1936. In all, approximately 2,500 barbiturates have been synthesized, and 50 barbiturates have been used clinically.

The barbiturates can be classified as long-acting (such as barbital and phenobarbital), medium- to short-acting (such as butabarbital, amobarbital, pentobarbital, and secobarbital), and ultrashort-acting (such as thiopental and hexobarbital). Long-acting barbiturates are useful as sedatives in chronic anxiety but are relatively poor hypnotics. Medium- to-short-acting barbiturates are useful in the treatment of acute and chronic anxiety. Commonly used barbiturates are represented in Table 11.

Phenobarbital is relatively ineffective in acute anxiety but effective in chronic anxiety. Medium-length barbiturates are also effective in chronic anxiety and can produce a dramatic antianxiety effect in an acute anxiety attack. Sometimes a patient will derive a sense of control over episodes of acute anxiety from the knowledge that he has a few barbiturate tablets in his pocket and can control an anxiety attack if it develops. This sense of control both prevents the development of anticipatory anxiety and allows the patient to overcome his fears.

Table 11. *Commonly Used Barbiturates**

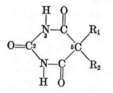

Group and Drug	Side Chains			Hypnotic Dose (gm.)
	R₁	R₂	N₃	
Ultrashort-Acting Group†				
Thiopental (Pentothal)	Ethyl	1-Methylbutyl	H,S replaces O on C₂	Intravenous anesthesia
Thiamylal (Surital)	Allyl	1-Methylbutyl	H,S replaces O on C₂	Intravenous anesthesia
Hexobarbital (Evipal)	Methyl	Cyclohexenyl	1-Methyl	Intravenous anesthesia
Short-Acting Group‡				
Secobarbital (Seconal)	Allyl	1-Methylbutyl		0.1
Pentobarbital (Nembutal)	Ethyl	1-Methylbutyl		0.1
Butabarbital (Butisol)	Ethyl	n-Butyl		0.1
Amobarbital (Amytal)	Ethyl	Iso-Amyl		0.1–0.2
Long-Acting Group§				
Barbital (Veronal)	Ethyl	Ethyl		0.3–0.5
Phenobarbital (Luminal)	Ethyl	Phenyl		0.1–0.2
Mephobarbital (Mebaral)	Ethyl	Phenyl		0.1–0.2

* Trade names in parentheses.
† Effects last less than two hours.
‡ Effects last less than eight hours.
§ Effects last more than eight hours.

The relative efficacy of minor tranquilizers and barbiturates is discussed elsewhere. The argument for the use of barbiturates concentrates on their inexpensiveness, the argument against their use is the real danger of habituation and their lethal effect in overdoses—as little as ten tablets, taken along with alcohol, can cause death. In elderly persons barbiturates can cause a paradoxical confusion.

Barbiturates are useful in inducing sleep in cases of ordinary insomnia. If the insomnia consists only of difficulty in falling asleep, 0.1- to 0.2-mg. doses of pentobarbital or secobarbital may be tried. Barbiturates have also been used as anticonvulsants and anesthetics and in neurological and electroencephalogram diagnosis.

Thiopental and amytal (so-called "truth serums") have been used to induce narcosis. While in this state, some neurotic patients can be encouraged to re-experience the traumatic event or events precipitating their symptoms during an interview. This abreaction brings relief from the symptoms. Although this method has been used in treating war neuroses and other traumatic neuroses, it is a specialized technique, regarded by some as controversial and/or dangerous, and in any case it is not generally used in group psychotherapy.

Another specialized use of medium-acting barbiturates, such as intravenous amobarbital (400 to 600 mg. in 10 cc. of water), is the control of acute psychosis or panic, barbiturate treatment being added to the usual antipsychotic drugs. Most such episodes can be well controlled with antipsychotic medication or diazepam or both, but occasionally barbiturates are used.

As noted earlier, the barbiturates are no substitute for the phenothiazines in schizophrenic patients and have no antipsychotic effect. Barbiturates were shown to be inferior to meprobamate in about half the studies reported above and inferior to chlordiazepoxide in most of the studies. Extreme caution should be used when prescribing barbiturates to depressed patients because of the potential lethal effects of these drugs.

Patients easily develop tolerance to barbiturates, and dosage must be increased to continue to produce the same effect. In addition to the hazard of addiction, idiosyncratic side effects may be encountered with barbiturate use. It must be remembered that barbiturates and alcohol are mutually potentiating. These drugs are highly lethal and should be dispensed only in small quantities to psychiatric patients. It has been reported clinically that occasionally patients can become more depressed on barbiturates, but the drug's role in this has not been clearly defined. On occasion, one will see a patient who has taken small doses of barbiturates for many years without ill effect. It is sometimes wise not to alter this equilibrium without positive indication that the change may be useful.

The most common situation to arise in group therapy involving prescription of barbiturates would probably be requests for medication to combat daytime anxiety or insomnia at night. If the anxiety or insomnia relates to an incipient schizophrenic or depressive episode, definitive treatment of the emerging disease is mandatory. Correct diagnosis and vigorous treatment are important in controlling the psychosis and preventing destructive behavior or suicide.

Patients often request sleeping medication or sedatives in instances when there is no clear indication. These requests can be dealt with in the group psychotherapy process by discussing the patient's anxiety and his reasons for desiring a "gift" of medication from the therapist.

Nonbarbiturate Sedatives

Glutethimide (Doriden®, Ciba) is structurally related to the barbiturates. It has been used widely as a hypnotic and a daytime sedative. Like barbiturates, glutethimide is addicting and is very lethal in large doses. It should be prescribed with the same vigilance that is exercised in the prescription of barbiturates.

Methyprylon (Noludar®, Roche) is similar in structure to glutethimede, and, like glutethimide, it is used as both a hypnotic and a daytime sedative. It is addicting and can be lethal in large doses.

Ethinamate (Valmid®, Lilly) is a reliable hypnotic with a very brief duration of action, the drug is, therefore, unsatisfactory as a daytime sedative. Like other sedatives, ethinamate is addicting, and, like other sedatives, it has been involved in fatal suicide attempts.

Ethchlorvynol (Placidyl®, Abbott) is useful as both a hypnotic and a daytime sedative. Both addiction and high-dose lethal effects have been reported.

Chloral hydrate is the oldest hypnotic, having been introduced into medicine in 1869. It is a relatively short-acting drug that is useful in initial insomnia, but it has less value as a daytime sedative. As with the other drugs discussed, addiction may occur with chloral hydrate, and overdoses may be fatal.

Paraldehyde is another traditional hypnotic, first introduced into medicine in 1882. It shares the sedative and hypnotic properties, as well as the overdose toxicity and habituation, of the other sedatives. It is not generally used for daytime sedation because it causes an unpleasant breath odor.

Psychomotor Stimulants

Amphetamine was first introduced into clinical practice in 1935 for the treatment of narcolepsy, a condition for which amphetamine is still indicated. The drug was found to produce a transient euphoria, which led to its widespread use in the treatment of depressive illness. Later, other agents were synthesized in order to obtain greater central stimulatory properties with less peripheral activity. These agents include *methamphetamine* (Methedrine®, Burroughs Wellcome; Desoxyn®, Abbott) and *methylphenidate* (Ritalin®, Ciba).

In general, these drugs have little value in the treatment of severe depression. In all well-controlled efficacy studies, amphetamine has been found no more effective than a placebo; indeed, in some studies patients treated with psychomotor stimulants have become worse. Methylphenidate was found to be of only slightly more value than a placebo in one study of mildly depressed patients. These drugs have never been demonstrated to be effective antidepressants in any adult population, whether general practice patients, depressed outpatients, or depressed inpatients. However, uncontrolled clinical experience suggests that some patients may benefit from these drugs. The possibility therefore exists that controlled studies have not identified the type of patient who is helped by psychomotor stimulants.

There is some clinical evidence that stimulants may be of some use in the first few days of tricyclic antidepressant treatment to provide an initial mood elevation during the lag period that precedes antidepressant action of the tricyclic.

Side effects of amphetamine and the other psychomotor stimulants include jitteriness, irritability, palpitations, postamphetamine fatigue, dejection, and, at high doses, a paranoia-like psychosis. Other side effects of amphetamine reflect its indirect sympathomimetic activity: dryness of the mouth, sweating, tremor, hyperreflexia, insomnia, tachycardia, and anorexia. Agitation and anxiety may become more prominent in a patient with schizophrenic disease. There is also a danger of hypertensive crises, particularly when amphetamine is injected intravenously in patients on monoamine oxidase inhibitors. Finally, it should be remembered that the psychomotor stimulants have a definite liability for abuse.

Chronic amphetamine abuse is often associated with irritability, restlessness, insomnia, and weight loss. But the most striking syndrome of chronic amphetamine abuse is the amphetamine psychosis, which often resembles a florid paranoid schizophrenia. This syndrome can be induced in normal people by administering high doses of the drug. Such conditions are characterized by paranoid ideation and visual and auditory hallucinations, which may occur in clear consciousness. Often the amphetamine psychosis will disappear in a few days after withdrawal of the drug.

Patients can become tolerant to amphetamine and take very large quantities without serious risk. In spite of this, amphetamine can be stopped suddenly without fear of the usual withdrawal symptoms, the sweating, restlessness, hallucinations, etc., that are seen with narcotic or barbiturate withdrawal. Persons coming off an amphetamine high often experience postamphetamine depres-

Table 12.   *Other Sedatives*

Drug	Structure	Hypnotic Dose
Glutethimide (Doriden)		0.5–1.0 gm.
Methyprylon (Noludar)		0.25–0.5 gm.
Chloral hydrate	$Cl_3C \cdot CH \cdot OH$	0.5–2.0 gm.
Paraldehyde		3–8 ml.
Ethinamate (Valmid)		0.5–1.0 gm.
Ethchlorvynol (Placidyl)		0.5–1.0 gm.

sion. In some cases this depression can be serious enough to lead to suicide. Despite the development of tolerance, amphetamine overdose can cause death.

The rate of excretion of amphetamine is markedly influenced by the pH of the urine. The drug is rapidly excreted in patients with acid urine and very slowly excreted by those with alkaline urine. Using labeled amphetamine, one of the authors (J. M. D.) has demonstrated that the disappearance of the drug from blood under alkaline urine conditions is very slow—a half-life of 24 to 36 hours, as contrasted with a half-life of 9 to 12 hours when the urine is acid. Under alkaline urine conditions a much greater proportion of amphetamine is metabolized to such products as hippuric acid and hydroxy-

amphetamine, but with acid urine most of the amphetamine is excreted as is. Table 12 lists sedatives and stimulants in current use.

OTHER DRUG TREATMENTS

Doxepin (Sinequan®, Pfizer) is a new drug that is claimed to have both antidepressant and antianxiety properties. This drug represents an important new class, the dibenzoxepines, which has some structural similarity to the tricyclic antidepressants but no real similarity to any of the minor tranquilizers. Doxepin has been evaluated for clinical efficacy in a series of double-blind controlled studies and has been found to be superior to a placebo in several studies, equal to or

Table 13. *Controlled Evaluations of Doxepin*

No. of Studies in Which Doxepin Was:	Population				
	Anxiety	Depression	Anxiety and Depression	Other	Total
Better than:					
Placebo	2	1	1	1	5
Chlordiazepoxide	1	—	—	—	1
Amitriptyline	—	—	1	—	1
Equal to:					
Chlordiazepoxide	1	—	—	—	1
Diazepam	2	—	1	—	3
Amitriptyline	—	—	1	—	1
Amitriptyline and Perphenazine	—	—	2	1	3
Better in 150-mg. Dose than in 75-mg. Dose	—	—	1	—	1

better than chlordiazepoxide, and equal in effectiveness to diazepam, amitriptyline, and an amitriptyline-perphenazine combination. Table 13 presents a summary of these studies.

Although it is true that many new drugs are initially greeted with enthusiasm and later turn out to be less effective than initial proponents claimed, the evidence for the therapeutic efficacy of doxepin is considerable. This drug is a promising agent. A better definition of its usefulness is awaited in treating severe depression in comparison with tricyclics, in treating the anxious outpatient in comparison with minor tranquilizers, and, especially, in treating depressed and anxious outpatients, where both of the drug's properties could be useful.

Benactyzine has been combined with meprobamate in a compound marketed as Deprol® (Wallace), which has both antianxiety and mild antidepressant properties. The compound has been used with some success in mild outpatient anxiety and depression.

Antidepressants have been found useful in the treatment of a phobic anxiety syndrome; this is discussed in more detail under antidepressant drugs (Klein, 1964).

Antipsychotic drugs have been shown to be equal to minor tranquilizers in a few studies of patients with anxiety. Chlorpromazine was shown to be equal to mepro-

bamate in one study and inferior to diazepam in two studies. Trifluoperazine was inferior to diazepam in two studies. Prochlorperazine was equal to meprobamate in one study but inferior in another study. Fluphenazine was equal to chlordiazepoxide in one study and inferior in a second study. Haloperidol was equal to chlordiazepoxide in one study.

Many factors could influence these results, and for various methodological reasons, the authors cannot reach any firm conclusions about the efficacy of phenothiazines as antianxiety drugs. Empirically, it seems that in some studies the phenothiazines are equal to the so-called minor tranquilizers in antianxiety properties, and in other studies they are inferior in the treatment of outpatients with nonpsychotic illnesses. The differential lack of effectiveness of the phenothiazines with outpatients may be due to side effects, for many nonpsychotic outpatients are alarmed by phenothiazine's side effects, believing them to be manifestations of their illness.

The authors disagree with the viewpoint that phenothiazine derivatives and minor tranquilizers act on the same illness continuum. The contention of the authors is that the phenothiazines, thioxanthenes, and butyrophenones are antipsychotic in action, but drugs of the meprobamate and chlordiazepoxide families are not. This is a clinically important distinction. Nevertheless, residents and medical students are taught in one Eastern medical school that the phenothiazines are major antianxiety drugs, the benzodiazepines are moderate antianxiety drugs, and meprobamate is for mild anxiety. This approach is scientifically unsound and may lead to poor medical treatment. It has never been demonstrated that chlordiazepoxide is better for moderate anxiety and meprobamate better for mild anxiety. Furthermore, minor tranquilizers have not been shown to be effective in the treatment of schizophrenia. Because of the aforementioned erroneous philosophy, then, many schizophrenics without severe anxiety may receive ineffective treatment unless the physician has concluded, as a result, for example, of some mental gymnastics, that he can use phenothiazines in these patients because they have severe "unconscious anxiety."

Antipsychotic drugs are the chemotherapy of choice for schizophrenia in particular and for psychosis in general. The minor tranquilizers are indicated for some cases of outpatient nonpsychotic anxiety. However, it is important to remember that some outpatients do much better on phenothiazines and that a few schizophrenics benefit from minor tranquilizers. The general principle of antipsychotic drugs for psychotics and antianxiety drugs for nonpsychotic outpatients is tempered by the observation that there is considerable variation in patient response to various drugs; an empirical trial is, therefore, indicated for many patients.

REFERENCES

Caffey, E. M., Jr., Diamond, L. S., Frank, T. V., Grasberger, J. C., Herman, L., Klett, C. J., and Rothstein, C. Discontinuation or reduction of chemotherapy in chronic schizophrenics. J. Chronic Dis., *17:* 347, 1964.

Caffey, E. M., Jr., and Klett, C. J. Side effects and laboratory findings during combined drug therapy of chronic schizophrenics. Dis. Nerv. Syst., *28:* 370, 1961.

Casey, J. F., Bennett, I. F., Lindley, C. J., Hollister, L. E., Gordon, M. H., and Springer, N. N. Drug therapy in schizophrenia. A controlled study of the relative effectiveness of chlorpromazine, promazine, phenobarbital, and placebo. Arch. Gen. Psychiat., *2:* 210, 1960.

Casey, J. F., Hollister, L. E., Klett, C. J., Lasky, J. J., and Caffey, E. M., Jr. Combined drug therapy of chronic schizophrenics. Controlled evaluation of placebo, dextro-amphetamine, imipramine, isocarboxazid and trifluoperazine added to maintenance doses of chlorpromazine. Amer. J. Psychiat., *117:* 997, 1961.

Casey, J. F., Lasky, J. J., Klett, C. J., and Hollister, L. E. Treatment of schizophrenic reaction with phenothiazine derivatives. A comparative study of chlorpromazine, triflupromazine, mepazine, prochlorperazine, perphenazine, and phenobarbital. Amer. J. Psychiat., *117:* 97, 1960.

Cole, J. O., and Davis, J. M. Antidepressant drugs. In *Comprehensive Textbook of Psychiatry*, p. 1263, A. M. Freedman and H. I. Kaplan, editors. Williams & Wilkins, Baltimore, 1967.

Cole, J. O., and Davis, J. M. Antipsychotic drugs. In *The Schizophrenic Syndrome*, p. 478, L. Bellak and L. Loeb, editors. Grune & Stratton, New York, 1969.

Cole, J. O., Goldberg, S. C., and Davis, J. M. Drugs in the treatment of psychosis: controlled studies. In *Psychiatric Drugs*, p. 153, P. Solomon, editor. Grune & Stratton, New York, 1966.

Crane, G. E. Iproniazid (Marsilid) phosphate, a therapeutic agent for mental disorders and debilitating disease. Psychiat. Res. Rep. Amer. Psychiat. Assoc., *8:* 142, 1957.

Crane, G. E. A review of clinical literature on haloperidol. Int. J. Neuropsychiat., *31 (Suppl. 1):* S110, 1967.

Curry, S. H., Davis, J. M., Janowsky, D. S., and Marshall, J. H. L. Factors affecting chlorpromazine plasma levels in psychiatric patients. Arch. Gen. Psychiat., *22:* 209, 1970.

Curry, S. H., Marshall, J. H. L., Davis, J. M., and Janowsky, D. S. Chlorpromazine plasma levels and effects. Arch. Gen. Psychiat., *22:* 289, 1970.

Daneman, E. A. Imipramine in office management of depressive reactions. A double blind clinical study. Dis. Nerv. Syst., *22:* 213, 1961.

Daneman, E. A. Double blind study with diazepam, chlordiazepoxide and placebo in the treatment of psychoneurotic anxiety. J. Med. Assoc. Georgia, *53:* 55, 1964.

Davis, J. M. Efficacy of tranquilizing and antidepressant drugs. Arch. Gen. Psychiat., *13:* 552, 1965.

Davis, J. M., Bartlett, E., and Termini, B. A. Overdose of psychotropic drugs: a review. Dis. Nerv. Syst., *20:* 157, 1968.

Davis, J. M., Lerman, G. L. and Schildkraut, J. J. Drugs used in the treatment of depression. In *Psychopharmacology. A Review of Progress 1957–1967*, p. 719, D. H. Efron, editor. United States Government Printing Office, Washington, D. C., 1968.

Evangelakis, M. G. De-institutionalization of patients. Dis. Nerv. Syst., *22:* 26, 1961.

Gardos, G., DiMascio, A., Salzman, C., and Shader, R. J. Differential actions of chlordiazepoxide and oxazepam on hostility. Arch. Gen. Psychiat., *181:* 757, 1968.

Goldberg, S. C. Prediction of response to antipsychotic drugs. In *Psychopharmacology. A Review of Progress 1957–1967*, p. 1101, D. H. Efron, editor. United States Government Printing Office, Washington, D. C., 1968.

Goldberg, S. C., Cole, J. O., and Klerman, G. L. Differential prediction of improvement under three phenothiazines. In *Prediction of Response to Pharmacotherapy*, p. 69, J. R. Wittenborn and P. R. A. May, editors. Charles C Thomas, Springfield, Ill., 1966.

Gorham, D. R., and Pokorny, A. D. Effects of a phenothiazine and/or group psychotherapy with schizophrenics. Dis. Nerv. Syst., *25:* 77, 1964.

Greenblatt, M., Solomon, M. H., Evans, A. S., and Brooks, G. W., editors. Drug and social therapy. In *Chronic Schizophrenia*, Charles C Thomas, Springfield, Ill., 1965.

Grinspoon, L., Ewalt, J. R., and Shader, R. Psychotherapy and pharmacotherapy in chronic schizophrenia. Amer. J. Psychiat., *124:* 1645, 1968.

Hollister, L. E., Caffey, E. M., Jr., and Klett, C. J. Abnormal symptoms, signs and laboratory tests during treatment with phenothiazine derivatives. Clin. Pharmacol. Ther., *1:* 284, 1960.

Hollister, L. E., Overall, J. E., Johnson, M. H., Shelton, J., Kimbell, I., Jr., and Brunse, A. Amitriptyline alone and combined with perphenazine in newly admitted depressed patients. J. Nerv. Ment. Dis., *142:* 460, 1966.

Honigfeld, G., Rosenblum, M. P., Blumenthal, I. J., Lambert, H. L., and Roberts, A. J. Behavioral improvement in the older schizophrenic patient: drug and social therapies. J. Amer. Geriat. Soc., *13:* 57, 1965.

Jacobs, M. A., Globus, G., and Heim, E. Reduction in symptomatology in ambulatory patients. The combined effects of a tranquilizer and psychotherapy. Arch. Gen. Psychiat., *15:* 45, 1966.

King, P. D. Controlled study of group psychotherapy in schizophrenics receiving chlorpromazine. Psychiat. Dig., *24:* 21, 1963.

Klein, D. F. Delineation of two drug-responsive anxiety syndromes. Psychopharmacologia, *5:* 397, 1964.

Klein, D. F., and Davis, J. M. *Diagnosis and Drug Treatment of Psychiatric Disorders*. Williams & Wilkins, Baltimore, 1969.

Kline, N. S. Clinical experience with iproniazid (Marsilid). J. Clin. Exp. Psychopath., *19 (Suppl. 1):* 72, 1958.

Kline, N. S. Depression: its diagnosis and treatment. Mod. Probl. Pharmacopsychiat., *3:* 1, 1969.

Kline, N. S., and Davis, J. M. Therapeutic efficacy of the phenothiazines and other antipsychotic agents. In *Drugs and the Brain*, p. 173, P. Black, editor. Johns Hopkins Press, Baltimore, 1969.

Lasky, J. J., Klett, C. J., Caffey, E. M., Bennett J. L., Rosenblum, M. P., and Hollister, L. E. Drug treatment of schizophrenic patients. A comparative evaluation of chlorpromazine, chlorprothixene, fluphenazine, reserpine, thioridazine and triflupromazine. Dis. Nerv. Syst., *23:* 98, 1962.

Lipman, R. S., Hammer, H. M., Bernardes, J. F., Park, L. C., and Cole, J. O. Patient report of significant life situation events. Methodological implications for outpatient drug evaluation. Dis. Nerv. Syst., *26:* 586, 1965.

Lorr, M., McNair, D. M., and Weinstein G. J. Early effects of chlordiazepoxide (Librium) used with psychotherapy. J. Psychiat. Res., *1:* 257, 1963.

May, P. R., and Tuma, A. H. Treatment of schizophrenia. An experimental study of five treatment methods. Brit. J. Psychiat., *111:* 503, 1965.

Michaux, M. H., Kurland, A. A., and Agallianos, D. Chlorpromazine, chlordiazepoxide and chlorpromazine-imipramine treatment of newly hospitalized acutely ill psychiatric patients. Curr. Ther. Res., *8:* 117, 1966.

National Institute of Mental Health-Psychopharmacology Service Center Collaborative Study Group. Phenothiazine treatment in acute schizophrenia, effectiveness. Arch. Gen. Psychiat., *10:* 246, 1964.

National Institute of Mental Health-Psychopharmacology Service Center Collaborative Study Group. Clinical effects of three phenothiazines in "acute" schizophrenia. Publication Report No. 6, United States Public Health Service, Bethesda, Md., 1966.

Overall, J. E., Hollister, L. E., Honigfeld, G., Kimbell, I. H., Jr., Meyer, F., Bennett, J. L., and Caffey, E. M., Jr. Comparison of acetophenazine with perphenazine in schizophrenics: demonstration of differential effects based on computer-derived diagnostic models. Clin. Pharmacol. Ther., *4:* 200, 1963.

Overall, J. E., Hollister, L. E., Meyer, F., Kimbell, I., Jr., and Shelton, J. Imipramine and thioridazine in depressed and schizophrenic patients. Are there specific antidepressant drugs? J. A. M. A., *189:* 605, 1964.

Rickels, K., Cattell, R. B., Weise, C., Gray, B., Yee, R., Mallin, A. and Aaronson, H. G.

Controlled psychopharmacological research in private psychiatric practice. Psychopharmacologia, *9:* 288, 1966.

Rickels, K., Jenkins, B. W., Zamostein, B., Raad, E., and Kanther, M. Pharmacotherapy in neurotic depression. Differential population responses. J. Nerv. Ment. Dis., *145:* 475, 1967.

Schiele, B. C., Vestre, N. D., and Stein, K. E. A comparison of thioridazine, trifluoperazine, chlorpromazine, and placebo: a double-blind controlled study on the treatment of chronic, hospitalized, schizophrenic patients. J. Clin. Exp. Psychopath., *23:* 151, 1961.

Simpson, G. M., Admin, M., and Kunz, E. Withdrawal effects of phenothiazines. Compr. Psychiat., *6:* 347, 1965.

Wheatley, D. Chlordiazepoxide trial. A report from the General Practitioner Research Group, prepared for the Psychopharmacology Service Center. National Institute of Mental Health, Washington, D. C., 1963.

5

Phoenix Houses: Therapeutic Communities for Drug Addicts

Mitchell S. Rosenthal, M.D. and D. Vincent Biase, Ph.D.

INTRODUCTION

Experience over the past ten years in different parts of the United States has shown that drug addiction can be treated effectively. Although a few psychotherapists have reported success in treating addicts individually, most of the reports have come from therapeutic community facilities such as Synanon in California, Daytop Village in New York, and the Addiction Research Center in Puerto Rico. We believe that Boorstein's statement—in Boorstein (1967) —about legal offenders in general applies particularly to drug addicts: "At the present time, the only approach to the problem which can possibly deal with the numbers involved and the ego defects present is the Therapeutic Community."

In fact, regardless of the availability of other treatment methods, the therapeutic community appears to be the most effective means of rehabilitating addicts. Successful treatment is possible only in a small community setting where each member is committed to eradicating antisocial and criminal behavior, with emotional support and consistent positive reinforcement provided by peers and staff.

PHOENIX HOUSE PROGRAMS

One such program is the Phoenix House program of the Addiction Services Agency (ASA) of the City of New York. Addicts come into the program through 12 neighhood storefront units called Phoenix Centers, which are manned by former addicts, and through recruiting programs at correctional institutions. The Phoenix Centers offer encouragement and counseling and, like the Phoenix Houses, a tumultuous but effective form of group therapy called encounters. Candidates for Phoenix House programs usually spend from one to three months in a center program while they break the drug habit.

Characteristics of Residents

When an addict is ready to commit himself to an intensified residential rehabilitation program, he may be admitted to a Phoenix House. Successful treatment usually takes 12 to 18 months, after which the person is transferred to an ASA Phoenix Re-entry House for 6 to 12 months for the final phases of social and vocational rehabilitation. Each Phoenix House has 70 to 80 residents, 20 to 30 per cent of them women. The residents have been drug abusers for an average of ten years. Their mean age is around 27, although we have had a boy as young as 10 and a man as old as 73 in the program.

Most of the residents have records of arrest; 85 per cent of the men and 60 per cent of the women have been arrested, with averages of four and two convictions. Ninety per cent of the women and 53 per cent of the men have no regular occupation. Few have gone beyond eleventh grade in school.

Facilities

There are a number of Phoenix Houses, all located in neighborhoods that have high rates of drug abuse. The houses actually are four- or five-story tenements, which have been renovated largely by Phoenix House work crews. When ASA acquires one of the buildings, either by purchase or lease, it sends in a crew of members to put the building in shape, except for work such as plumbing or wiring that requires skilled, licensed technicians. Some of the work crew camp out in the building until it becomes habitable, and others come during the day to help. Other Phoenix House members canvass the neighborhood for contributions of furnishings, money, and help. The responses have been tremendous. For example, members solicited $125,000 for one house. In addition, various groups and individuals in the neighborhood joined in to help with the renovation work.

ADVANTAGES OF RESIDENTIAL TREATMENT

Having treatment take place where drug problems flourish has many therapeutic advantages. One is that the helping resource is easily accessible and highly visible to those who need it most. We have found that the number recruited into a Phoenix Center

program is greater where the center is adjacent to a Phoenix House; the neighborhood addicts notice the improvement in the house residents and see hope for themselves.

In turn, the Phoenix House resident can contrast his new, more orderly life style with the squalid and unproductive modes of living of the neighborhood drug abusers. We believe that his recognition and appreciation of the differences represent a milestone in his emotional growth. Such awareness enhances his sense of identity and shows him that he is able to move upward in the social scale.

Although we assign clients to Phoenix Houses away from their own neighborhoods, to lessen the risk of their lapsing into their old ways with their old cronies, drug users can usually recognize one another. Thus the residents know that a "fix" is not too far away, but knowing that and choosing not to get one has proved to be a strengthening factor to them. It should be noted that new residents are not permitted to have visitors or to leave the house unaccompanied until they have been in the program for at least two months and have demonstrated some responsibility. To check for relapses into drug use, each week we test a random sample of one fifth of the population of each house, using thin-layer chromatography analysis of urine. During a recent three-month period, all the analyses yielded negative results.

STAFF

Each Phoenix House has three paid staff members: a director and two assistant directors, one a man and one a woman. They all have experienced and overcome some serious problem, such as addiction, alcoholism, or mental illness, and have been free of symptoms for several years. A number of them are graduates of similar programs, such as Synanon, and others have risen through the ranks of ASA programs. In addition to the paid staff, each house has two coordinators and seven department heads; they are house residents who have progressed to positions of authority. All of them, plus residents who are considered senior members because of the responsibility they have demonstrated, serve as role models for the other residents.

The lack of identity that characterizes the addict can best be overcome by giving him a role model he can identify with, understand, respect, and emulate. The Phoenix House leaders make excellent models because of their own experiences. Not only can they establish rapport readily, but they also personify a success that the new member can hope to achieve. The status system in a Phoenix House is based not on what a member attained before he entered the program but on what he accomplishes while in it.

Within the therapeutic community framework, those who are role models demonstrate alternative, positive ways of coping with stresses. They do so not in the neutral, didactic fashion of the Freudian therapist but in self-revealing, involved, and involving transactions with the community's members. Everything is out in the open; the members know practically everything there is to know about one another, contrasting with the typical "staff-patient" disparity of personal knowledge.

RULES AND PENALTIES

In each house the rules are strictly enforced. The street-culture code of "no squealing" is forbidden; each member has the duty to see that the rules are observed. All infractions are penalized, justly but severely. A member may be required to wear a sign or even have his head shorn, to remind himself and the others that deviance will not be tolerated. Penalties are determined by the director, although he may consult the members. The most severe punishment is to be ousted. So far, only two members have been forced to leave a community—one for repeatedly threatening physical harm to others, and the other for assaulting a fellow resident with a chair, although he was later readmitted. Informal penalties are imposed by the members on those who try to upset the therapeutic community system: the tough guy or rebel who seeks to enlist others in antiauthoritarian maneuvers is socially isolated.

COMMUNITY MEETINGS

The entire community meets at least once a day, usually after breakfast or lunch. The meeting is a structured session, not a free discussion group, and is led by one of the directors or coordinators. It usually consists of a report on important local or national news, on house activities and projects, and on visitors who are scheduled to observe the program. Problems concerning the entire community are handled in formal "bitch sessions" moderated by the staff, and special meetings may be called at any time to discuss rule violations or poor behavior.

ENCOUNTERS

Individual and interpersonal difficulties are usually handled through a form of group therapy called encounters. Each resident takes part in at least three encounters a week. An encounter consists of 8 to 12 members engaging in what might be called a verbal street fight: screaming and yelling and even profanity are encouraged, to heighten the emotional intensity. Laughter, rage, tears, and compassion pour forth. Nothing is barred, except dishonesty and physical violence. No topic is taboo, but the emphasis is on present behavior, not past. No member is immune, but no one is forced to participate.

Kinds of Encounters

The house coordinators arrange the encounters, balancing the group in terms of the members' articulateness, insight, and seniority, and putting together those who have been building up interpersonal pressures. Members may ask to be put into an encounter with certain others, or the coordinators may rig certain groupings—for example, by bringing together a hostile member with those who are the targets of his hostility. Encounters rarely include the same individuals twice in a row; the participants are changed to avoid a stagnant pecking order and reciprocal contracts. Such verbal or tacit contracts—for example, "If you won't mention my habitual lateness, I won't say anything about your constant swearing"—can be made with perhaps a dozen people, but hardly with the whole community.

Floor Encounter. There are two types of encounters. The basic one, called a floor encounter, is especially useful for newcomers. Emotional catharsis is the main goal, and the accuracy of the confrontation or interpretation is not important. The floor encounter is a training ground for newcomers to loosen up and toughen up psychologically, and to learn the encounter maneuvers. There is no appointed leader, but an unofficial leader often emerges from the interaction.

Tutorial Encounter. The tutorial encounter is for experienced participants, and is directed by a senior member or a staff person. The leader commands a powerful force in the group, and unleashes it on each member in turn. The tutorial sessions are both educational and cathartic, for each participant is enjoined to observe group processes and individual styles of defense.

How Encounters Work

Encounters address themselves to the problem of ignorance, in the psychological rather than the intellectual sense. Behavior that is antisocial, amoral, self-defeating, or immature is considered "stupid," and that attitude is expressed vividly and repeatedly during an encounter. The attack is directed toward past or present stupid behavior and also toward the ensuing rationalization and denial; it is amazing how quickly a member's façade of bravado, self-righteousness, or justification crumbles under the blistering scrutiny of the group.

The only effective defense is honesty, and the target member, once stripped of his pretenses, is open to learning healthier ways of reacting and behaving. Frequently the group will give him a suggestion to follow. For example, a member who has been generally sloppy in his appearance will be told to try being especially neat for a week, starting by shining his shoes and cutting his hair. A member who has been acting depressed may be told to go through the motions of being pleasant and enjoying activities. The group does not offer or accept reasons for a member's stupid behavior, but will tell him, "Maybe after you've been doing the right thing for a while, you'll understand why you used to screw things up."

There are rules to prevent members from taking the license of the encounter into other situations. Outside the encounters, they are expected to speak and act politely and to demonstrate social awareness. Following an encounter there is usually a social gathering, which serves as a decompression device. A member who has just been subjected to attack can get human first aid; he finds that the others still relate to him as a person, regardless of what went on in the encounter. Some of the areas covered in it may be talked over in the social gathering, but in a more restrained fashion than in the encounter.

WORK AND EDUCATIONAL PROGRAMS

The encounters are an important element of the treatment program, but the work and educational programs are also important. Each member is assigned to work in one of the seven departments. Job changes are frequent; the department heads readily arrange promotions, demotions, and transfers, sometimes to separate certain individuals or bring together others in order to highlight and resolve personality clashes. The important consideration is to keep each member active and involved and aware of his identity in the house community.

The sense of community is also enhanced by having the residents pool their welfare stipends toward the operating expenses of the house; each member then receives from 50 cents to 3 dollars a week for spending money, depending on his progress. The pooling of members' funds, plus what they contribute in work and solicit in money and goods, greatly increases their personal investment in the program. It also lowers the agency's cost to about 10 dollars a day for each resident.

Work Assignments

The work assignments in four of the seven departments—service, building, kitchen-commissary, and supply—are concerned with the physical operations and upkeep of the house. The administration department maintains all personnel records, census totals, and files of correspondence and administrative memos. The archives department is responsible for taking photographs and compiling scrapbooks of clippings about Phoenix House activities, as well as keeping bulletin boards and other house information records current. The education department conducts a variety of programs in which house members are both teachers and learners. It also maintains a library of fiction and nonfiction, and the department members are responsible for procuring and cataloguing the books and encouraging the residents to use them.

Education Programs

The education programs primarily are in the form of five types of seminars.

Seminars. The department seminars are lectures on topics of general interest given by members assigned to the department; they research their own topics, which include personality development, basic psychological principles, and proper English usage. The individual seminar is a talk given by a house member on a subject of his own choosing; when he needs or asks for assistance in preparing material, members of the education department provide close guidance.

The concept seminar is a free discussion based on an idea taken out of context from literature, philosophy, religion, or psychology: the idea is written on a blackboard, and the participants are invited to give their interpretations of it. It is designed to stimulate conceptual thinking and expression. In the impromptu-speaking seminar, a participant is given a topic for a five- to ten-minute talk, and allowed only a few minutes to collect his thoughts. Afterward the others offer constructive criticism of his speech. The fifth seminar is a debate, following the traditional collegiate rules. Two pairs of members are assigned the positive or negative side of an issue and given a set length of time to prepare their arguments and rebuttals. The debates encourage objective, analytic thinking and expression.

EVALUATION

House members are tested and evaluated periodically to ascertain their educational growth, and the results are recorded in their educational history charts. That chart, along with other records of personal development, accompanies the member when he completes the Phoenix House program and advances to a re-entry house for the final stages of resocialization and vocational training. As of 1969 ASA operated two re-entry houses serving a total of 72 residents. The re-entry program takes from 6 to 12 months, depending on the type of vocational training involved.

REFERENCES

Bassin, A. Daytop village. Psychol. Today, *2:* 48, 1968.

Calof, J. A study of four voluntary treatment and rehabilitation programs for New York City's narcotics addicts. Community Service Society of New York, New York, 1967.

Dole, V. P., and Nyswander, M. A. Medical treatment for diacetylmorphine (heroin) addiction. J.A.M.A., *193:* 646, 1965.

Einstein, S., and Jones, F. Group therapy with adolescent addicts. In *Drug Addiction in Youth*, p. 132. E. Harms, editor. Pergamon Press, New York, 1965.

Wallach, C., Jerez, E., and Blinick, G. Pregnancy and menstrual function in narcotics addicts treated with methadone. Amer. J. Obstet. Gynec., *105:* 1226, 1969.

Wikler, A. Conditioning factors in opiate addiction and relapse. In *Narcotics*, p. 85. D. M. Wilner and G. G. Kassebaum, editors. McGraw-Hill, New York, 1965.

Zucker, A. H. Group psychotherapy and the nature of drug addiction. Int. J. Psychother., *11:* 209, 1961.

Glossary*

Aberration, mental. Pathological deviation from normal thinking. Mental aberration is not related to a person's intelligence. *See also* Mental illness.

Abreaction. A process by which repressed material, particularly a painful experience or a conflict, is brought back to consciousness. In the process of abreacting, the person not only recalls but relives the repressed material, which is accompanied by the appropriate affective response. *See also* Catharsis.

Accelerated interaction. An alternate term for marathon group session that was introduced by one of its co-developers, Frederick Stoller. *See also* Group marathon.

Accountability. The responsibility a member has for his actions within a group and the need to explain to other members the motivations for his behavior.

Acid. Slang for lysergic acid diethylamide (LSD).

Acrophobia. Fear of high places.

Acting out. An action rather than a verbal response to an unconscious instinctual drive or impulse that brings about temporary partial relief of inner tension. Relief is attained by reacting to a present situation as if it were the situation that originally gave rise to the drive or impulse. *See also* Therapeutic crisis.

Actional-deep approach. Group procedure in which communication is effected through various forms of nonverbal behavior as well as or in place of language to produce character change. It is a technique used in psychodrama. *See also*

* Edited by Ernesto A. Amaranto, M.D.

Actional-superficial approach, Activity group therapy, Verbal-deep approach, Verbal-superficial approach.

Actional-superficial approach. Group procedure in which specific activities and verbal communication are used for limited goals. Verbal interchange and patient-to-patient interaction are of relatively minor therapeutic significance, and the groups are usually large. *See also* Actional-deep approach, Verbal-deep approach, Verbal-superficial approach.

Action group (A-group). Group whose purpose is to discuss a problem—community, industrial, or organizational—and to formulate a program of action. Emphasis is put on problem-solving rather than on developing awareness of self and group process. *See also* T-group.

Active therapist. Type of therapist who makes no effort to remain anonymous but is forceful and expresses his personality definitively in the therapy setting. *See also* Passive therapist.

Activity group therapy. A type of group therapy introduced and developed by S. R. Slavson and designed for children and young adolescents, with emphasis on emotional and active interaction in a permissive, nonthreatening atmosphere. The therapist stresses reality-testing, ego-strengthening, and action interpretation. *See also* Actional-deep approach; Activity-interview method; Bender, Lauretta; Play therapy.

Activity-interview method. Screening and diagnostic technique used with children. *See also* Activity group therapy.

Actualization. Process of mobilizing one's potentialities or making them concrete. *See also* Individuation.

I

Adaptational approach. An approach used in analytic group therapy. Consonant with Sandor Rado's formulations on adaptational psychodynamics, the group focuses on the maladaptive patterns used by patients in the treatment sessions, on how these patterns developed, and on what the patients must do to overcome them and stabilize their functioning at self-reliant, adult levels. New methods of adaptation are practiced by the group members in the therapeutic sessions and later in their regular interpersonal relationships. *See also* Social adaptation.

Adapted Child. In transactional analysis, the primitive ego state that is under the parental influence. The adapted Child is dependent, unexpressive, and constrained. *See also* Natural Child.

Adler, Alfred (1870–1937). Viennese psychiatrist and one of Freud's original followers. Adler broke off from Freud and introduced and developed the concepts of individual psychology, inferiority complex, and overcompensation. A pioneer in group psychotherapy, he believed that the sharing of problems takes precedence over confidentiality. He also made contributions in the understanding of group process. *See also* Individual psychology, Masculine protest.

Adolescence. Period of growth from puberty to maturity. The beginning of adolescence is marked by the appearance of secondary sexual characteristics, usually at about age 12, and the termination is marked by the achievement of sexual maturity at about age 20. *See also* Psychosexual development.

Adult. In transactional analysis, an ego state oriented toward objective, autonomous data-processing and estimating. It is essentially a computer, devoid of feeling. It is also known as neopsychic function.

Affect. Emotional feeling tone attached to an object, idea, or thought. The term includes inner feelings and their external manifestations. *See also* Inappropriate affect, Mood.

Affect, blunted. A disturbance of affect manifested by dullness of externalized feeling tone. Observed in schizophrenia, it is one of that disorder's fundamental symptoms, according to Eugen Bleuler.

Affection phase. Last stage of group treatment. In this phase the members experience reasonable equality with the therapist and dwell on affectionate contact with each other in a give-and-take atmosphere rather than dwelling on dependency or aggression. *See also* Inclusion phase, Power phase.

Affective interaction. Interpersonal experience and exchange that are emotionally charged.

Affectualizing. In transactional analysis, the expression of emotions or feelings in group or individual treatment as part of a pasttime or game. It is distinguished from the expression of authentic feelings, which are characteristic of intimacy.

Afro-American. American Negro of African ancestry. This term has significance for blacks who seek a deeper and more positive sense of identity with their African heritage. *See also* Black separatism.

After-session. Group meeting of patients without the therapist. It is held immediately after a regular therapist-led session. *See also* Alternate session, Premeeting.

Agency. The striving and need to achieve in a person. Agency manifests itself in self-protection, the urge to master, self-expansion, and repression of thought, feeling, and impulse. *See also* Communion.

Aggression. Forceful, goal-directed behavior that may be verbal or physical. It is the motor counterpart of the affects of rage, anger, and hostility.

Aggressive drive. Destructive impulse directed at oneself or another. It is also known as the death instinct. According to contemporary psychoanalytic psychology, it is one of the two basic drives; sexual drive is the other one. Sexual drive operates on the pleasure-pain principle, whereas aggressive drive operates on the repetition-compulsion principle. *See also* Aggression, Libido theory.

Agitation. State of anxiety associated with severe motor restlessness.

Agnosia. Disturbance of perception characterized by inability to recognize a stimulus and interpret the significance of its memory impressions. It is observed in patients with organic brain disease and in certain schizophrenics, hysterics, and depressed patients.

Agoraphobia. Fear of open places. *See also* Claustrophobia.

Agranulocytosis. A rare, serious side effect, occurring with some of the psychotropic drugs. The condition is characterized by sore throat, fever, a sudden sharp decrease in white blood cell count, and a marked reduction in number of granulocytes.

A-group. *See* Action group.

Alcoholics Anonymous (A.A.) An organization of alcoholics formed in 1935. It uses certain group methods, such as inspirational-supportive techniques, to help rehabilitate chronic alcoholics.

Algophobia. Fear of pain.

Allergic jaundice. *See* Jaundice, allergic.

Alliance. *See* Therapeutic alliance, Working alliance.

Allport's group relations theory. Gordon W. Allport's theory that a person's behavior is influenced by his personality and his need to conform to social forces. It illustrates the interrelationship between group therapy and social psychology. For example, dealing with bigotry in a therapy group enhances the opportunity for therapeutic experiences because it challenges the individual patient's need to conform to earlier social determinants or to hold on to familiar but restrictive aspects of his personality.

Alternate session. Scheduled group meeting held without the therapist. Such meetings are held on a regular basis in between therapist-led sessions. Use of this technique was originated by Alexander Wolf. *See also* After-session, Premeeting.

Alternating role. Pattern characterized by periodic switching from one type of behavior to another. For example, in a group, alternating role is observed among members who switch from the role of the recipient of help to the giver of help.

Alternating scrutiny. *See* Shifting attention.

Altruism. Regard for and dedication to the welfare of others. The term was originated by Auguste Comte (1798–1857), a French philosopher. In psychiatry the term is closely linked with ethics and morals. Freud recognized altruism as the only basis for the development of community interest; Bleuler equated it with morality.

Ambivalence. Presence of strong and often overwhelming simultaneous contrasting attitudes, ideas, feelings, and drives toward an object, person, or goal. The term was coined by Eugen Bleuler, who differentiated three types: affective, intellectual, and ambivalence of the will.

Amnesia. Disturbance in memory manifested by partial or total inability to recall past experiences.

Amphetamine. A central nervous system stimulant. Its chemical structure and action are closely related to ephedrine and other sympathomimetic amines. *See also* Sympathomimetic drug.

Anal erotism. *See* Anal phase.

Anal phase. The second stage in psychosexual development. It occurs when the child is between the ages of one and three. During this period the infant's activities, interests, and concerns are centered around his anal zone, and the pleasurable experience felt around this area is called anal erotism. *See also* Genital phase, Infantile sexuality, Latency phase, Oral phase, Phallic phase.

Analysis. *See* Psychoanalysis.

Analysis in depth. *See* Psychoanalysis.

Analysis of transference. *See* Psychoanalysis.

Analytic psychodrama. Psychotherapy method in which a hypothesis is tested on a stage to verify its validity. The analyst sits in the audience and observes. Analysis of the material is made immediately after the scene is presented.

Anchor. Point at which the patient settles down to the analytic work involved in the therapeutic experience.

Antianxiety drug. Drug used to reduce pathological anxiety and its related symptoms without influencing cognitive or perceptual disturbance. It is also known as a minor tranquilizer and a psycholeptic drug. Meprobamate derivatives and diazepoxides are typical antianxiety drugs.

Anticholinergic effect. Effect due to a blockade of the cholinergic (parasympathetic and somatic) nerves. It is often seen as a side effect of phenothiazine therapy. Anticholinergic effects include dry mouth and blurred vision. *See also* Paralytic ileus.

Antidepressant drug. Drug used in the treatment of pathological depression. It is also known as a thymoleptic drug and a psychic energizer. The two main classes of antidepressant drugs are the tricyclic drugs and the monoamine oxidase inhibitors. *See also* Hypertensive crisis, Monoamine oxidase inhibitor, Tinnitus, Tricyclic drug.

Antimanic drug. Drug, such as lithium, used to alleviate the symptoms of mania. Lithium is particularly effective in preventing relapses in manic-depressive illness. Other drugs with antimanic effects are haloperidol and chlorpromazine.

Antiparkinsonism drug. Drug used to relieve the symptoms of parkinsonism and the extrapyramidal side effects often induced by antipsychotic drugs. The antiparkinsonism drug acts by diminishing muscle tone and involuntary movements. Antiparkinsonism agents include benztropine, procyclidine, biperiden, and trihexphenidyl. *See also* Cycloplegia, Mydriasis.

Antipsychotic drug. Drug used to treat psychosis, particularly schizophrenia. It is also known as a major tranquilizer and a neuroleptic drug. Phenothiazine derivatives, thioxanthene derivatives, and butyrophenone derivatives are typical antipsychotic drugs. *See also* Autonomic side effect, Dyskinesia, Extrapyramidal effect, Major tranquilizer, Parkinsonismlike effect, Reserpine, Tardive oral dyskinesia.

Antirepression device. Technique used in encounter groups and therapeutic groups to break through the defense of repression. In encounter groups, such techniques are frequently nonverbal and involve physical contact between group members. In therapeutic groups, dream analysis, free association, and role-playing are some antirepression techniques.

Anxiety. Unpleasurable affect consisting of psychophysiological changes in response to an intrapsychic conflict. In contrast to fear, the danger or threat in anxiety is unreal. Physiological changes consist of increased heart rate, disturbed breathing, trembling, sweating, and vasomotor changes. Psychological changes consist of an uncomfortable feeling of impending danger accompanied by overwhelming awareness of being powerless, inability to perceive the unreality of the threat, prolonged feeling of tension, and exhaustive readiness for the expected danger. *See also* Basic anxiety, Fear.

Apathetic withdrawal. *See* Withdrawal.

Apathy. Want of feeling or affect; lack of interest and emotional involvement in one's surroundings. It is observed in certain types of schizophrenia and depression.

Apgar scores. Measurements taken one minute and five minutes after birth to determine physical normality in the neonate. The scores are based on color, respiratory rate, heart beat, reflex action, and muscle tone. Used routinely, they are particularly useful in detecting the effects on the infant of drugs taken by the pregnant mother.

Aphasia. Disturbance in speech due to organic brain disorder. It is characterized by inability to express thoughts verbally. There are several types of aphasia: (1) motor aphasia—inability to speak, although understanding remains; (2) sensory aphasia—inability to comprehend the meaning of words or use of objects; (3) nominal aphasia—difficulty in finding the right name for an object; (4) syntactical aphasia—inability to arrange words in proper sequence.

Apperception. Awareness of the meaning and significance of a particular sensory stimulus as modified by one's own experiences, knowledge, thoughts, and emotions. *See also* Perception.

Archeopsychic function. *See* Child.

Arteriosclerotic cardiovascular disease. A metabolic disturbance characterized by degenerative changes involving the blood vessels of the heart and other arteries, mainly the arterioles. Fatty plaques, deposited within the blood vessels, gradually obstruct the flow of blood. Organic brain syndrome may develop when cerebral arteries are involved in the degenerative process.

Ataractic drug. *See* Major tranquilizer.

Ataxia. Lack of coordination, either physical or mental. In neurology it refers to loss of muscular coordination. In psychiatry the term intrapsychic ataxia refers to lack of coordination between feelings and thoughts; the disturbance is found in schizophrenia.

Atmosphere. *See* Therapeutic atmosphere.

Attention. Concentration; the aspect of consciousness that relates to the amount of effort exerted in focusing on certain aspects of an experience.

Attitude. Preparatory mental posture with which one receives stimuli and reacts to them. Group therapy often involves itself in defining for the group members their attitudes that have unconsciously dominated their reactions.

Auditory hallucination. False auditory sensory perception.

Authenticity. Quality of being authentic, real, and valid. In psychological functioning and personality, it applies to the conscious feelings, perceptions, and thoughts that a person expresses and communicates. It does not apply to the deeper, unconscious layers of the personality. *See also* Honesty.

Authority figure. A real or projected person in a position of power; transferentially, a projected parent.

Authority principle. The idea that each member of an organizational hierarchy tries to comply with the presumed or fantasied wishes of those above him while those below him try to comply with his wishes. *See also* Hierarchical vector, Political therapist, Procedural therapist.

Autism. *See* Autistic thinking.

Autistic thinking. A form of thinking in which the thoughts are largely narcissistic and egocentric, with emphasis on subjectivity rather than objectivity and without regard for reality. The term is used interchangeably with autism and dereism. *See also* Narcissism.

Autoerotism. Sexual arousal of self without the participation of another person. The term, introduced by Havelock Ellis, is at present used interchangeably with masturbation. In psychoanalysis, autoerotism is considered a primitive phase in object-relationship development, preceding the narcissistic stage. In narcissism there is a love object, but there is no love object in autoerotism.

Autonomic side effect. Disturbance of the autonomic nervous system, both central and peripheral. It may be a result of the use of anti-psychotic drugs, particularly the phenothiazine derivatives. The autonomic side effects include hypotension, hypertension, blurred vision, nasal congestion, and dryness of the mouth. *See also* Mydriasis.

Auxiliary ego. In psychodrama, a person, usually a member of the staff, trained to act out different roles during a psychodramatic session to intensify the therapeutic situation. The trained auxiliary ego may represent an important figure in the patient's life. He may express the patient's unconscious wishes and attitudes or portray his unacceptable self. He may represent a delusion, hallucination, symbol, ideal, animal, or object that makes the patient's psychodramatic world real, concrete, and tangible. *See also* Ego model Hallucinatory psychodrama, Mirror, Multiple double.

Auxiliary therapist. Co-therapist. *See also* Co-therapy.

Back-home group. Collection of persons that a patient usually lives with, works with, and socializes with. It does not include the members of his therapy group. *See also* Expanded group.

Bag. Slang for area of classification, interest, or skill. Bringing together members of a group with different bags makes it initially difficult to achieve a feeling of group cohesiveness but later provides the potential for more productive interchange and deeper cohesiveness.

Basic anxiety. As conceptualized by Karen Horney, the mainspring from which neurotic trends get their intensity and pervasiveness. Basic anxiety is characterized by vague feelings of loneliness, helplessness, and fear of a potentially hostile world. *See also* Anxiety, Fear.

Basic skills training. The teaching of leadership functions, communication skills, the use of group processes, and other interpersonal skills. National Training Laboratories' groups include this training as part of the T-group process. *See also* East-Coast-style T-group.

Behavioral group psychotherapy. A type of group therapy that focuses on overt and objectively observable behavior rather than on thoughts and feelings. It aims at symptomatic improvement and the elimination of suffering and maladaptive habits. Various conditioning and anxiety-eliminating techniques derived from learning theory are combined with didactic discussions and techniques adapted from other systems of treatment.

Behind-the-back technique. An encounter group procedure in which a patient talks about himself and then turns his back and listens while the other participants discuss him as if he were physically absent. Later he "returns" to the group to participate in further discussions of his problems.

Bender, Lauretta (1897–). American psychiatrist who has done extensive work in the fields of child psychiatry, neurology, and psychology. She employed group therapy, particularly activity group therapy, with inpatient children in the early 1940's.

Berne, Eric (1910–1970). American psychiatrist. He was the founder of transactional analysis, which is used in both individual and group therapy. *See also* Transactional group psychotherapy.

Bestiality. Sexual deviation in which a person engages in sexual relations with an animal.

Bieber, Irving (1908–). American psychiatrist and psychoanalyst who has done extensive work in the field of homosexuality. He originated the first major scientific study of male homosexuality published as *Homosexuality; A Psychoanalytic Study.*

Bio-energetic group psychotherapy. A type of group therapy developed by Alexander Lowen that directly involves the body and mobilizes energy processes to facilitate the expression of feeling. Verbal interchange and a variety of exercises are designed to improve and coordinate physical functioning with mental functioning.

Bion, Walter R. British psychoanalyst of the Kleinian school. He introduced concepts dealing largely with the group as a whole. He was one of the European workers who demonstrated the use of open wards in mental hospitals and who developed the concept of therapeutic milieu. *See also* Leaderless therapeutic group, Pairing, Therapeutic community.

Bisexuality. Existence of the qualities of both sexes in the same person. Freud postulated that both biologically and psychologically the sexes differentiated from a common core, that differentiation between the two sexes was relative rather than absolute, and that regression to the common core occurs to varying degrees in both normal and abnormal conditions. An adult person who engages in bisexual behavior is one who is sexually attracted to and has contact with members of both sexes. He is also known in lay terms as an AC-DC person. *See also* Heterosexuality, Homosexuality, Latent homosexuality, Overt homosexuality.

Black separatism. Philosophy that blacks, in order to develop a positive identity, must establish cultural, socioeconomic, and political systems that are distinctively black and separate from white systems. *See also* Afro-American.

Blank screen. Neutral backdrop on which the patient projects a gamut of transferential irrationalities. The passivity of the analyst allows him to act as a blank screen.

Blind self. The behavior, feelings, and motivations of a person known to others but not to himself. The blind self is one quadrant of the Johari Window, a diagrammatic concept of human behavior. *See also* Hidden self, Public self, Undeveloped potential.

Blind spot. Area of someone's personality that he is totally unaware of. These unperceived areas are often hidden by repression so that he can avoid painful emotions. In both group and individual therapy, such blind spots often appear obliquely as projected ideas, intentions, and emotions.

Blind walk. A technique used in encounter groups to help a member experience and develop trust. As a group exercise, each member picks a partner; one partner closes his eyes, and the other leads him around, keeping him out of dangerous places. The partners then reverse roles. Later, the group members discuss their reactions to the blind walk.

Blocking. Involuntary cessation of thought processes or speech because of unconscious emotional factors. It is also known as thought deprivation.

Blunted affect. *See* Affect, blunted.

Body-contact-exploration maneuver. Any physical touching of another person for the purpose of becoming more aware of the sensations and emotions aroused by the experience. The technique is used mainly in encounter groups.

Boundary. Physical or psychological factor that separates relevant regions in the group structure. An external boundary separates the group from the external environment. A major internal boundary distinguishes the group leader from the members. A minor internal boundary separates individual members or subgroups from one another.

Brainwashing. Any technique designed to manipulate human thought or action against the desire, will, or knowledge of the person involved. It usually refers to systematic efforts to indoctrinate nonbelievers. *See also* Dog-eat-dog period, Give-up-itis.

Breuer, Josef (1842–1925). Viennese physician with wide scientific and cultural interests. His collaboration with Freud in studies of cathartic therapy were reported in *Studies on Hysteria* (1895). He withdrew as Freud proceeded to introduce psychoanalysis, but he left important imprints on that discipline, such as the concepts of the primary and secondary process.

Brill, A. A. (1874–1948). First American analyst (1908). Freud gave him permission to translate several of his most important works. He was active in the formation of the New York Psychoanalytic Society (1911) and remained in the forefront of propagators of psychoanalysis as a lecturer and writer throughout his life.

Brooding compulsion. *See* Intellectualization.

Bull session. Informal group meeting at which members discuss their opinions, philosophies, and personal feelings about situations and people. Such groups are leaderless, and no attempt is made to perceive group process, but the cathartic value is often great. It is also known as a rap session.

Burned-out anergic schizophrenic. A chronic schizophrenic who is apathetic and withdrawn, with minimal florid psychotic symptoms but with persistent and often severe schizophrenic thought processes.

Burrow, Trigant L. (1875–1951). American student of Freud and Jung who coined the term group analysis and later developed a method called phyloanalysis. Much of Burrow's work was based on his social views and his opinion that individual psychotherapy places the therapist in too authoritarian a role to be therapeutic. He formed groups of patients, students, and colleagues who, living together in a camp, analyzed their interactions.

Catalepsy. *See* Cerea flexibilitas.

Cataphasia. *See* Verbigeration.

Cataplexy. Temporary loss of muscle tone, causing weakness and immobilization. It can be precipitated by a variety of emotional states.

Catecholamine. Monoamine containing a catechol group that has a sympathomimetic property. Norepinephrine, epinephrine, and dopamine are common catecholamines.

Category method. Technique used in structured interactional group psychotherapy. Members are asked to verbally rate one another along a variety of parameters—such as appearance, intelligence, and relatedness.

Catharsis. Release of ideas, thoughts, and repressed materials from the unconscious, accompanied by an affective emotional response and release of tension. Commonly observed in the course of treatment, both individual and group, it can also occur outside therapy. *See also* Abreaction, Bull session, Conversational catharsis.

Cathexis. In psychoanalysis, a conscious or unconscious investment of the psychic energy of a drive in an idea, a concept, or an object.

Cerea flexibilitas. Condition in which a person maintains the body position he is placed into. It is a pathological symptom observed in severe cases of catatonic schizophrenia. It is also known as waxy flexibility or catalepsy.

Chain-reaction phenomenon. Group therapy situation in which information is passed from one group to another, resulting in a loss of confidentiality. This phenomenon is common when members of different groups socialize together.

Chemotherapy. *See* Drug therapy.

Child. In transactional analysis, an ego state that is an archaic relic from an early period of the person's life. It is also known as archeopsychic function. *See also* Adapted Child, Natural Child.

Chlorpromazine. A phenothiazine derivative used primarily as an antipsychotic agent and in the treatment of nausea and vomiting. The drug was synthesized in 1950 and was used in psychiatry for the first time in 1952. At present, chlorpromazine is one of the most widely used drugs in medical practice.

Circumstantiality. Disturbance in the associative thought processes in which the patient digresses into unnecessary details and inappropriate thoughts before communicating the central idea. It is observed in schizophrenia, obsessional disturbances, and certain cases of epileptic dementia. *See also* Tangentiality, Thought process disorder.

Clarification. In transactional analysis, the attainment of Adult control by a patient who understands what he is doing, knows what parts of his personality are involved in what he is doing, and is able to control and decide whether or not to continue his games. Clarification contributes to stability by assuring the patient that his hidden Parent and Child ego states can be monitored by his Adult ego state. *See also* Decontamination, Interpretation.

Class method. Group therapy method that is lecture-centered and designed to enlighten patients as to their condition and provide them with motivations. Joseph Pratt, a Boston physician, first used this method at the turn of the century to help groups of tuberculous patients understand their illness. *See also* Didactic technique, Group bibliotherapy, Mechanical group therapy.

Claustrophobia. Fear of closed places. *See also* Agoraphobia.

Client-centered psychotherapy. A form of psychotherapy, formulated by Carl Rogers, in which the patient or client is believed to possess the ability to improve. The therapist merely helps him clarify his own thinking and feeling. The client-centered approach in both group and individual therapy is democratic, unlike the psychotherapist-centered treatment methods. *See also* Group-centered psychotherapy, Nondirective approach.

Closed group. Treatment group into which no new members are permitted once it has begun the treatment process. *See also* Open group.

Clouding of consciousness. Disturbance of consciousness characterized by unclear sensory perceptions.

Coexistent culture. Alternative system of values, perceptions, and patterns for behavior. The group experience leads to an awareness of other systems as legitimate alternatives to one's own system.

Cognition. Mental process of knowing and becoming aware. One of the ego functions, it is closely associated with judgment. Groups that study their own processes and dynamics use more cognition than do encounter groups, which emphasize emotions. It is also known as thinking.

Cohesion. *See* Group cohesion.

Cold turkey. Abrupt withdrawal from opiates without the benefit of methadone or other drugs. The term was originated by drug addicts to describe their chills and consequent goose flesh. This type of detoxification is generally used by abstinence-oriented therapeutic communities.

Collaborative therapy. A type of marital therapy in which treatment is conducted by two therapists, each of whom sees one spouse. They may confer occasionally or at regular intervals. This form of treatment affords each analyst a double view of his patient—the way in which one patient reports to his analyst and the way in which the patient's mate sees the situation as reported to the analyst's colleague. *See also* Combined therapy, Concurrent therapy, Conjoint therapy, Family therapy, Group marital therapy, Marriage therapy, Quadrangular therapy, Square interview.

Collective experience. The common emotional experiences of a group of people. Identification, mutual support, reduction of ego defenses, sibling transferences, and empathy help integrate the individual member into the group and accelerate the therapeutic process. S. R. Slavson, who coined the phrase, warned against letting the collective experience submerge the individuality of the members or give them an opportunity to escape from their own autonomy and responsibility.

Collective family transference neurosis. A phenomenon observed in a group when a member projects irrational feelings and thoughts onto other members as a result of transferring the family psychopathology from early childhood into the therapeutic group situation. The interpretation and analysis of this phenomenon is one of the cornerstones of psychoanalytic group therapy. *See also* Lateral transference, Multiple transference.

Collective unconscious. Psychic contents outside the realm of awareness that are common to mankind in general, not to one person in particular. Jung, who introduced the term, believed that the collective unconscious is inherited and derived from the collective experience of the species. It transcends cultural differences and explains the analogy between ancient mythological ideas and the primitive archaic projections observed in some patients who have never been exposed to these ideas.

Coma. A profound degree of unconsciousness with minimal or no detectable responsiveness to stimuli. It is seen in conditions involving the brain—such as head injury, cerebral hemorrhage, thrombosis and embolism, and cerebral infection—in such systemic conditions as diabetes, and in drug and alcohol intoxication. In psychiatry, comas may be seen in severe catatonic states.

Coma vigil. A profound degree of unconsciousness in which the patient's eyes remain open but there is minimal or no detectable evidence of responsiveness to stimuli. It is seen in acute brain syndromes secondary to cerebral infection.

Combined therapy. A type of psychotherapy in which the patient is in both individual and group treatment with the same or two different therapists. In marriage therapy, it is the combination of married couples group therapy with either individual sessions with one spouse or conjoint sessions with the marital pair. *See also* Collaborative therapy, Concurrent therapy, Conjoint therapy, Co-therapy, Family therapy, Group marital therapy, Marriage therapy, Quadrangular therapy, Square interview.

Coming on. A colloquial term used in transactional analysis groups to label an emerging ego state. For example, when a patient points his finger and says "should," he is coming on Parent.

Command automation. Condition closely associated with catalepsy in which suggestions are followed automatically.

Command negativism. *See* Negativism.

Common group tension. Common denominator of tension arising out of the dominant unconscious fantasies of all the members in a group.

Each member projects his unconscious fantasy onto the other members and tries to manipulate them accordingly. Interpretation by the group therapist plays a prominent role in bringing about change.

Communion. The union of one living thing with another or the participation of a person in an organization. It is a necessary ingredient in individual and group psychotherapy and in sensitivity training. Both the leader-therapist and the patient-trainee must experience communion for a successful learning experience to occur. *See also* Agency.

Communion-oriented group psychotherapy. A type of group therapy that focuses on developing a spirit of unity and cohesiveness rather than on performing a task.

Community. *See* Therapeutic community.

Community psychiatry. Psychiatry focusing on the detection, prevention, and early treatment of emotional disorders and social deviance as they develop in the community rather than as they are perceived and encountered at large, centralized psychiatric facilities. Particular emphasis is placed on the environmental factors that contribute to mental illness.

Compensation. Conscious or, usually, unconscious defense mechanism by which a person tries to make up for an imagined or real deficiency, physical or psychological or both.

Competition. Struggle for the possession or use of limited goods, concrete or abstract. Gratification for one person largely precludes gratification for another.

Complementarity of interaction. A concept of bipersonal and multipersonal psychology in which behavior is viewed as a response to stimulation and interaction replaces the concept of reaction. Each person in an interactive situation plays both a provocative role and a responsive role.

Complex. A group of inter-related ideas, mainly unconscious, that have a common affective tone. A complex strongly influences the person's attitudes and behavior. *See also* God complex, Inferiority complex, Mother Superior complex, Oedipus complex.

Composition. Make-up of a group according to

sex, age, race, cultural and ethnic background, and psychopathology.

Compulsion. Uncontrollable impulse to perform an act repetitively. It is used as a way to avoid unacceptable ideas and desires. Failure to perform the act leads to anxiety. *See also* Obsession.

Conation. That part of a person's mental life concerned with his strivings, instincts, drives, and wishes as expressed through his behavior.

Concretization of living. As used in psychodrama, the actualization of life in a therapeutic setting, integrating time, space, reality, and cosmos.

Concurrent therapy. A type of family therapy in which one therapist handles two or more members of the same family but sees each member separately. *See also* Collaborative therapy, Combined therapy, Conjoint therapy, Family therapy, Group marital therapy, Marriage therapy, Quadrangular therapy, Square interview.

Conditioning. Procedure designed to alter behavioral potential. There are two main types of conditioning—classical and operant. Classical or Pavlovian conditioning pairs two stimuli—one adequate, such as offering food to a dog to produce salivation, and the other inadequate, such as ringing a bell, which by itself does not have an effect on salivation. After the two stimuli have been paired several times, the dog responds to the inadequate stimulus (ringing of bell) by itself. In operant conditioning, a desired activity is reinforced by giving the subject a reward every time he performs the act. As a result, the activity becomes automatic without the need for further reinforcement.

Confabulation. Unconscious filling of gaps in memory by imagining experiences that have no basis in fact. It is common in organic brain syndromes. *See also* Paramnesia.

Confidentiality. Aspect of medical ethics in which the physician is bound to hold secret all information given him by the patient. Legally, certain states do not recognize confidentiality and can require the physician to divulge such information if needed in a legal proceeding. In group psychotherapy this ethic is adhered to by the members as well as by the therapist.

Confirmation. In transactional analysis, a re-

confrontation that may be undertaken by the patient himself. *See also* Confrontation.

Conflict. Clash of two opposing emotional forces. In a group, the term refers to a clash between group members or between the group members and the leader, a clash that frequently reflects the inner psychic problems of individual members. *See also* Extrapsychic conflict, Intrapsychic conflict.

Conflict-free area. Part of one's personality or ego that is well-integrated and does not cause any conflicts, symptoms, or displeasure. Conflict-free areas are usually not analyzed in individual analysis, but they become obvious in the interaction of an analytic group, where they can then be analyzed.

Confrontation. Act of letting a person know where one stands in relationship to him, what one is experiencing, and how one perceives him. Used in a spirit of deep involvement, this technique is a powerful tool for changing relationships; used as an attempt to destroy another person, it can be harmful. In group and individual therapy, the value of confrontation is likely to be determined by the therapist. *See also* Encounter group, Existential group psychotherapy.

Confusion. Disturbance of consciousness manifested by a disordered orientation in relation to time, place, or person.

Conjoint therapy. A type of marriage therapy in which a therapist sees the partners together in joint sessions. This situation is also called triadic or triangular, since two patients and one therapist work together. *See also* Collaborative therapy, Combined therapy, Concurrent therapy, Family therapy, Group marital therapy, Marriage therapy, Quadrangular therapy, Square interview.

Conscious. One division of Freud's topographical theory of the mind. The content of the conscious is within the realm of awareness at all times. The term is also used to describe a function of organic consciousness. *See also* Preconscious, Unconscious.

Consciousness. *See* Sensorium.

Consensual validation. The continuous comparison of the thoughts and feelings of group members toward one another that tend to modify and correct interpersonal distortions. The term was introduced by Harry Stack Sullivan. Previously, Trigant Burrow referred to consensual observation to describe this process, which results in effective reality-testing.

Contact situation. Encounter between individual persons or groups in which the interaction patterns that develop represent the dynamic interplay of psychological, cultural, and socioeconomic factors.

Contagion. Force that operates in large groups or masses. When the level of psychological functioning has been lowered, some sudden upsurge of anxiety can spread through the group, speeded by a high degree of suggestibility. The anxiety gradually mounts to panic, and the whole group may be simultaneously affected by a primitive emotional upheaval.

Contamination. In transactional analysis, a state in which attitudes, prejudices, and standards that originate in a Parent or Child ego state become part of the Adult ego state's information and are treated as accepted facts. *See also* Clarification, Decontamination.

Contemporaneity. Here-and-now.

Contract. Explicit, bilateral commitment to a well-defined course of action. In group or individual therapy, the therapist-patient contract is to attain the treatment goal.

Conversational catharsis. Release of repressed or suppressed thoughts and feelings in group and individual psychotherapy as a result of verbal interchange.

Conversion. An unconscious defense mechanism by which the anxiety that stems from an intrapsychic conflict is converted and expressed in a symbolic somatic symptom. Seen in a variety of mental disorders, it is particularly common in hysterical neurosis.

Cooperative therapy. *See* Co-therapy.

Co-patients. Members of a treatment group exclusive of the therapist and the recorder or observer. Co-patients are also known as patient peers.

Coprolalia. The use of vulgar, obscene, or dirty words. It is observed in some cases of schizophrenia. The word is derived from the Greek words *kopros* (excrement) and *lalia* (talking). *See also* Gilles de la Tourette's disease.

Corrective emotional experience. Re-exposure, under favorable circumstances, to an emotional situation that the patient could not handle in the past. As advocated by Franz Alexander, the therapist temporarily assumes a particular role to generate the experience and facilitate reality-testing.

Co-therapy. A form of psychotherapy in which more than one therapist treat the individual patient or the group. It is also known as combined therapy, cooperative therapy, dual leadership, multiple therapy, and three-cornered therapy. *See also* Role-divided therapy, Splitting situation.

Counterdependent person. *See* Nontruster.

Countertransference. Conscious or unconscious emotional response of the therapist to the patient. It is determined by the therapist's inner needs rather than by the patient's needs, and it may reinforce the patient's earlier traumatic history if not checked by the therapist.

Co-worker. Professional or paraprofessional who works in the same clinical or institutional setting.

Creativity. Ability to produce something new. Silvano Arieti describes creativity as the tertiary process, a balanced combination of primary and secondary processes, whereby materials from the id are used in the service of the ego.

Crisis-intervention group psychotherapy. Group therapy aimed at decreasing or eliminating an emotional or situational crisis.

Crisis, therapeutic. *See* Therapeutic crisis.

Crystallization. In transactional analysis, a statement of the patient's position from the Adult of the therapist to the Adult of the patient. *See also* Ego state.

Cultural conserve. The finished product of the creative process; anything that preserves the values of a particular culture. Without this repository of the past, man would be forced to create the same forms to meet the same situations day after day. The cultural conserve also entices new creativity.

Cultural deprivation. Restricted participation in the culture of the larger society.

Current material. Data from present interpersonal experiences. *See also* Genetic material.

Cyclazocine. A narcotic antagonist that blocks the effects of heroin but does not relieve heroin craving. It has been used experimentally with a limited number of drug addicts in research programs.

Cycloplegia. Paralysis of the muscles of accommodation in the eye. It is observed at times as an autonomic side effect of phenothiazine and antiparkinsonism drugs.

Dance therapy. Nonverbal communication through rhythmic body movements, used to rehabilitate people with emotional or physical disorders. Pioneered by Marian Chase in 1940, this method is used in both individual and group therapy.

Data. *See* Current material, Genetic material.

Death instinct. *See* Aggressive drive.

Decision. In transactional analysis, a childhood commitment to a certain existential position and life style. *See also* Script analysis.

Decompensation. In medical science, the failure of normal functioning of an organ, as in cardiac decompensation; in psychiatry, the breakdown of the psychological defense mechanisms that maintain the person's optimal psychic functioning. *See also* Depersonalization.

Decontamination. In transactional analysis, a process whereby a person is freed of Parent or Child contaminations. *See also* Clarification.

Defense mechanism. Unconscious intrapsychic process. Protective in nature, it is used to relieve the anxiety and conflict arising from one's impulses and drives. *See also* Compensation, Conversion, Denial, Displacement, Dissociation, Idealization, Identification, Incorporation, Intellectualization, Introjection, Projection, Rationalization, Reaction formation, Regression, Repression, Sublimation, Substitution, Symbolization, Undoing.

Defensive emotion. Strong feeling that serves as a screen for a less acceptable feeling, one that would cause a person to experience anxiety if it appeared. For example, expressing the emotion of anger is often more acceptable to a group member than expressing the fear that his anger covers up. In this instance, anger is defensive.

Déjà entendu. Illusion of auditory recognition. *See also* Paramnesia.

Déjà vu. Illusion of visual recognition in which a new situation is incorrectly regarded as a repetition of a previous experience. *See also* Paramnesia.

Delirium. A disturbance in the state of consciousness that stems from an acute organic reaction characterized by restlessness, confusion, disorientation, bewilderment, agitation, and affective lability. It is associated with fear, hallucinations, and illusions.

Delusion. A false fixed belief not in accord with one's intelligence and cultural background. Types of delusion include:
Delusion of control. False belief that one is being manipulated by others.
Delusion of grandeur. Exaggerated concept of one's importance.
Delusion of infidelity. False belief that one's lover is unfaithful; it is derived from pathological jealousy.
Delusion of persecution. False belief that one is being harrassed.
Delusion of reference. False belief that the behavior of others refers to oneself; a derivation from ideas of reference in which the patient falsely feels that he is being talked about by others.
Delusion of self-accusation. False feeling of remorse.
Paranoid delusion. Oversuspiciousness leading to false persecutory ideas or beliefs.

Dementia. Organic loss of mental functioning.

Denial. An unconscious defense mechanism in which an aspect of external reality is rejected. At times it is replaced by a more satisfying fantasy or piece of behavior. The term can also refer to the blocking of awareness of internal reality. It is one of the primitive or infantile defenses.

Dependence on therapy. Patient's pathological need for therapy, created out of the belief that he cannot survive without it.

Dependency. A state of reliance on another

for psychological support. It reflects needs for security, love, protection, and mothering.

Dependency phase. *See* Inclusion phase.

Depersonalization. Sensation of unreality concerning oneself, parts of oneself, or one's environment. It is seen in schizophrenics, particularly during the early stages of decompensation. *See also* Decompensation.

Depression. In psychiatry, a morbid state characterized by mood alterations, such as sadness and loneliness; by low self-esteem associated with self-reproach; by psychomotor retardation and, at times, agitation; by withdrawal from interpersonal contact and, at times, a desire to die; and by such vegetative symptoms as insomnia and anorexia. *See also* Grief.

Derailment. *See* Tangentiality.

Derealization. Sensation of distorted spatial relationships. It is seen in certain types of schizophrenia.

Dereism. Mental activity not concordant with logic or experience. This type of thinking is commonly observed in schizophrenic states.

Detoxification. Removal of the toxic effects of a drug. It is also known as detoxication. *See also* Cold turkey, Methadone.

Diagnostic and Statistical Manual of Mental Disorders. A handbook for the classification of mental illnesses. Formulated by the American Psychiatric Association, it was first issued in 1952 (DSM-I). The second edition (DSM-II), issued in 1968, correlates closely with the World Health Organization's *International Classification of Diseases.*

Dialogue. Verbal communication between two or more persons.

Didactic psychodrama. Psychodrama used as a teaching method. It is used with persons involved in the care of psychiatric patients to teach them how to handle typical conflicts.

Didactic technique. Group therapeutic method given prominence by J. M. Klapman that emphasizes the tutorial approach. The group therapist makes use of outlines, texts, and visual aids to teach the group about themselves and their functioning. *See also* Class method, Group bibliotherapy, Mechanical group therapy.

Differentiation. *See* Individuation.

Dilution of transference. Partial projection of irrational feelings and reactions onto various group members and away from the leader. Some therapists do not believe that dilution of transference occurs. *See also* Multiple transference, Transference.

Dipsomania. Morbid, irrepressible compulsion to drink alcoholic beverages.

Directive-didactic approach. Group therapy approach characterized by guided discussions and active direction by the therapist. Various teaching methods and printed materials are used, and autobiographical material may be presented. Such an approach is common with regressed patients in mental institutions.

Discussion model of group psychotherapy. A type of group therapy in which issues, problems, and facts are deliberated, with the major emphasis on rational understanding.

Disinhibition. Withdrawal of inhibition. Chemical substances such as alcohol can remove inhibitions by interfering with functions of the cerebral cortex. In psychiatry, disinhibition leads to the freedom to act on one's own needs rather than to submit to the demands of others.

Displacement. An unconscious defense mechanism by which the affective component of an unacceptable idea or object is transferred to an acceptable one.

Disposition. Sum total of a person's inclinations as determined by his mood.

Dissociation. An unconscious defense mechanism by which an idea is separated from its accompanying affect, as seen in hysterical dissociative states; an unconscious process by which a group of mental processes are split off from the rest of a person's thinking, resulting in an independent functioning of this group of processes and thus a loss of the usual inter-relationships.

Distortion. Misrepresentation of reality. It is based on historically determined motives.

Distractability. Inability to focus one's attention.

Diversified reality. A condition in a treatment situation that provides various real stimuli with which the patient may interact. In a group, the term refers to the variety of personalities of the co-members, in contrast with the one personality of the analyst in the dyadic relationship.

Doctor-patient relationship. Human interchange that exists between the person who is sick and the person who is selected because of training and experience to heal.

Dog-eat-dog period. Early stage of Communist brainwashing of American prisoners during the Korean War. During this period, as described by former Army psychiatrist William Mayer, the Communists encouraged each prisoner to be selfish and to do only what was best for himself. *See also* Give-up-itis.

Dominant member. The patient in a group who tends to monopolize certain group sessions or situations.

Double. *See* Mirror.

Double-bind. Two conflicting communications from another person. One message is usually non-verbal and the other verbal. For example, parents may tell a child that arguments are to be settled peacefully and yet battle with each other constantly. The concept was formulated by Gregory Bateson.

Double-blind study. A study in which one or more drugs and a placebo are compared in such a way that neither the patient nor the persons directly or indirectly involved in the study know which is being given to the patient. The drugs being investigated and the placebo are coded for identification.

Dream. Mental activity during sleep that is experienced as though it were real. A dream has both a psychological and a biological purpose. It provides an outlet for the release of instinctual impulses and wish fulfillment of archaic needs and fantasies unacceptable in the real world. It permits the partial resolution of conflicts and the healing of traumata too overwhelming to be dealt with in the waking state. And it is the guardian of sleep, which is indispensable for the proper functioning of mind and body during the waking state. *See also* Hypnagogic hallucination, Hypnopompic hallucination, Paramnesia.

Dreamy state. Altered state of consciousness likened to a dream situation. It is accompanied by hallucinations—visual, auditory, and olfactory—and is believed to be associated with temporal lobe lesions. *See also* Marijuana.

Drive. A mental constituent, believed to be genetically determined, that produces a state of tension when it is in operation. This tension or state of psychic excitation motivates the person into action to alleviate the tension. Contemporary psychoanalysts prefer to use the term drive rather than Freud's term, instinct. *See also* Aggressive drive, Instinct, Sexual drive.

Drop-out. Patient who leaves group therapy against the therapist's advice.

Drug therapy. The use of chemical substances in the treatment of illness. It is also known as chemotherapy. *See also* Maintenance drug therapy.

DSM. *See Diagnostic and Statistical Manual of Mental Disorders.*

Dual leadership. *See* Co-therapy.

Dual therapy. *See* Co-therapy.

Dyad. A pair of persons in an interactional situation—such as husband and wife, mother and father, co-therapists, or patient and therapist.

Dyadic session. Psychotherapeutic session involving only two persons, the therapist and the patient.

Dynamic reasoning. Forming all the clinical evidence gained from free-associative anamnesis into a psychological reconstruction of the patient's development. It is a term used by Franz Alexander.

Dyskinesia. Involuntary, stereotyped, rhythmic muscular activity, such as a tic or a spasm. It is sometimes observed as an extrapyramidal side effect of antipsychotic drugs, particularly the phenothiazine derivatives. *See also* Tardive oral dyskinesia.

Dystonia. Extrapyramidal motor disturbance consisting of uncoordinated and spasmodic movements of the body and limbs, such as arching of the back and twisting of the body and neck. It is observed as a side effect of phenothiazine drugs and other major tranquilizers. *See also* Tardive oral dyskinesia.

East-Coast-style T-group. Group that follows the traditional National Training Laboratories orientation by developing awareness of group process. The first T-groups were held in Bethel, Maine. *See also* Basic skills training, West-Coast-style T-group.

Echolalia. Repetition of another person's words or phrases. It is a psychopathological symptom observed in certain cases of schizophrenia, particularly the catatonic types. Some authors consider this behavior to be an attempt by the patient to maintain a continuity of thought processes. *See also* Gilles de la Tourette's disease.

Echopraxia. Imitation of another person's movements. It is a psychopathological symptom observed in some cases of catatonic schizophrenia.

Ecstasy. Affect of intense rapture.

Ego. One of the three components of the psychic apparatus in the Freudian structural framework. The other two components are the id and the superego. Although the ego has some conscious components, many of its operations are automatic. It occupies a position between the primal instincts and the demands of the outer world, and it therefore serves to mediate between the person and external reality. In so doing, it performs the important functions of perceiving the needs of the self, both physical and psychological, and the qualities and attitudes of the environment. It evaluates, coordinates, and integrates these perceptions so that infernal demands can be adjusted to external requirements. It is also responsible for certain defensive functions to protect the person against the demands of the id and the superego. It has a host of functions, but adaptation to reality is perhaps the most important one. *See also* Reality-testing.

Ego-coping skill. Adaptive method or capacity developed by a person to deal with or overcome a psychological or social problem.

Ego defense. *See* Defense mechanism.

Ego ideal. Part of the ego during its development that eventually fuses with the superego. It is a social as well as a psychological concept, reflecting the mutual esteem as well as the disillusionment in child-parent and subsequent relationships.

Egomania. Pathological self-preoccupation or self-centeredness. *See also* Narcissism.

Ego model. A person on whom another person patterns his ego. In a group, the therapist or a healthier member acts as an ego model for members with less healthy egos. In psychodrama, the auxiliary ego may act as the ego model.

Ego state. In Eric Berne's structural analysis, a state of mind and its related set of coherent behavior patterns. It includes a system of feelings directly related to a given subject. There are three ego states—Parent, Adult, and Child.

Eitingon, Max (1881–1943). Austrian psychoanalyst. An emissary of the Zurich school, he gained fame as the first person to be analyzed by Freud—in a few sessions in 1907. Later he became the first chief of the Berlin Psychoanalytic Clinic, a founder of the Berlin Psychoanalytic Institute, and a founder of the Palestine Psychoanalytic Society.

Elation. Affect characterized by euphoria, confidence, and enjoyment. It is associated with increased motor activity.

Electrocardiographic effect. Change seen in recordings of the electrical activity of the heart. It is observed as a side effect of phenothiazine derivatives, particularly thioridazine.

Electroconvulsive treatment. *See* Shock treatment.

Emotion. *See* Affect.

Emotional deprivation. Lack of adequate and appropriate interpersonal or environmental experiences or both, usually in the early developmental years. Emotional deprivation is caused by poor mothering or by separation from the mother.

Emotional insight. *See* Insight.

Emotional support. Encouragement, hope, and inspiration given to one person by another. Members of a treatment group often empathize with a patient who needs such support in order to try a new mode of behavior or to face the truth.

Empathy. Ability to put oneself in another person's place, get into his frame of reference, and understand his feelings and behavior objectively. It is one of the major qualities in a successful therapist, facilitator, or helpful group member. *See also* Sympathy.

Encounter group. A form of sensitivity training that emphasizes the experiencing of individual relationships within the group and minimizes intellectual and didactic input. It is a group that focuses on the present rather than concerning itself with the past or outside problems of its members. J. L. Moreno introduced and developed the idea of the encounter group in 1914. *See also* Here-and-now approach, Intervention laboratory, Nonverbal interaction, Task-oriented group.

Encountertapes. Tape recordings designed to provide a group with guidelines for progressive interaction in the absence of a leader. They are copyrighted by the Bell & Howell Company and are available commercially from their Human Development Institute in Atlanta, Georgia.

Epileptic dementia. A form of epilepsy that is accompanied by progressive mental and intellectual impairment. Some believe that the circulatory disturbances during epileptic attacks cause nerve cell degeneration and lead to dementia.

Epinephrine. A sympathomimetic agent. It is the chief hormone secreted by the adrenal medulla. In a state of fear or anxiety, the physiological changes stem from the release of epinephrine. Also known as adrenaline, it is related to norepinephrine, a substance presently linked with mood disturbances in depression.

Eros. *See* Sexual drive.

Erotomania. Pathological preoccupation with sexual activities or fantasies.

Esalen massage. A particular type of massage taught and practiced at the Esalen Institute, a growth center at Big Sur, California. The massage lasts between one and a half and three hours and is intended to be an intimate, loving communion between the participants. A variation is the massage of one person by a group. The massage is given without words.

Ethnocentrism. Conviction that one's own group is superior to other groups. It impairs one's ability to evaluate members of another group realistically or to communicate with them on an open, equal, and person-to-person basis.

Euphoria. An altered state of consciousness characterized by an exaggerated feeling of well-being that is inappropriate to apparent events. It is often associated with opiate, amphetamine, or alcohol abuse.

Evasion. Act of not facing up to or of strategically eluding something. It consists of suppressing an idea that is next in a thought series and replacing it with another idea closely related to it. Evasion is also known as paralogia and perverted logic.

Exaltation. Affect consisting of intense elation and feelings of grandeur.

Exhibitionism. A form of sexual deviation characterized by a compulsive need to expose one's body, particularly the genitals.

Existential group psychotherapy. A type of group therapy that puts the emphasis on confrontation, primarily in the here-and-now interaction, and on feeling experiences rather than on rational thinking. Less attention is put on patient resistances. The therapist is involved on the same level and to the same degree as the patients. *See also* Encounter group.

Expanded group. The friends, immediate family, and interested relatives of a group therapy patient. They are the people with whom he has to relate outside the formal therapy group. *See also* Back-home group.

Experiencing. Feeling emotions and sensations as opposed to thinking; being involved in what is happening rather than standing back at a distance and theorizing. Encounter groups attempt to bring about this personal involvement.

Experiential group. *See* Encounter group.

Experiential stimulator. Anything that stimulates an emotional or sensory response. Several techniques, many of them nonverbal, have been developed for encounter groups to accomplish this stimulation. *See also* Behind-the-back technique, Blind walk.

Extended family therapy. A type of family therapy that involves family members, beyond the nuclear family, who are closely associated with it and affect it. *See also* Network, Social network therapy, Visitor.

Exteropsychic function. *See* Parent.

Extrapsychic conflict. Conflict that arises between the person and his environment. *See also* Intrapsychic conflict.

Extrapyramidal effect. Bizarre, involuntary motor movement. It is a central nervous system side effect sometimes produced by antipsychotic drugs. *See also* Dyskinesia.

Extratherapeutic contact. Contact between group members outside of a regularly scheduled group session.

Facilitator. Group leader. He may be the therapist or a patient who emerges during the course of an encounter and who channels group interaction. He is also known as the session leader.

Fag hag. Slang, derogatory expression often used by homosexuals to describe a woman who has become part of a homosexual social circle and has assumed a central role as a mother figure.

Family neurosis. Emotional maladaptation in which a person's psychopathology is unconsciously inter-related with that of the other members of his family.

Family therapy. Treatment of a family in conflict. The whole family meets as a group with the therapist and explores its relationships and process. The focus is on the resolution of current reactions to one another rather than on individual members. *See also* Collaborative therapy, Combined therapy, Concurrent therapy, Conjoint therapy, Extended family therapy, Group marital therapy, Marriage therapy, Quadrangular therapy, Square interview.

Fantasy. Day dream; fabricated mental picture or chain of events. A form of thinking dominated by unconscious material and primary processes, it seeks wish-fulfillment and immediate solutions to conflicts. Fantasy may serve as the matrix for creativity or for neurotic distortions of reality.

Father surrogate. Father substitute. In psychoanalysis, the patient projects his father image onto another person and responds to that person unconsciously in an inappropriate and unrealistic manner with the feelings and attitudes he had toward the original father.

Fausse reconnaissance. False recognition. *See also* Paramnesia.

Fear. Unpleasurable affect consisting of psychophysiological changes in response to a realistic threat or danger to one's existence. *See also* Anxiety.

Federn, Paul (1871–1950). Austrian psychoanalyst, one of Freud's earliest followers, and the last survivor of the original Wednesday Evening Society. He made important original contributions to psychoanalysis—such as the concepts of flying dreams and ego feeling—and was instrumental in saving the minutes of the Vienna Psychoanalytic Society for subsequent publication.

Feedback. Expressed response by one person or a group to another person's behavior. *See also* Sociometric feedback, Transaction.

Feeling-driven group. A group in which little or no attention is paid to rational processes, thinking, or cognition and where the expression of all kinds of emotion is rewarded. *See also* Affectualizing, Encounter group, Existential group psychotherapy.

Ferenczi, Sandor (1873–1933). Hungarian psychoanalyst, one of Freud's early followers, and a brilliant contributor to all aspects of psychoanalysis. His temperament was more romantic than Freud's, and he came to favor more active and personal techniques, to the point that his adherence to psychoanalysis during his last years was questioned.

Field theory. Concept postulated by Kurt Lewin that a person is a complex energy field in which all behavior can be conceived of as a change in some state of the field during a given unit of time. Lewin also postulated the presence within the field of psychological tensions—states of readiness or preparation for action. The field theory is concerned essentially with the present field, the here-and-now. The theory has been applied by various group psychotherapists.

Fliess, Wilhelm (1858–1928). Berlin nose and throat specialist. He shared an early interest with Freud in the physiology of sex and entered into a prolonged correspondence that figures importantly in the records of Freud's self-analysis. Freud was influenced by Fliess's concept of bisexuality and his theory of the periodicity of the sex functions.

Focal-conflict theory. Theory elaborated by Thomas French in 1952 that explains the current behavior of a person as an expression of his method of solving currently experienced personality conflicts that originated very early in his life. He constantly resonates to these early-life conflicts.

Focused exercise. Technique used particularly in encounter groups to help participants break through their defensive behavior and express such specific emotional reactions as anger, affection, and joy. A psychodrama, for instance, may focus on a specific problem that a group member is having with his wife. In playing out both his part and her part, he becomes aware of the emotion he has been blocking.

Folie à deux. Emotional illness shared by two persons. If it involves three persons, it is referred to as *folie à trois*, etc.

Forced interaction. Relationship that occurs in a group when the therapist or other members demand that a particular patient respond, react, and be active. *See also* Structured interactional group psychotherapy.

Ford negative personal contacts with Negroes scale. A scale that measures whites' negative social contacts with blacks. *See also* Kelley desegregation scale, Rosander anti-Negro behavior scale, Steckler anti-Negro scale, Steckler anti-white scale.

Ford negative personal contacts with whites scale. A scale that measures blacks' negative personal contacts with whites. It helps assess the extent to which negative social contacts influence prejudiced attitudes, thus contributing to the theoretical basis for the employment of interracial group experiences to reduce prejudice. *See also* Kelley desegregation scale, Rosander anti-Negro behavior scale, Steckler anti-Negro scale, Steckler anti-white scale.

Formal operations. Jean Piaget's label for the complete development of a person's logical thinking capacities.

Foulkes, S. H. (1923–   ). English psychiatrist and one of the organizers of the group therapy movement in Great Britain. His work combines Moreno's ideas—the here-and-now, the socio-genesis, the social atom, the psychological network—with psypchoanalytic views. He stresses the importance of group-as-a-whole phenomena. *See also* Group analytic psychotherapy, Network.

Free association. Investigative psychoanalytic technique devised by Freud in which the patient seeks to verbalize, without reservation or censor, the passing contents of his mind. The conflicts that emerge while fulfilling this task constitute resistances that are the basis of the analyst's interpretations. *See also* Antirepression device, Conflict.

Free-floating anxiety. Pervasive, unrealistic fear that is not attached to any idea or alleviated by symptom substitution. It is observed particularly in anxiety neurosis, although it may be seen in some cases of latent schizophrenia.

Freud, Sigmund (1856–1939). Austrian psychiatrist and the founder of psychoanalysis. With Josef Breuer, he explored the potentialities of cathartic therapy, then went on to develop the analytic technique and such fundamental concepts of mental phenomena as the unconscious, infantile sexuality, repression, sublimation, superego, ego, and id formation and their applications throughout all spheres of human behavior.

Fulfillment. Satisfaction of needs that may be either real or illusory.

Future projection. Psychodrama technique wherein the patient shows in action how he thinks his future will shape itself. He, sometimes with the assistance of the director, picks the point in time, the place, and the people, if any, he expects to be involved with at that time.

Galactorrhea. Excessive or spontaneous flow of milk from the breast. It may be a result of the endocrine influence of phenothiazine drugs.

Gallows transaction. A transaction in which a person with a self-destructive script smiles while narrating or engaging in a self-destructive act. His smile evokes a smile in the listener, which is in essence an encouragement for self-destruction. *See also* Hamartic script.

Game. Technique that resembles a traditional game in being physical or mental competition conducted according to rules but that is used in the group situation as an experiential learning device. The emphasis is on the process of the game rather than on the objective of the game. A game in Eric Berne's transactional analysis refers to an orderly sequence of social maneuvers with an ulterior motive and resulting in a psychological payoff for the players. *See also* Hit-and-run game, Million-dollar game, Pastime, Survival, Transactional group psychotherapy.

Game analysis. In transactional analysis, the analysis of a person's social interactions that are not honest and straightforward but are contaminated with pretenses for personal gain. *See also* Script analysis, Structural analysis.

Genetic material. Data out of the personal history of the patient that are useful in developing an understanding of the psychodynamics of his present adaptation. *See also* Current material.

Genital phase. The final stage of psychosexual development. It occurs during puberty. In this stage the person's psychosexual development is so organized that he can achieve sexual gratification from genital-to-genital contact and has the capacity for a mature, affectionate relationship with someone of the opposite sex. *See also* Anal phase, Infantile sexuality, Latency phase, Oral phase, Phallic phase.

Gestalt therapy. Type of psychotherapy that emphasizes the treatment of the person as a whole—his biological component parts and their organic functioning, his perceptual configuration, and his inter-relationships with the outside world. Gestalt therapy, developed by Frederic S. Perls, can be used in either an individual or a group therapy setting. It focuses on the sensory awareness of the person's here-and-now experiences rather than on past recollections or future expectations. Gestalt therapy employs role-playing and other techniques to promote the patient's growth process and to develop his full potential. *See also* Nonverbal interaction.

Gilles de la Tourette's disease. A rare illness that has its onset in childhood. The illness, first described by a Paris physician, Gilles de la Tourette, is characterized by involuntary muscular movements and motor incoordination accompanied by echolalia and coprolalia. It is considered by some to be a schizophrenic condition.

Give-up-itis. Syndrome characterized by a giving up of the desire to live. The alienation, isolation, withdrawal, and eventual death associated with this disease syndrome were experienced by many American prisoners during the Korean War, particularly in the early stages of Communist brainwashing. *See also* Dog-eat-dog period.

Go-around. Technique used in group therapy, particularly in structured interactional group psychotherapy, in which the therapist requires that each member of the group respond to another member, a theme, an association, etc. This procedure encourages participation of all members in the group.

God complex. A belief, sometimes seen in therapists, that one can accomplish more than is humanly possible or that one's word should not be doubted. The God complex of the aging psychoanalyst was first discussed by Ernest Jones, Freud's biographer. *See also* Mother Superior complex.

Gould Academy. Private preparatory school in Bethel, Maine, that has been used during summers as the site of the human relations laboratories run by the National Educational Association.

Grief. Alteration in mood and affect consisting of sadness appropriate to a real loss. *See also* Depression.

Group. *See* Therapeutic group.

Group action technique. Technique used in group work to help the participants achieve skills in interpersonal relations and improve their capacity to perform certain tasks better on the job or at home; technique, often involving physical interaction, aimed at enhancing involvement or communion within a new group.

Group analysand. A person in treatment in a psychoanalytically oriented group.

Group analytic psychotherapy. A type of group therapy in which the group is used as the principal therapeutic agent and all communications and relationships are viewed as part of a total field of interaction. Interventions deal primarily with group forces rather than with individual forces. S. H. Foulkes applied the term to his treatment procedure in 1948. It is also known as therapeutic group analysis. *See also* Phyloanalysis, Psychoanalytic group psychotherapy.

Group apparatus. Those people who preserve order and ensure the survival of a group. The internal apparatus deals with members' proclivities in order to maintain the structure of the group and strengthen cohesion. The therapist usually serves as his own apparatus in a small therapy group; in a courtroom, a bailiff ensures internal order. The external apparatus deals with the environment in order to minimize the threat of external pressure. The therapist usually acts as his own external apparatus by setting the time and place for the meetings and making sure that outsiders do not interfere; in a war, combat forces act as the external apparatus.

Group bibliotherapy. A form of group therapy that focuses on the use of selected readings as stimulus material. Outside readings and oral presentations of printed matter by therapist and patients are designed to encourage verbal interchange in the sessions and to hold the attention of severely regressed patients. This approach is used in the treatment of large groups of institutionalized patients. *See also* Class method, Didactic technique, Mechanical group therapy.

Group-centered psychotherapy. A short-term, nonclinical form of group therapy developed by followers of Carl Rogers and based on his client-centered method of individual treatment. The therapist maintains a nonjudgmental attitude, clarifies the feelings expressed in the sessions, and communicates empathic understanding and respect. The participants are not diagnosed, and uncovering techniques are not employed.

Group climate. Atmosphere and emotional tone of a group therapy session.

Group cohesion. Effect of the mutual bonds between members of a group as a result of their concerted effort for a common interest and purpose. Until cohesiveness is achieved, the group cannot concentrate its full energy on a common task. *See also* Group growth.

Group dynamics. Phenomena that occur in groups; the movement of a group from its inception to its termination. Interactions and interrelations among members and between the members and the therapist create tension, which maintains a constantly changing group equilibrium. The interactions and the tension they create are highly influenced by individual members' psychological make-up, unconscious instinctual drives, motives, wishes, and fantasies. The understanding and effective use of group dynamics is essential in group treatment. It is also known as

group process. *See also* Group mobility, Psychodynamics.

Group grope. Belittling reference to procedures used in certain encounter groups. The procedures are aimed at providing emotional release through physical contact.

Group growth. Gradual development of trust and cohesiveness in a group. It leads to awareness of self and of other group process and to more effective coping with conflict and intimacy problems. *See also* Group cohesion.

Group history. Chronology of the experiences of a group, including group rituals, group traditions, and group themes.

Group inhibition. *See* Group resistance.

Group marathon. Group meeting that usually lasts from eight to 72 hours, although some sessions last for a week. The session is interrupted only for eating and sleeping. The leader works for the development of intimacy and the open expression of feelings. The time-extended group experience culminates in intense feelings of excitement and elation. Group marathon was developed by George Bach and Frederick Stoller. *See also* Accelerated interaction, Nude marathon, Too-tired-to-be-polite phenomenon.

Group marital therapy. A type of marriage therapy that makes use of a group. There are two basic techniques: (1) Inviting the marital partner of a group member to a group session. The other group members are confronted with the neurotic marriage pattern, which gives them new insights and awareness. (2) Placing a husband and wife together in a traditional group of patients. This method seems indicated if the spouses are unable to achieve meaningful intimacy because they fear the loss of their individual identity at an early phase of the marriage, before a neurotic equilibrium is established. *See also* Collaborative therapy, Combined therapy, Concurrent therapy, Conjoint therapy, Family therapy, Quadrangular therapy, Square interview.

Group mind. Autonomous and unified mental life in an assemblage of people bound together by mutual interests. It is a concept used by group therapists who focus on the group as a unit rather than on the individual members.

Group mobility. Spontaneity and movement in

the group brought about by changes in the functions and roles of individual members, relative to their progress. *See also* Group dynamics.

Group-on-group technique. Device used in T-groups wherein one group watches another group in action and then gives feedback to the observed group. Frequently, one group breaks into two sections, each taking turns in observing the other. The technique is intended to sharpen the participants' observation of individual behavior and group process.

Group phenomenon. *See* Group dynamics.

Group pressure. Demand by group members that individual members submit and conform to group standards, values, and behavior.

Group process. *See* Group dynamics.

Group psychotherapy. A type of psychiatric treatment that involves two or more patients participating together in the presence of one or more psychotherapists, who facilitate both emotional and rational cognitive interaction to effect changes in the maladaptive behavior of the members. *See also* Behavioral group psychotherapy, Bio-energetic group psychotherapy, Client-centered psychotherapy, Communion-oriented group psychotherapy, Crisis-intervention group psychotherapy, Existential group psychotherapy, Group analytic psychotherapy, Group bibliotherapy, Group-centered psychotherapy, Individual therapy, Inspirational-supportive group psychotherapy, Psychoanalytic group psychotherapy, Repressive-inspirational group psychotherapy, Social network therapy, Structured interactional group psychotherapy, Traditional group therapy, Transactional group psychotherapy.

Group resistance. Collective natural aversion of the group members toward dealing with unconscious material, emotions, or old patterns of defense.

Group ritual. Tradition or activity that any group establishes to mechanize some of its activities.

Group stimulus. Effect of several group members' communicating together. Each member has a stimulating effect on every other member, and the total stimulation is studied for therapeutic purposes. *See also* Transactions.

Group therapy. *See* Group psychotherapy.

Group tradition. Activity or value established historically by a group. It determines in part the group's manifest behavior.

Group value. Relative worth or standard developed by and agreed on by the members of a group.

Guilt. Affect associated with self-reproach and need for punishment. In psychoanalysis, guilt refers to a neurotic feeling of culpability that stems from a conflict between the ego and the superego. It begins developmentally with parental disapproval and becomes internalized as conscience in the course of superego formation. Guilt has normal psychological and social functions, but special intensity or absence of guilt characterizes many mental disorders, such as depression and antisocial personality. Some psychiatrists distinguish shame as a less internalized form of guilt.

Gustatory hallucination. False sense of taste.

Hallucination. A false sensory perception without a concrete external stimulus. It can be induced by emotional and by organic factors, such as drugs and alcohol. Common hallucinations involve sights or sounds, although any of the senses may be involved. *See also* Auditory hallucination, Gustatory hallucination, Hypnagogic hallucination, Hypnopompic hallucination, Kinesthetic hallucination, Lilliputian hallucination, Tactile hallucination, Visual hallucination.

Hallucinatory psychodrama. A type of psychodrama wherein the patient portrays the voices he hears and the visions he sees. Auxiliary egos are often called on to enact the various phenomena expressed by the patient and to involve him in interaction with them, so as to put them to a reality test. The intended effect on the patient is called psychodramatic shock.

Hallucinogenic drug. *See* Psychotomimetic drug.

Hamartic script. In transactional analysis, a life script that is self-destructive and tragic in character. *See also* Gallows transaction, Script, Script antithesis, Script matrix.

Healthy identification. Modeling of oneself, consciously or unconsciously, on another person who has sound psychic make-up. The identification has constructive purposes. *See also* Imitation.

Herd instinct. Desire to belong to a group and to participate in social activities. Wilfred Trotter used the term to indicate the presence of a hypothetical social instinct in man. In psychoanalysis, herd instinct is viewed as a social phenomenon rather than as an instinct. *See also* Aggressive drive, Sexual drive.

Here-and-now. Contemporaneity. *See also* There-and-then.

Here-and-now approach. A technique that focuses on understanding the interpersonal and intrapersonal responses and reactions as they occur in the on-going treatment session. Little or no emphasis is put on past history and experiences. *See also* Encounter group, Existential group psychotherapy.

Heterogeneous group. A group that consists of patients from both sexes, a wide age range, differing psychopathologies, and divergent socioeconomic, racial, ethnic, and cultural backgrounds. *See also* Homogeneous group.

Heterosexuality. Sexual attraction or contact between opposite-sex persons. The capacity for heterosexual arousal is probably innate, biologically programmed, and triggered in very early life, perhaps by olfactory modalities, as seen in lower animals. *See also* Bisexuality, Homosexuality.

Hidden self. The behavior, feelings, and motivations of a person known to himself but not to others. It is a quadrant of the Johari Window, a diagrammatic concept of human behavior. *See also* Blind self, Public self, Undeveloped potential.

Hierarchical vector. Thrust of relating to the other members of a group or to the therapist in a supraordinate or subordinate way. It is the opposite of relating as peers. It is also known as vertical vector. *See also* Authority principle, Horizontal vector, Political therapist.

Hit-and-run game. Hostile or nonconstructive aggressive activity indiscriminately and irresponsibly carried out against others. *See also* Game, Million dollar game, Survival.

Homogeneous group. A group that consists of patients of the same sex, with similarities in their psychopathology, and from the same age range and socioeconomic, racial, ethnic, and cultural background. *See also* Heterogeneous group.

Homosexuality. Sexual attraction or contact between same-sex persons. Some authors distinguish two types: overt homosexuality and latent homosexuality. *See also* Bisexuality, Heterosexuality, Inversion, Lesbianism.

Homosexual panic. Sudden, acute onset of severe anxiety, precipitated by the unconscious fear or conflict that one may be a homosexual or act out homosexual impulses. *See also* Homosexuality.

Honesty. Forthrightness of conduct and uprightness of character; truthfulness. In therapy, honesty is a value manifested by the ability to communicate one's immediate experience, including inconsistent, conflicting, or ambivalent feelings and perceptions. *See also* Authenticity.

Hook. In transactional analysis, to switch one's transactions to a new ego state. For example, a patient's Adult ego state is hooked when he goes to the blackboard and draws a diagram.

Horizontal vector. Thrust of relating to the therapist or other members of the group as equals. It is also known as peer vector. *See also* Authority principle, Hierarchical vector, Political therapist.

House encounter. Group meeting of all the persons in a treatment facility. Such a meeting is designed to deal with specific problems within the therapeutic community that affect its functioning, such as poor morale and poor job performances.

Hydrotherapy. External or internal use of water in the treatment of disease. In psychiatry, the use of wet packs to calm an agitated psychotic patient was formerly a popular treatment modality.

Hyperactivity. Increased muscular activity. The term is commonly used to describe a disturbance found in children that is manifested by constant restlessness and movements executed at a rapid rate. The disturbance is believed to be due to brain damage, mental retardation, emotional disturbance, or physiological disturbance. It is also known as hyperkinesis.

Hyperkinesis. *See* Hyperactivity.

Hypermnesia. Exaggerated degree of retention and recall. It is observed in schizophrenia, the manic phase of manic-depressive illness, organic brain syndrome, drug intoxication induced by amphetamines and hallucinogens, hypnosis, and febrile conditions. *See also* Memory.

Hypertensive crisis. Severe rise in blood pressure that can lead to intracranial hemorrhage. It is occasionally seen as a side effect of certain antidepressant drugs.

Hypnagogic hallucination. False sensory perception that occurs just before falling asleep. *See also* Hypnopompic hallucination.

Hypnodrama. Psychodrama under hypnotic trance. The patient is first put into a hypnotic trance. During the trance he is encouraged to act out the various experiences that torment him.

Hypnopompic hallucination. False sensory perception that occurs just before full wakefulness. *See also* Hypnagogic hallucination.

Hypnosis. Artificially induced alteration of consciousness of one person by another. The subject responds with a high degree of suggestibility, both mental and physical, during the trancelike state.

Hypochondriasis. Exaggerated concern with one's physical health. The concern is not based on real organic pathology.

Hypotension, orthostatic. *See* Orthostatic hypotension.

Hysterical anesthesia. Disturbance in sensory perception characterized by absence of sense of feeling in certain areas of the body. It is observed in certain cases of hysterical neurosis, particularly the conversion type, and it is believed to be a defense mechanism.

Id. Part of Freud's concept of the psychic apparatus. According to his structural theory of mental functioning, the id harbors the energy that stems from the instinctual drives and desires of a person. The id is completely in the unconscious realm, unorganized and under the influence of the primary processes. *See also* Conscious, Ego, Preconscious, Primary process, Superego, Unconscious.

Idealization. A defense mechanism in which a person consciously or, usually, unconsciously overestimates an attribute or an aspect of another person.

Ideas of reference. Misinterpretation of incidents and events in the outside world as having a direct personal reference to oneself. Occasionally observed in normal persons, ideas of reference are frequently seen in paranoid patients. *See also* Projection.

Ideational shield. An intellectual, rational defense against the anxiety a person would feel if he became vulnerable to the criticisms and rejection of others. As a result of his fear of being rejected, he may feel threatened if he criticizes another person—an act that is unacceptable to him. In both group and individual therapy, conditions are set up that allow the participants to lower this ideational shield.

Identification. An unconscious defense mechanism in which a person incorporates into himself the mental picture of an object and then patterns himself after this object; seeing oneself as like the person used as a pattern. It is distinguished from imitation, a conscious process. *See also* Healthy identification, Imitation, Role.

Identification with the aggressor. An unconscious process by which a person incorporates within himself the mental image of a person who represents a source of frustration from the outside world. A primitive defense, it operates in the interest and service of the developing ego. The classical example of this defense occurs toward the end of the oedipal stage, when the male child, whose main source of love and gratification is the mother, identifies with his father. The father represents the source of frustration, being the powerful rival for the mother; the child cannot master or run away from his father, so he is obliged to identify with him. *See also* Psychosexual development.

Idiot. *See* Mental retardation.

I-It. Philosopher Martin Buber's description of damaging interpersonal relationships. If a person treats himself or another person exclusively as an object, he prevents mutuality, trust, and growth. When pervasive in a group, I-It relationships prevent human warmth, destroy cohesiveness, and retard group process. *See also* I-Thou.

Ileus, paralytic. *See* Paralytic ileus.

Illusion. False perception and misinterpretation of an actual sensory stimulus.

Illustration. In transactional analysis, an anecdote, simile, or comparison that reinforces a confrontation or softens its potentially undesirable effects. The illustration may be immediate or remote in time and may refer to the external environment or to the internal situation in the group.

Imbecile. *See* Mental retardation.

Imitation. In psychiatry, a conscious act of mimicking another person's behavior pattern. *See also* Healthy identification, Identification.

Impasse. *See* Therapeutic impasse.

Improvement scale. In transactional analysis, a quantitative specification of a patient's position in terms of improvement in the course of therapy.

Improvisation. In psychodrama, the acting out of problems without prior preparation.

Impulse. Unexpected, instinctive urge motivated by conscious and unconscious feelings over which the person has little or no control. *See also* Drive, Instinct.

Inappropriate affect. Emotional tone that is out of harmony with the idea, object, or thought accompanying it.

Inclusion phase. Early stage of group treatment. In this phase, each group member's concern focuses primarily on belonging and being accepted and recognized, particularly by the therapist. It is also known as the dependency stage. *See also* Affection phase, Power phase.

Incorporation. An unconscious defense mechanism in which an object representation is assimilated into oneself through symbolic oral ingestion. One of the primitive defenses, incorporation is a special form of introjection and is the primary mechanism in identification.

Individual psychology. Holistic theory of personality developed by Alfred Adler. Personality development is explained in terms of adaptation to the social milieu (life style), strivings toward perfection motivated by feelings of inferiority, and the interpersonal nature of the person's problems. Individual psychology is applied in

group psychotherapy and counseling by Adlerian practitioners.

Individual therapy. A type of psychotherapy in which a professionally trained psychotherapist treats one patient who either wants relief from disturbing symptoms or improvement in his ability to cope with his problems. This one therapist–one patient relationship, the traditional dyadic therapeutic technique, is opposed to other techniques that deal with more than one patient. *See also* Group psychotherapy, Psychotherapy.

Individuation. Differentiation; the process of molding and developing the individual personality so that it is different from the rest of the group. *See also* Actualization.

Infantile dynamics. Psychodynamic integrations, such as the Oedipus complex, that are organized during childhood and continue to exert unconsciously experienced influences on adult personality.

Infantile sexuality. Freudian concept regarding the erotic life of infants and children. Freud observed that, from birth, infants are capable of erotic activities. Infantile sexuality encompasses the overlapping phases of psychosexual development during the first five years of life and includes the oral phase (birth to 18 months), when erotic activity centers around the mouth; the anal phase (ages one to three), when erotic activity centers around the rectum; and the phallic phase (ages two to six), when erotic activity centers around the genital region. *See also* Psychosexual development.

Inferiority complex. Concept, originated by Alfred Adler, that everyone is born with inferiority or a feeling of inferiority secondary to real or fantasied organic or psychological inadequacies. How this inferiority or feeling of inferiority is handled determines a person's behavior in life. *See also* Masculine protest.

Infra reality. Reduced actuality that is observed in certain therapeutic settings. For example, according to J. L. Moreno, who coined the term, the contact between doctor and patient is not a genuine dialogue but is an interview, research situation, or projective test.

Injunction. In transactional analysis, the instructions given by one ego state to another, usually the Parent ego state to the Child ego state, that become the basis of the person's life script decisions. *See also* Permission, Program, Role, Script analysis.

Inner-directed person. A person who is self-motivated and autonomous and is not easily guided or influenced by the opinions and values of other people. *See also* Other-directed person.

Insight. Conscious awareness and understanding of one's own psychodynamics and symptoms of maladaptive behavior. It is highly important in effecting changes in the personality and behavior of a person. Most therapists distinguish two types: (1) intellectual insight—knowledge and awareness without any change of maladaptive behavior; (2) emotional or visceral insight—awareness, knowledge, and understanding of one's own maladaptive behavior, leading to positive changes in personality and behavior.

Inspirational-supportive group psychotherapy. A type of group therapy that focuses on the positive potential of members and stresses reinforcement for accomplishments or achievements. *See also* Alcoholics Anonymous.

Instinct. A biological, species-specific, genetically determined drive to respond in an automatic, complex, but organized way to a particular stimulus. *See also* Drive, Impulse.

Institute of Industrial Relations. A department of the Graduate School of Business Administration at the University of California at Los Angeles. It has conducted sensitivity training laboratories for business and professional people for nearly 20 years.

Insulin coma therapy. A form of psychiatric treatment originated by Manfred Sakel in which insulin is administered to the patient to produce coma. It is used in certain types of schizophrenia. *See also* Shock treatment.

Intellectual insight. *See* Insight.

Intellectualization. An unconscious defense mechanism in which reasoning or logic is used in an attempt to avoid confrontation with an objectionable impulse or affect. It is also known as brooding or thinking compulsion.

Intelligence. Capacity for understanding, recalling, mobilizing, and integrating constructively what one has learned and for using it to meet new situations.

Intensive group process. Group process designed to evoke a high degree of personal interaction and involvement, often accompanied by the expression of strong or deep feelings.

Interaction. *See* Transaction.

Interpersonal conflict. *See* Extrapsychic conflict.

Interpersonal psychiatry. Dynamic-cultural system of psychoanalytic therapy based on Harry Stack Sullivan's interpersonal theory. Sullivan's formulations were couched in terms of a person's interactions with other people. In group psychotherapy conducted by practitioners of this school, the focus is on the patients' transactions with one another.

Interpersonal skill. Ability of a person in relationship with others to express his feelings appropriately, to be socially responsible, to change and influence, and to work and create. *See also* Socialization.

Interpretation. A psychotherapeutic technique used in psychoanalysis, both individual and group. The therapist conveys to the patient the significance and meaning of his behavior, constructing into a more meaningful form the patient's resistances, defenses, transferences, and symbols (dreams). *See also* Clarification.

Interpretation of Dreams, The. Title of a book by Freud. Published in 1899, this work was a major presentation not only of Freud's discoveries about the meaning of dreams—hitherto regarded as outside scientific interest—but also of his concept of a mental apparatus that is topographically divided into unconscious, preconscious, and conscious areas.

Interracial group. *See* Heterogeneous group.

Intervention laboratory. Human relations laboratory, such as an encounter group or training group, especially designed to intervene and resolve some group conflict or crisis.

Intrapersonal conflict. *See* Intrapsychic conflict.

Intrapsychic ataxia. *See* Ataxia.

Intrapsychic conflict. Conflict that arises from the clash of two opposing forces within oneself.

It is also known as intrapersonal conflict. *See also* Extrapsychic conflict.

Introjection. An unconscious defense mechanism in which a psychic representation of a loved or hated object is taken into one's ego system. In depression, for example, the emotional feelings related to the loss of a loved one are directed toward the introjected mental representation of the loved one. *See also* Identification, Incorporation.

Inversion. Synonym for homosexuality. Inversion was the term used by Freud and his predecessors. There are three types: absolute, amphigenous, and occasional. *See also* Homosexuality, Latent homosexuality, Overt homosexuality.

I-Thou. Philosopher Martin Buber's conception that man's identity develops from true sharing by persons. Basic trust can occur in a living partnership in which each member identifies the particular real personality of the other in his wholeness, unity, and uniqueness. In groups, I-Thou relationships promote warmth, cohesiveness, and constructive group process. *See also* I-It.

Jamais vu. False feeling of unfamiliarity with a real situation one has experienced. *See also* Paramnesia.

Jaundice, allergic. Yellowish staining of the skin and deeper tissues accompanied by bile in the urine secondary to a hypersensitivity reaction. An obstructive type of jaundice, it is occasionally detected during the second to fourth week of phenothiazine therapy.

Johari Window. A schematic diagram used to conceptualize human behavior. It was developed by Joseph (Jo) Luft and Harry (Hari) Ingham at the University of California at Los Angeles in 1955. The diagram is composed of quadrants, each representing some aspect of a person's behavior, feelings, and motivations. *See also* Blind self, Hidden self, Public self, Undeveloped potential.

Jones, Ernest (1879–1958). Welsh psychoanalyst and one of Freud's early followers. He was an organizer of the American Psychoanalytic Association in 1911 and the British Psychoanalytical Society in 1919 and a founder and long-time editor of the journal of the International Psychoanalytical Association. He was the author of many valuable works, the most important of which is his three-volume biography of Freud.

Judgment. Mental act of comparing or evaluating choices within the framework of a given set of values for the purpose of electing a course of action. Judgment is said to be intact if the course of action chosen is consistent with reality; judgment is said to be impaired if the chosen course of action is not consistent with reality.

Jung, Carl Gustav (1875–1961). Swiss psychiatrist and psychoanalyst. He founded the school of analytic psychology. *See also* Collective unconscious.

Karate-chop experience. A technique used in encounter groups to elicit aggression in timid or inhibited participants in a humorous way. The timid one stands facing a more aggressive member. Both make violent pseudokarate motions at each other, without making physical contact but yelling "Hai!" as loudly as possible at each stroke. After this exercise, the group members discuss the experience.

Kelley desegregation scale. A scale designed to measure the attitudes of whites toward blacks in the area of school integration. The scale provides a rough measure of racial prejudice and may be of help in ascertaining the effects on prejudice of participation in an interracial group. *See also* Ford negative personal contacts with Negroes scale, Ford negative personal contacts with whites scale, Rosander anti-Negro behavior scale, Steckler anti-Negro scale, Steckler anti-white scale.

Kinesthetic hallucination. False perception of muscular movement. An amputee may feel movement in his missing limb; this phenomenon is also known as phantom limb.

Kinesthetic sense. Sensation in the muscles as differentiated from the senses that receive stimulation from outside the body.

Kleptomania. Pathological compulsion to steal. In psychoanalytic theory, it originates in the infantile stage of psychosexual development.

Latency phase. Stage of psychosexual development extending from age five to the beginning of adolescence at age 12. Freud's work on ego psychology showed that the apparent cessation of sexual preoccupation during this period stems from a strong, aggressive blockade of libidinal and sexual impulses in an effort to avoid the dangers of the oedipal relationships. During the latency period, boys and girls are inclined to choose friends and join groups of their own sex. *See also* Identification with the aggressor, Psychosexual development.

Latent homosexuality. Unexpressed conscious or unconscious homoerotic wishes that are held in check. Freud's theory of bisexuality postulated the existence of a constitutionally determined, though experientially influenced, instinctual masculine-feminine duality. Normally, the opposite-sex component is dormant, but a breakdown in the defenses of repression and sublimation may activate latent instincts and result in overt homoeroticism. Many writers have questioned the validity of a universal latent homoeroticism. *See also* Bisexuality, Homosexuality, Overt homosexuality.

Lateral transference. Projection of long-range attitudes, values, and emotions onto the other members of the treatment group rather than onto the therapist. The patient sees other members of the group, co-patients, and peers in terms of his experiences in his original family. *See also* Collective family transference neurosis, Multiple transference.

Leaderless therapeutic group. An extreme form of nondirective group, conducted primarily for research purposes, such as the investigations of intragroup tensions by Walter R. Bion. On occasion, the therapist interacts verbally in a nonauthoritarian manner, but he generally functions as a silent observer—withholding explanations, directions, and support.

Leadership function. *See* Leadership role.

Leadership role. Stance adopted by the therapist in conducting a group. There are three main leadership roles: authoritarian, democratic, and laissez-faire. Any group—social, therapeutic, training, or task-oriented—is primarily influenced by the role practiced by the leader.

Leadership style. *See* Leadership role.

Lesbianism. Female homosexuality. About 600 B.C. on the island of Lesbos in the Aegean Sea, the poetess Sappho encouraged young women to engage in mutual sex practices. Lesbianism is also known as Sapphism. *See also* Bisexuality,

Homosexuality, Latent homosexuality, Overt homosexuality.

Lewin, Kurt (1890–1946). German psychologist who emigrated to the United States in 1933. His work on the field theory has been useful in the experimental study of human behavior in a social situation. He was one of the early workers who helped develop the National Training Laboratories.

Libido theory. Freudian theory of sexual instinct, its complex process of development, and its accompanying physical and mental manifestations. Before Freud's introduction and completion of the dual-instinct theory (sexual and aggressive) in 1920, all instinctual manifestations were related to the sexual instinct, making for some confusion at that time. Current psychoanalytic practice assumes the existence of two instincts: sexual (libido) and aggressive (death). *See also* Aggressive drive, Sexual drive.

Life instinct. *See* Sexual drive.

Life lie. A contrary-to-fact conviction around which a person structures his life philosophy and attitudes.

Life line. A group technique in which each member is asked to draw a line representing his life, beginning with birth and ending with death. Comparison and discussion usually reveal that the shape and slope of the lines are based on a variety of personally meaningful parameters, such as maturity and academic achievement.

Lifwynn Foundation. Organization established by Trigant Burrow in 1927 as a social community in which the participants examined their interactions in the daily activities in which they were engaged. Lifwynn is currently under the direction of Hans Syz, M.D., in Westport, Conn.

Lilliputian hallucination. False perception that persons are reduced in size. *See also* Micropsia.

Lobotomy. Neurosurgical procedure in which one or more nerve tracts in a lobe of the cerebrum are severed. Prefrontal lobotomy is the ablation of one or more nerve tracts in the prefrontal area of the brain. It is used in the treatment of certain severe mental disorders that do not respond to other treatments.

Locus. Place of origin.

Logorrhea. Copious, pressured, coherent speech. It is observed in manic-depressive illness, manic type. Logorrhea is also known as tachylogia, verbomania, and volubility.

LSD (lysergic acid diethylamide). A potent psychotogenic drug discovered in 1942. LSD produces psychoticlike symptoms and behavior changes—including hallucinations, delusions, and time-space distortions.

Lysergic acid diethylamide. *See* LSD.

Macropsia. False perception that objects are larger than they really are. *See also* Micropsia.

Maintenance drug therapy. A stage in the course of chemotherapy. After the drug has reached its maximal efficacy, the dosage is reduced and sustained at the minimal therapeutic level that will prevent a relapse or exacerbation.

Major tranquilizer. Drug that has antipsychotic properties. The phenothiazines, thioxanthenes, butyrophenones, and reserpine derivatives are typical major tranquilizers, which are also known as ataractics, neuroleptics, and antipsychotics. *See also* Dystonia, Minor tranquilizer.

Maladaptive way. Poorly adjusted or pathological behavior pattern.

Mannerism. Stereotyped involuntary activity that is peculiar to a person.

MAO inhibitor. *See* Monoamine oxidase inhibitor.

Marathon. *See* Group marathon.

Marijuana. Dried leaves and flowers of *Cannabis sativa* (Indian hemp). It induces somatic and psychic changes in man when smoked or ingested in sufficient quantity. The somatic changes include increased heart rate, rise in blood pressure, dryness of the mouth, increased appetite, and occasional nausea, vomiting, and diarrhea. The psychic changes include dreamy-state level of consciousness, disruptive chain of ideas, perceptual disturbances of time and space, and alterations of mood. In strong doses, marijuana can produce hallucinations and, at times, paranoid ideas and suspiciousness. It is also known as pot, grass, weed, tea, and Mary Jane.

Marital counseling. Process whereby a trained counselor helps married couples resolve problems that arise and trouble them in their relationship. The theory and techniques of this approach were first developed in social agencies as part of family casework. Husband and wife are seen by the same worker in separate and joint counseling sessions, which focus on immediate family problems.

Marital therapy. *See* Marriage therapy.

Marriage therapy. A type of family therapy that involves the husband and the wife and focuses on the marital relationship, which affects the individual psychopathology of the partners. The rationale for this method is the assumption that psychopathological processes within the family structure and in the social matrix of the marriage perpetuate individual pathological personality structures, which find expression in the disturbed marriage and are aggravated by the feedback between partners. *See also* Collaborative therapy, Combined therapy, Concurrent therapy, Conjoint therapy, Family therapy, Group marital therapy, Marital counseling, Quadrangular therapy, Square interview.

Masculine identity. Well-developed sense of gender affiliation with males.

Masculine protest. Adlerian doctrine that depicts a universal human tendency to move from a passive and feminine role to a masculine and active role. This doctrine is an extension of his ideas about organic inferiority. It became the prime motivational force in normal and neurotic behavior in the Adlerian system. *See also* Adler, Alfred; Inferiority complex.

Masculinity-femininity scale. Any scale on a psychological test that assesses the relative masculinity or femininity of the testee. Scales vary and may focus, for example, on basic identification with either sex or preference for a particular sex role.

Masochism. A sexual deviation in which sexual gratification is derived from being maltreated by the partner or oneself. It was first described by an Austrian novelist, Leopold von Sacher-Masoch (1836–1895). *See also* Sadism, Sadomasochistic relationship.

Masturbation. *See* Autoerotism.

Mattress-pounding. A technique used in encounter groups to mobilize repressed or suppressed anger. A group member vents his resentments by beating the mattress with his fists and yelling. Frequently, the mattress becomes in fantasy a hated parent, sibling, or spouse. After this exercise, the group members discuss their reactions. *See also* Pillow-beating.

Maximal expression. Utmost communication. In psychodrama, it is the outcome of an involved sharing by the group of the three portions of the session: the warm-up, the action, and the postaction. During the action period the patient is encouraged to express all action and verbal communication to the limit. To this end, delusions, hallucinations, soliloquies, thoughts, and fantasies are allowed to be part of the production.

Mechanical group therapy. A form of group therapy that makes use of mechanical devices. As applied in the early 1950's, it required neither a group nor a therapist. An example of this form of therapy is the playing of brief recorded messages over the loudspeaker system of a mental hospital; the same statement, bearing on some elementary principle of mental health, is frequently repeated to secure general acceptance. *See also* Class method, Didactic technique, Group bibliotherapy.

Megalomania. Morbid preoccupation with expansive delusions of power and wealth.

Melancholia. Old term for depression that is rarely used at the present time. As used in the term involutional melancholia, it refers to a morbid state of depression and not to a symptom.

Memory. Ability to revive past sensory impressions, experiences, and learned ideas. Memory includes three basic mental processes: registration—the ability to perceive, recognize, and establish information in the central nervous system; retention—the ability to retain registered information; and recall—the ability to retrieve stored information at will. *See also* Amnesia, Hypermnesia, Paramnesia.

Mental aberration. *See* Aberration, mental.

Mental illness. Psychiatric disease included in the list of mental disorders in the *Diagnostic and Statistical Manual of Mental Disorders* published by the American Psychiatric Association and in the *Standard Nomenclature of Diseases and Operations* approved by the American Medical Association.

Mental retardation. Subnormal general intellectual functioning, which may be evident at birth or may develop during childhood. Learning, social adjustment, and maturation are impaired, and emotional disturbance is often present. The degree of retardation is commonly measured in terms of I.Q.: borderline (68–85), mild (52–67), moderate (36–51), severe (20–35), and profound (under 20). Obsolescent terms that are still used occasionally are idiot (mental age of less than three years), imbecile (mental age of three to seven years), and moron (mental age of eight years).

Methadone. Methadone hydrochloride, a long-acting synthetic narcotic developed in Germany as a substitute for morphine. It is used as an analgesic and in detoxification and maintenance treatment of opiate addicts.

Methadone maintenance treatment. Long-term use of methadone on a daily basis to relieve narcotic craving and avert the effects of narcotic drugs.

Micropsia. False perception that objects are smaller than they really are. *See also* Lilliputian hallucination, Macropsia.

Milieu therapy. Treatment that emphasizes appropriate socioenvironmental manipulation for the benefit of the patient. The setting for milieu therapy is usually the psychiatric hospital.

Million-dollar game. Group game designed to explore the psychological meaning of money and to encourage free, creative thinking. The group is told that it has a million dollars, which is to be used productively in any way, as long as the endeavor actively involves all members of the group. *See also* Game, Hit-and-run game, Survival.

Minnesota Multiphasic Personality Inventory. Questionnaire type of psychological test for ages 16 and over with 550 true-false statements that are coded in 14 scales, ranging from a social scale to a schizophrenia scale. Group and individual forms are available.

Minor tranquilizer. Drug that diminishes tension, restlessness, and pathological anxiety without any antipsychotic effect. Meprobamate and diazepoxides are typical minor tranquilizers, which are also known as psycholeptics. *See also* Major tranquilizer.

Minutes of the Vienna Psychoanalytic Society. Diary of Freud's Wednesday Evening Society (after 1910, the Vienna Psychoanalytic Society) as recorded by Otto Rank, the paid secretary between 1906 and 1915.

Mirror. In psychodrama, the person who represents the patient, copying his behavior and trying to express his feelings in word and movement, showing the patient as if in a mirror how other people experience him. The mirror may exaggerate, employing techniques of deliberate distortion in order to arouse the patient to come forth and change from a passive spectator into an active participant. The mirror is also known as the double. *See also* Auxiliary ego.

Mirroring. A group process by which a person sees himself in the group by the reflections that come back to him in response to the way he presents himself. The image may be true or distorted, depending on the level of truth at which the group is functioning at the time. Mirroring has been used as an exercise in encounter group therapy and as a laboratory procedure in the warming-up period of the psychodrama approach.

Mixed-gender group. *See* Heterogeneous group.

MMPI. *See* Minnesota Multiphasic Personality Inventory.

Mobility. *See* Group mobility.

Monoamine oxidase inhibitor. Agent that inhibits the enzyme monoamine oxidase (MAO), which oxidizes such monoamines as norepinephrine and serotonin. Some of the MAO inhibitors are highly effective as antidepressants. *See also* Tricyclic drug.

Monomania. Morbid mental state characterized by preoccupation with one subject. It is also known as partial insanity.

Mood. Feeling tone that is experienced by a person internally. Mood does not include the external expression of the internal feeling tone. *See also* Affect.

Mood swing. Oscillation of a person's emotional feeling tone between periods of euphoria and depression.

Moron. *See* Mental retardation.

Moses and Monotheism. Title of a book by Freud published in 1939. In this book, Freud undertook a historical but frankly speculative reconstruction of the personality of Moses and examined the concept of monotheism and the abiding effect of the patriarch on the character of the Jews. One of Freud's last works, it bears the imprint of his latter-day outlook and problems.

Mother Superior complex. Tendency of a therapist to play the role of the mother in his relations with his patients. The complex often leads to interference with the therapeutic process. *See also* God complex.

Mother surrogate. Mother substitute. In psychoanalysis, the patient projects his mother image onto another person and responds to that person unconsciously in an inappropriate and unrealistic manner with the feelings and attitudes he had toward the original mother.

Motivation. Force that pushes a person to act to satisfy a need. It implies an incentive or desire that influences the will and causes the person to act.

Mourning. *See* Grief.

Multibody situation. Group situation. The term was originally used in the description of the evolution of social interaction in human beings from narcissism through the dyadic relationship to the three-body constellation of the Oedipus complex to the multibody situation prevailing in groups.

Multiple double. Several representations of the patient, each portraying a part of him—one as he is now, another as he was (for instance, five years ago), another at a crucial moment in his life (for example, when his mother died), a fourth how he may be 20 years hence. The multiple representations of the patient are presented in sequence, each continuing where the last left off. *See also* Auxiliary ego.

Multiple ego states. Many psychological stages, relating to different periods of one's life or to different depths of experience. These states may be of varying degrees of organization and complexity, and they may or may not be capable of being called to awareness consecutively or simultaneously.

Multiple interaction. Group behavior in which many members participate in the transactions, both verbal and nonverbal, at any one moment in the session.

Multiple intragroup transference. *See* Multiple transference.

Multiple reactivity. A phenomenon in which many group members respond in a variety of ways to the provocative role or stimulation afforded by one patient's behavior.

Multiple therapy. *See* Co-therapy.

Multiple transferences. Feelings and attitudes originally held toward members of one's family that become irrationally attached to the therapist and various group members simultaneously. *See also* Collective family transference neurosis, Lateral transference.

Mutism. *See* Stupor.

Mutual support. Expressions of sympathy, understanding, and affection that group members give to one another. *See also* Pairing.

Mydriasis. Dilatation of the pupil. The condition sometimes occurs as an autonomic side effect of phenothiazine and antiparkinsonism drugs.

Nalline test. The use of Nalline, a narcotic antagonist, to determine abstinence from opiates. An injection of Nalline precipitates withdrawal symptoms if opiates have been used recently. The most important use for Nalline, however, is as an antidote in the treatment of opiate overdose.

Narcissism. Self-love. It is linked to autoerotism but is devoid of genitality. The word is derived from Narcissus, a Greek mythology figure who fell in love with his own reflected image. In psychoanalytic theory, it is divided into primary narcissism and secondary narcissism. Primary narcissism refers to the early infantile phase of object relationship development, when the child has not differentiated himself from the outside world. All sources of pleasure are unrealistically recognized as coming from within himself, giving him a false sense of omnipotence.

Secondary narcissism is the type of narcissism that results when the libido once attached to external love objects is redirected back to the self. *See also* Autistic thinking, Autoerotism.

Narcotic hunger. A physiological craving for a drug. It appears in abstinent narcotic addicts.

National Training Laboratories. Organization started in 1947 at Bethel, Maine, to train professionals who work with groups. Interest in personal development eventually led to sensitivity training and encounter groups. The organization is now called the NTL Institute for Applied Behavioral Science. *See also* Basic skills training, East Coast style T-group.

Natural Child. In transactional analysis, the autonomous, expressive, archaic Child ego state that is free from parental influence. *Se also* Adapted Child.

Natural group. Group that tends to evolve spontaneously in human civilization, such as a kinship, tribal, or religious group. In contrast are various contrived groups or aggregates of people who meet for a relatively brief time to achieve some goal.

Negativism. Verbal or nonverbal opposition to outside suggestions and advice. It is also known as command negativism.

Neologism. New word or condensation of several words formed by patient in an effort to express a highly complex idea. It is often seen in schizophrenia.

Neopsychic function. *See* Adult.

Network. The persons in the patient's environment with whom he is most intimately connected. It frequently includes the nuclear family, the extended family, the orbit of relatives and friends, and work and recreational contacts. S. H. Foulkes believes that this dynamically interacting network has a fundamental significance in the production of illness in the patient. *See also* Extended family therapy, Social network therapy, Visitor.

Neuroleptic. *See* Antipsychotic drug, Major tranquilizer.

Neurosis. Mental disorder characterized by anxiety. The anxiety may be experienced and expressed directly, or, through an unconscious psychic process, it may be converted, displaced, or somatized. Although neuroses do not manifest depersonalization or overt distortion of reality, they can be severe enough to impair a person's functioning. The neuroses, also known as psychoneuroses, include the following types: anxiety neurosis, hysterical neurosis, phobic neurosis, obsessive-compulsive neurosis, depressive neurosis, neurasthenic neurosis, depersonalization neurosis, and hypochondriacal neurosis.

Nondirective approach. Technique in which the therapist follows the lead of the patient in the interview rather than introducing his own theories and directing the course of the interview. This method is applied in both individual and group therapy, such as Carl Rogers' client-centered and group-centered therapy. *See also* Passive therapist.

Nontruster. A person who has a strong unfilled need to be nurtured but whose early experience was one of rejection or overprotection. As a defense against repetition of this experience, he develops an overly strong show of independence. Sometimes this independence is manifested in group therapy by a member's constant rejection of support and of attempts by other members to get close to him. *See also* Outsider.

Nonverbal interaction. Technique used without the aid of words in encounter groups to promote communication and intimacy and to bypass verbal defenses. Many exercises of this sort are carried out in complete silence; in others, the participants emit grunts, groans, yells, cries, or sighs. Gestalt therapy pays particular attention to nonverbal expression.

Norepinephrine. A catecholamine that functions as a neurohumoral mediator liberated by postganglionic adrenergic nerves. It is also present in the adrenal medulla and in many areas in the brain, with the highest concentration in the hypothalamus. A disturbance in the metabolism of norepinephrine is considered to be an important factor in the etiology of depression. *See also* Serotonin.

Nuclear family. Immediate members of a family, including the parents and the children. *See also* Extended family therapy, Network, Social network therapy, Visitor.

Nuclear group member. *See* Therapist surrogate.

Nude marathon. Encounter group in which members assemble for an emotional experience of prolonged duration (from a minimum of eight hours to a couple of days), with the added factor of physical nakedness as members go about their activities. The theory is that clothes are themselves defenses against openness, that they connote limiting roles and result in stereotyped responses from others, and that they allow participants to avoid facing conflicts about their own bodies. *See also* Group marathon, Sensory-experiential group.

Nymphomania. Morbid, insatiable need in women for sexual intercourse. *See also* Satyriasis.

Observer. Person who is included but is generally not an active participant in therapy sessions. His observations are later discussed in posttherapy meetings with the staff or supervisor. *See also* Recorder.

Observer therapist. *See* Passive therapist.

Obsession. Persistent idea, thought, or impulse that cannot be eliminated from consciousness by logical effort. *See also* Compulsion.

Oedipus complex. A distinct group of associated ideas, aims, instinctual drives, and fears that are generally observed in children when they are from three to six years of age. During this period, which coincides with the peak of the phallic phase of psychosexual development, the child's sexual interest is attached chiefly to the parent of the opposite sex and is accompanied by aggressive feelings and wishes for the parent of the same sex. One of Freud's most important concepts, the Oedipus complex was discovered in 1897 as a result of his self-analysis. *See also Totem and Taboo.*

Ogre. In structural analysis, the Child ego state in the father that supersedes the nurturing Parent and becomes a pseudo-Parent.

One-gender group. *See* Homogeneous group.

Open group. Treatment group in which new members are continuously added as other members leave. *See also* Closed group.

Oral dyskinesia, tardive. *See* Tardive oral dyskinesia.

Oral phase. The earliest stage in psychosexual development. It lasts through the first 18 months of life. During this period, the oral zone is the center of the infant's needs, expression, and pleasurable erotic experiences. It has a strong influence on the organization and development of the child's psyche. *See also* Anal phase, Genital phase, Infantile sexuality, Latency phase, Phallic phase.

Orientation. State of awareness of one's relationships and surroundings in terms of time, place, and person.

Orthostatic hypotension. Reduction in blood pressure brought about by a shift from a recumbent to an upright position. It is observed as a side effect of several psychotropic drugs.

Other-directed person. A person who is readily influenced and guided by the attitudes and values of other people. *See also* Inner-directed person.

Outsider. In group therapy, a member who feels alienated and isolated from the group. Such a person has usually experienced repetitive rejection in his early life and is wary of trusting people in the present. Often much effort is required by the group and the therapist before the outsider trusts someone. *See also* Nontruster.

Overt homosexuality. Behaviorally expressed homoeroticism as distinct from unconsciously held homosexual wishes or conscious wishes that are held in check. *See also* Homosexuality, Latent homosexuality.

Pairing. Term coined by Walter R. Bion to denote mutual support between two or more group members who wish to avoid the solution of their problems. The term is often used more loosely to denote an attraction between two group members.

Panic. An acute, intense attack of anxiety associated with personality disorganization. Some writers use the term exclusively for psychotic episodes of overwhelming anxiety. *See also* Homosexual panic.

Pantomime. Gesticulation; psychodrama without the use of words.

Paralogia. *See* Evasion.

Paralytic ileus. Intestinal obstruction of the nonmechanical type, secondary to paralysis of the bowel wall, that may lead to fecal retention.

It is a rare anticholinergic side effect of phenothiazine therapy.

Paramnesia. Disturbance of memory in which reality and fantasy are confused. It is observed in dreams and in certain types of schizophrenia and organic brain syndromes. *See also* Confabulation, Déjà entendu, Déjà vu, Fausse reconnaissance, Jamais vu, Retrospective falsification.

Paranoid delusion. *See* Delusion.

Parent. In transactional analysis, an ego state borrowed from a parental figure. It is also known as exteropsychic function.

Parental rejection. Denial of affection and attention to a child by one or both parents. The child in turn develops great affect hunger and hostility, which is directed either outwardly in the form of tantrums, etc., or inwardly toward himself in the form of allergies, etc.

Parkinsonism. Syndrome characterized by rhythmical muscular tremors known as pill rolling accompanied by spasticity and rigidity of movement, propulsive gait, droopy posture, and masklike facies. It is usually seen in later life as a result of arteriosclerotic changes in the basal ganglia.

Parkinsonismlike effect. Symptom that is a frequent side effect of antipsychotic drugs. Typical symptoms are motor retardation, muscular rigidity, alterations of posture, tremor, and autonomic nervous system disturbances. *See also* Phenothiazine derivative.

Partial insanity. *See* Monomania.

Passive therapist. Type of therapist who remains inactive but whose presence serves as a stimulus for the patient in the group or individual treatment setting. *See also* Active therapist, Leaderless therapeutic group, Nondirective approach.

Pastime. In transactional analysis, semistereotyped set of transactions dealing with a certain topic. Unlike Berne's term game, a pastime has no ulterior motive and no psychological payoff.

Patient peers. *See* Co-patients.

Patty-cake exercise. An encounter group technique that involves the palm-to-palm contact made by children in the game of patty-cake. This type of contact is familiar and does not usually arouse much anxiety in participants, yet it allows people to bypass verbal defenses in getting to know each other. After this exercise, the group members discuss their reactions. Also called Hand-dance.

Pecking order. Sequence of hierarchy or authority in an organization or social group. *See also* Hierarchical vector.

Peer co-therapist. Therapist who is equal in status to the other therapist treating a group and who relates to him on an equal level.

Peer-group phenomenon. Interaction or reaction of a person with a group of equals. These phenomena include activities he does within the group that he would probably not do individually outside the group.

Peer identification. Unconscious process that occurs in a group when one member incorporates within himself the qualities and attributes of another member. It usually occurs in members with low self-esteem who would like to feel at one with members who have improved.

Peer vector. *See* Horizontal vector.

Perception. Mental process by which data—intellectual, sensory, and emotional—are organized meaningfully. Through perception, a person makes sense out of the many stimuli that bombard him. It is one of the many ego functions. Therapy groups and T-groups aim to expand and alter perception in ways conducive to the development of the potential of each participant. *See also* Agnosia, Apperception, Clouding of consciousness, Ego, Hallucination, Hysterical anesthesia, Memory.

Perceptual expansion. Development of one's ability to recognize and interpret the meaning of sensory stimuli through associations with past experiences with similar stimuli. Perceptual expansion through the relaxation of defenses is one of the goals in both individual and group therapy.

Permission. In transactional analysis, a therapeutic transaction designed to permanently neutralize the parental injunctions.

Personal growth laboratory. A sensitivity training laboratory in which the primary emphasis is on each participant's potentialities for creativity, empathy, and leadership. In such a laboratory the facilitator encourages most modalities of experience and expression—such as art, sensory stimulation, and intellectual, emotional, written, oral, verbal, and nonverbal expression. *See also* National Training Laboratories.

Personality. Habitual configuration of behavior of a person, reflecting his physical and mental activities, attitudes, and interests and corresponding to the sum total of his adjustment to life.

Personality disorder. Mental disorder characterized by maladaptive patterns of adjustment to life. There is no subjective anxiety, as seen in neurosis, and no disturbance in the capacity to recognize reality, as seen in psychosis. The types of personality disorders include passive-aggressive, antisocial, schizoid, hysterical, paranoid, cyclothymic, explosive, obsessive-compulsive, asthenic, and inadequate.

Perversion. Deviation from the expected norm. In psychiatry it commonly signifies sexual perversion. *See also* Sexual deviation.

Perverted logic. *See* Evasion.

Peter Principle. Theory that man tends to advance to his level of incompetence. The idea was popularized in a book of the same name by Laurence J. Peter and Raymond Hull.

Phallic overbearance. Domination of another person by aggressive means. It is generally associated with masculinity in its negative aspects.

Phallic phase. The third stage in psychosexual development. It occurs when the child is from two to six years of age. During this period, the child's interest, curiosity, and pleasurable experiences are centered around the penis in boys and the clitoris in girls. *See also* Anal phase, Genital phase, Infantile sexuality, Latency phase, Oral phase.

Phantasy. *See* Fantasy.

Phantom limb. *See* Kinesthetic hallucination.

Phenothiazine derivative. Compound derived from phenothiazine. It is particularly known for its antipsychotic property. As a class, the phenothiazine derivatives are among the most widely used drugs in medical practice, particularly in psychiatry. Chlorpromazine, triflupromazine, fluphenazine, perphenazine, and thioridazine are some examples of phenothiazine derivatives. *See also* Anticholinergic effect, Autonomic side effect, Electrocardiographic effect, Mydriasis, Paralytic ileus, Parkinsonismlike effect.

Phobia. Pathological fear associated with some specific type of stimulus or situation. *See also* Acrophobia, Agoraphobia, Algophobia, Claustrophobia, Xenophobia, Zoophobia.

Phyloanalysis. A means of investigating disorders of human behavior, both individual and collective, resulting from impaired tensional processes that affected the organism's internal reaction as a whole. Trigant Burrow adopted the word to replace his earlier term, group analysis, which he first used in 1927 to describe the social participation of many persons in their common analysis. Because group analysis was confused with group psychotherapy of the analytic type, Burrow changed his nomenclature to phyloanalysis.

Pillow-beating. A technique used in encounter groups to elicit pent-up rage in a group member who needs to release it in a physical way. The member beats the pillow and yells angry words until he gets tired. The acceptance of his anger by the group is considered therapeutic. After this exercise, the group members discuss their reactions. *See also* Mattress-pounding.

Placebo. Inert substance prepared to resemble the active drug being tested in experimental research. It is sometimes used in clinical practice for a psychotherapeutic effect. The response to the placebo may represent the response due to the psychological effect of taking a pill and not to any pharmacological property.

Play therapy. Type of therapy used with children, usually of preschool and early latency ages. The patient reveals his problems on a fantasy level with dolls, clay, and other toys. The therapist intervenes opportunely with helpful explanations about the patient's responses and behavior in language geared to the child's comprehension. *See also* Activity group therapy.

Political therapist. A therapist who gives strong weight to the personalities of those above him as far as they impinge on his professional activities. He pays particular attention to the personal and historical aspects of authority. *See also* Authority principle, Hierarchical vector, Procedural therapist.

Popular mind. The primitive, fickle, suggestible, impulsive, uncritical type of mind that Le Bon felt was characteristic of the mass. He was referring to the unorganized crowds who lack leadership.

Postsession. *See* After-session.

Power phase. Second stage in group treatment. In this phase members start expressing anger and hostility—usually directed at the leader, sometimes directed at other members—in an attempt to achieve individuation and autonomy. *See also* Affection phase, Inclusion phase.

Pratt, Joseph H. Boston physician born in 1842 generally considered to be the first pioneer in group psychotherapy in America. He is known for his work with tuberculous patients (1900–1906). He formed discussion groups to deal with the physical aspects of tuberculosis. Later, these groups began discussing the emotional problems that stemmed from the illness. *See also* Class method.

Preconscious. In psychoanalysis, one of the three divisions of the psyche according to Freud's topographical psychology. The preconscious includes all ideas, thoughts, past experiences, and other memory impressions that can be consciously recalled with effort. *See also* Conscious, Unconscious.

Prefrontal lobotomy. *See* Lobotomy.

Prejudice. Adverse judgment or opinion formed without factual knowledge. Elements of irrational suspicion or hatred are often involved, as in racial prejudice.

Premeeting. Group meeting of patients without the therapist. It is held immediately before the regular therapist-led session and is also referred to as warming-up session and presession. *See also* After-session, Alternate session.

Preoccupation of thought. *See* Trend of thought.

Pressure cooker. Slang phrase to describe the high degree of group involvement and emotional pitch sought by certain intensive groups, such as marathon groups.

Primal father. Hypothetical head of the tribe. He is depicted by Freud in *Totem and Taboo* as slain by his sons, who subsequently devour him in a cannibalistic rite. Later, he is promoted to a god. The son who murders him is the prototype of the tragic hero, and the memory of the crime is perpetuated in the conscience of the individual and of the culture.

Primal scene. In psychoanalysis, the real or fantasied observation by a child of sexual intercourse, particularly between his parents.

Primary process. In psychoanalysis, the mental process directly related to the functions of the id and characteristic of unconscious mental activity. The primary process is marked by unorganized, illogical thinking and by the tendency to seek immediate discharge and gratification of instinctual demands. *See also* Secondary process.

Probe. An encounter technique designed for a specific purpose—for instance, to determine motivation for admission to treatment. The technique is commonly used in such drug rehabilitation centers as Odyssey House.

Procedural therapist. A therapist who places the most weight on the written word, on formal rules and regulations, and on the hierarchical system. *See also* Authority principle, Political therapist.

Process-centered group. Group whose main purpose is to study the dynamics of the group itself—how it operates and through what stages it progresses. Such groups often ask the question, "What's going on here?" rather than the encounter group question, "What are you experiencing or feeling?" *See also* Group analytic psychotherapy, Group-centered psychotherapy.

Program. In transactional analysis, the teaching by one of the parents of how best to comply with the script injunction.

Projection. Unconscious defense mechanism in which a person attributes to another the ideas, thoughts, feelings, and impulses that are part of his inner perceptions but that are unacceptable to him. Projection protects the person from anxiety arising from an inner conflict. By externalizing whatever is unacceptable, the person deals with it as a situation apart from himself. *See also* Blind spot, Future projection.

Projective method. Group treatment proce-

dure that uses the spontaneous creative work of the patients. For example, group members make and analyze drawings, which are often expressions of their underlying emotional problems.

Protagonist. In psychodrama, the patient who is the focal point of a psychodramatic session. He is asked to be himself, to portray his own private world on the stage.

Pseudoauthenticity. False or copied expression of thoughts and feelings.

Pseudocollusion. Sense of closeness, relationship, or cooperation that is not real but is based on transference.

Psychic determinism. Freudian adaptation of the concept of causality. It states that all phenomena or events have antecedent causes that operate on an unconscious level, beyond the control of the person involved.

Psychoactive drug. Drug that alters thoughts, feelings, or perceptions. Such a drug may help a person in either individual or group therapy overcome depression, anxiety, or rigidity of thought and behavior while he learns new methods of perceiving and responding.

Psychoanalysis. Freud's method of psychic investigation and form of psychotherapy. As a technique for exploring the mental processes, psychoanalysis includes the use of free association and the analysis and interpretation of dreams, resistances, and transferences. As a form of psychotherapy, it uses the investigative technique, guided by Freud's libido and instinct theories and by ego psychology, to gain insight into a person's unconscious motivations, conflicts, and symbols and thus to effect a change in his maladaptive behavior. Several schools of thought are loosely referred to as psychoanalytic at present. Psychoanalysis is also known as analysis in depth.

Psychoanalytically oriented group psychotherapy. *See* Psychoanalytic group psychotherapy.

Psychoanalytic group psychotherapy. A major method of group psychotherapy, pioneered by Alexander Wolf and based on the operational principles of individual psychoanalytic therapy. Analysis and interpretation of a patient's transferences, resistances, and defenses are modified to take place in a group setting. Although strictly designating treatment structured to produce significant character change, the term encompasses the same approach in groups conducted at more superficial levels for lesser goals. *See also* Collective family transference neurosis, Discussion model of group psychotherapy, Verbal-deep approach.

Psychoanalytic treatment. *See* Psychoanalysis.

Psychodrama. Psychotherapy method originated by J. L. Moreno in which personality make-up, interpersonal relationships, conflicts, and emotional problems are explored by means of dramatic methods. The therapeutic dramatization of emotional problems includes: (1) protagonist or patient, the person who presents and acts out his emotional problems with the help of (2) auxiliary egos, persons trained to act and dramatize the different aspects of the patient that are called for in a particular scene in order to help him express his feelings, and (3) director, leader, or therapist, the person who guides those involved in the drama for a fruitful and therapeutic session. *See also* Actional-deep approach, Analytic psychodrama, Concretization of living, Didactic psychodrama, Hallucinatory psychodrama, Hypnodrama, Improvisation, Maximal expression, Mirror, Re-enactment, Regressive-reconstructive approach, Role-playing, Role reversal, Self-realization.

Psychodramatic director. Leader of a psychodrama session. The director has three functions: producer, therapist, and analyst. As producer, he turns every clue the patient offers into dramatic action. As therapist, he attacks and shocks the patient at times, laughs and jokes with him at times, and becomes indirect and passive at times. As analyst, he interprets and elicits responses from the audience.

Psychodramatic shock. *See* Hallucinatory psychodrama.

Psychodynamics. Science of the mind, its mental processes, and affective components that influence human behavior and motivations. *See also* Group dynamics, Infantile dynamics.

Psychological defense system. *See* Defense mechanism.

Psychological procedure. Any technique intended to alter a person's attitude toward and

perception of himself and others. *See also* Group psychotherapy, Psychoanalysis, Psychotherapy.

Psychomotor stimulant. Drug that arouses the patient through its central excitatory and analeptic properties. Amphetamine and methylphenidate are drugs in this class.

Psychopathology. Branch of science that deals with morbidity of the mind.

Psychophysiological disorder. Mental disorder characterized by physical symptoms of psychic origin. It usually involves a single organ system innervated by the autonomic nervous system. The physiological and organic changes stem from a sustained emotional disturbance.

Psychosexual development. Maturation and development of the psychic phase of sexuality from birth to adult life. Its phases are oral, anal, phallic, latency, and genital. *See also* Identification with the aggressor, Infantile sexuality.

Psychosis. Mental disorder in which a person's mental capacity, affective response, and capacity to recognize reality, communicate, and relate to others are impaired enough to interfere with his capacity to deal with the ordinary demands of life. The psychoses are subdivided into two major classifications according to their origin—psychoses associated with organic brain syndromes and functional psychoses.

Psychosomatic illness. *See* Psychophysiological disorder.

Psychosurgery. *See* Lobotomy.

Psychotherapy. Form of treatment for mental illness and behavioral disturbances in which a trained person establishes a professional contract with the patient and through definite therapeutic communication, both verbal and nonverbal, attempts to alleviate the emotional disturbance, reverse or change maladaptive patterns of behavior, and encourage personality growth and development. Psychotherapy is distinguished from such other forms of psychiatric treatment as the use of drugs, surgery, electric shock treatment, and insulin coma treatment. *See also* Growth psychotherapy, Individual therapy, Psychoanalysis.

Psychotomimetic drug. Drug that produces psychic and behavioral changes that resemble psychosis. Unlike other drugs that can produce organic psychosis as a reaction, a psychotomimetic drug does not produce overt memory impairment. It is also known as a hallucinogenic drug. Lysergic acid diethylamide (LSD), tetrahydrocannabinol, and mescaline are examples of psychotomimetic drugs.

Psychotropic drug. Drug that affects psychic function and behavior. Also known as a phrenotropic drug, it may be classified as an antipsychotic drug, antidepressant drug, antimanic drug, antianxiety drug, or hallucinogenic drug. *See also* Agranulocytosis, Orthostatic hypotension.

Public self. The behavior, feelings, and motivations of a person known both to himself and to others. It is a quadrant of the Johari Window, a diagrammatic concept of human behavior. *See also* Blind self, Hidden self, Undeveloped potential.

Quadrangular therapy. A type of marital therapy that involves four people: the married pair and each spouse's therapist. *See also* Collaborative therapy, Combined therapy, Concurrent therapy, Conjoint therapy, Family therapy, Group marital therapy, Marriage therapy, Square interview.

Rank, Otto (1884–1939). Austrian psychoanalyst. He was one of Freud's earliest followers and the long-time secretary and recorder of the minutes of the Vienna Psychoanalytic Society. He wrote such fundamental works as *The Myth of the Birth of the Hero*. He split with Freud on the significance of the birth trauma, which he used as a basis of brief psychotherapy.

Rapport. Conscious, harmonious accord that usually reflects a good relationship between two persons. In a group, rapport is the presence of mutual responsiveness, as evidenced by spontaneous and sympathetic reaction to each other's needs, sentiments, and attitudes. *See also* Countertransference, Transference.

Rap session. *See* Bull session.

Rationalization. An unconscious defense mechanism in which an irrational behavior, motive, or feeling is made to appear reasonable. Ernest Jones introduced the term.

Reaction formation. An unconscious defense mechanism in which a person develops a socialized attitude or interest that is the direct antithesis of some infantile wish or impulse in the

unconscious. One of the earliest and most unstable defense mechanisms, it is closely related to repression; both are defenses against impulses or urges that are unacceptable to the ego.

Reality. The totality of objective things and factual events. Reality includes everything that is perceived by a person's special senses and is validated by other people.

Reality-testing. Fundamental ego function that consists of the objective evaluation and judgment of the world outside the self. By interacting with his animate and inanimate environment, a person tests its real nature as well as his own relation to it. How the person evaluates reality and his attitudes toward it are determined by early experiences with the significant persons in his life. *See also* Ego.

Recall. Process of remembering thoughts, words, and actions of a past event in an attempt to recapture what actually happened. It is part of a complex mental function known as memory. *See also* Amnesia, Hypermnesia.

Recathexis. In transactional analysis, the experiencing of different ego states.

Recognition. *See* Memory.

Reconstructive psychotherapy. A form of therapy that seeks not only to alleviate symptoms but to produce alterations in maladaptive character structures and to expedite new adaptive potentials. This aim is achieved by bringing into consciousness an awareness of and insight into conflicts, fears, inhibitions, and their derivatives. *See also* Psychoanalysis.

Recorder. Person who takes notes during the group or individual therapy session. Also referred to as the recorder-observer, he generally does not participate in therapy. *See also* Observer.

Re-enactment. In psychodrama, the acting out of a past experience as if it were happening in the present so that a person can feel, perceive, and act as he did the first time.

Registration. *See* Memory.

Regression. Unconscious defense mechanism in which a person undergoes a partial or total return to earlier patterns of adaptation. Regression is observed in many psychiatric conditions, particularly schizophrenia.

Regressive-reconstructive approach. A psychotherapeutic procedure in which regression is made an integral element of the treatment process. The original traumatic situation is reproduced to gain new insight and to effect significant personality change and emotional maturation. *See also* Psychoanalysis, Reconstructive psychotherapy.

Reik, Theodor (1888–1969). Psychoanalyst and early follower of Freud, who considered him one of his most brilliant pupils. Freud's book, *The Question of Lay Analysis* was written to defend Reik's ability to practice psychoanalysis without medical training. Reik made many valuable contributions to psychoanalysis on the subjects of religion, masochism, and technique. *See also* Third ear.

Relatedness. Sense of sympathy and empathy with regard to others; sense of oneness with others. It is the opposite of isolation and alienation.

Reparenting. A technique evolved in transactional analysis for the treatment of schizophrenia. The patient is first regressed to a Child ego state, and then missing Parent transactions are supplied and contaminations corrected.

Repeater. Group member who has had experience in another group.

Repetitive pattern. Continual attitude or mode of behavior characteristic of a person and performed mechanically or unconsciously.

Repression. An unconscious defense mechanism in which a person removes from consciousness those ideas, impulses, and affects that are unacceptable to him. A term introduced by Freud, it is important in both normal psychological development and in neurotic and psychotic symptom formation. Freud recognized two kinds of repression: (1) repression proper—the repressed material was once in the conscious domain; (2) primal repression—the repressed material was never in the conscious realm. *See also* Suppression.

Repressive-inspirational group psychotherapy. A type of group therapy in which discussion is intended to bolster patients' morale and help them avoid undesired feelings. It is used primarily with large groups of seriously regressed patients in institutional settings.

Reserpine. An alkaloid extracted from the root of the *Rauwolfia serpentina* plant. It is used primarily as an antihypertensive agent. It was formerly used as an antipsychotic agent because of its sedative effect.

Residential treatment facility. A center where the patient lives and receives treatment appropriate for his particular needs. A children's residential treatment facility ideally furnishes both educational and therapeutic experiences for the emotionally disturbed child.

Resistance. A conscious or unconscious opposition to the uncovering of the unconscious. Resistance is linked to underlying psychological defense mechanisms against impulses from the id that are threatening to the ego. *See also* Group resistance.

Resonance. Unconscious response determined by early life experiences. In a group, a member may respond by fantasizing at a particular level of psychosexual development when another member functions regressively at that level. The unconscious sounding board is constructed in the first five years of life. *See also* Focal-conflict theory.

Retardation. Slowness of development or progress. In psychiatry there are two types, mental retardation and psychomotor retardation. Mental retardation refers to slowness or arrest of intellectual maturation. Psychomotor retardation refers to slowness or slackened psychic activity or motor activity or both; it is observed in pathological depression.

Retention. *See* Memory.

Retrospective falsification. Recollection of false memory. *See also* Paramnesia.

Review session. Meeting in which each member reviews with the group his goals and progress in treatment. It is a technique used in structured interactional group psychotherapy.

Ritual. Automatic activity of psychogenic or cultural origin. *See also* Group ritual.

Role. Pattern of behavior that a person takes. It has its roots in childhood and is influenced by significant people with whom the person had primary relationships. When the behavior pattern conforms with the expectations and demands of other people, it is said to be a complementary role. If it does not conform with the demands and expectation of others, it is known as noncomplementary role. *See also* Identification, Injunction, Therapeutic role.

Role-divided therapy. Therapeutic arrangement in a co-therapy situation when each therapist takes on a specific function in treatment. For example, one therapist may take the role of a provocateur, while the other takes the role of a passive observer and interpreter. *See also* Splitting situation.

Role limit. Boundary placed on the therapist or the patient by virtue of his conscious position in the therapy group. The patient plays the patient, and the therapist plays the therapist; there is no reversal of roles.

Role model. In a therapeutic community or methadone program, an ex-addict who, because of his successful adjustment and similarity of experience with the patient population, becomes a source of positive identification and a tangible proof of success. *See also* Ego model.

Role-playing. Psychodrama technique in which a person is trained to function more effectively in his reality roles—such as employer, employee, student, and instructor. In the therapeutic setting of psychodrama, the protagonist is free to try and to fail in his role, for he is given the opportunity to try again until he finally learns new approaches to the situation he fears, approaches that he can then apply outside. *See also* Antirepression device.

Role reversal. Technique used in psychodrama whereby an auxiliary ego plays the role of the patient, and the patient plays the role of the other person. Distortions of interpersonal perception are thereby brought to the surface, explored, and corrected.

Role-training. *See* Role-playing.

Roll and rock. An encounter group technique that is used to develop trust in a participant. A person stands, with eyes closed, in a tight circle of group members and is passed around (rolled) from member to member. Then he is placed on his back on the floor, gently lifted by the group members, and rocked back and forth. He is then put back on the floor. After this exercise, the group members discuss their reactions.

Rosander anti-Negro behavior scale. A scale that measures white attitudes toward blacks by asking respondents what their behavior would be in various hypothetical situations involving black participants. The scale can be of aid in determining the degree of prejudice held by whites toward blacks and the influence of a group experience on such prejudices. *See also* Ford negative personal contacts with Negroes scale, Ford negative personal contacts with whites scale, Kelley desegregation scale, Steckler anti-Negro scale, Steckler anti-white scale.

Rosenberg self-esteem scale. A scale designed to measure a person's opinion of himself. Use of this scale gives the therapist a means of evaluating the effect a group experience has on a member's self-esteem.

Saboteur. One who obstructs progress within a group, either deliberately or unconsciously.

Sadism. A sexual deviation in which sexual gratification is achieved by inflicting pain and humiliation on the partner. Donatien Alphonse François de Sade (1740–1814), a French writer, was the first person to describe this condition. *See also* Masochism, Sadomasochistic relationship.

Sadomasochistic relationship. Relationship in which the enjoyment of suffering by one person and the enjoyment of inflicting pain by the other person are important and complementary attractions in their on-going relationship. *See also* Masochism, Sadism.

Satyriasis. Morbid, insatiable sexual needs or desires in men. It may be caused by organic or psychiatric factors. *See also* Nymphomania.

Schilder, Paul (1886–1940). American neuropsychiatrist. He started the use of group psychotherapy at New York's Bellevue Hospital, combining social and psychoanalytic principles.

Schizophrenia. Mental disorder of psychotic level characterized by disturbances in thinking, mood, and behavior. The thinking disturbance is manifested by a distortion of reality, especially by delusions and hallucinations, accompanied by fragmentation of associations that results in incoherent speech. The mood disturbance is manifested by inappropriate affective responses. The behavior disturbance is manifested by ambivalence, apathetic withdrawal, and bizarre activity. Formerly known as dementia praecox, schizophrenia as a term was introduced by Eugen Bleuler. The causes of schizophrenia remain unknown. The types of schizophrenia include simple type, hebephrenic type, catatonic type, paranoid type, schizo-affective type, childhood type, residual type, latent type, acute schizophrenic episode, and chronic undifferentiated type.

Schreber case. One of Freud's cases. It involved the analysis in 1911 of Daniel Paul Shreber's autobiographical account, *Memoirs of a Neurotic*, published in 1903. Analysis of these memoirs permitted Freud to decipher the fundamental meaning of paranoid processes and ideas, especially the relationship between repressed homosexuality and projective defenses.

Screening. Initial patient evaluation that includes medical and psychiatric history, mental status evaluation, and diagnostic formulation to determine the patient's suitability for a particular treatment modality.

Script. In transactional analysis, a complex set of transactions that are adaptations of infantile responses and experiences. The script is recurrent and operates on an unconscious level. It is the mold on which a person's life adaptation is based. *See also* Hamartic script.

Script analysis. The analysis of a person's life adaption—that is, his injunctions, decisions, and life scripts—and the therapeutic process that helps reverse the maladaptive behavior. It is the last phase in transactional analysis. *See also* Game analysis, Structural analysis.

Script antithesis. In transactional analysis, a therapeutic transaction designed to avert temporarily a tragic event in a script. *See also* Script, Script matrix.

Script matrix. Diagram used in transactional analysis to represent two parents and an offspring. It is useful in representing the genesis of life scripts. *See also* Script, Script antithesis.

Secondary process. In psychoanalysis, the mental process directly related to the functions of the ego and characteristic of conscious and preconscious mental activities. The secondary process is marked by logical thinking and by the tendency to delay gratification by regulation of discharge of instinctual demands. *See also* Primary process.

Sedative. Drug that produces a calming or relaxing effect through central nervous system depression. Some drugs with sedative properties are barbiturates, chloral hydrate, paraldehyde, and bromide.

Selective inattention. An aspect of attentiveness in which a person blocks out those areas that generate anxiety.

Self-analysis. Investigation of one's own psychic components. It plays a part in all analysis, although to a limited extent, since few are capable of sustaining independent and detached attitudes for it to be therapeutic.

Self-awareness. Sense of knowing what one is experiencing. For example, realizing that one has just responded with anger to another group member as a substitute for the anxiety felt when he attacked a vital part of one's self concept. Self-awareness is a major goal of all therapy, individual and group.

Self-discovery. In psychoanalysis, the freeing of the repressed ego in a person who has been brought up to submit to the wishes of the significant others around him.

Self-presentation. Psychodrama technique in which the patient plays the role of himself and of related persons (father, mother, brother, etc.) as he perceives them in a completely subjective manner.

Self-realization. Psychodrama technique in which the protagonist enacts, with the aid of a few auxiliary egos, the plan of his life, no matter how remote it may be from his present situation. For instance, an accountant who has been taking singing lessons, hoping to try out for a musical comedy part in summer stock, and planning to make the theatre his life's work can explore the effects of success in this venture and of possible failure and return to his old livelihood.

Sensation. Feeling or impression when the sensory nerve endings of any of the six senses—taste, touch, smell, sight, kinesthesia, and sound—are stimulated.

Sensitivity training group. Group in which members seek to develop self-awareness and an understanding of group processes rather than gain relief from an emotional disturbance. *See also* Encounter group, Personal growth laboratory, T-group.

Sensorium. Theoretical sensory center located in the brain that is involved with a person's awareness about his surroundings. In psychiatry, it is often referred to as consciousness.

Sensory-experiential group. An encounter group that is primarily concerned with the emotional and physical interaction of the participants. The experience itself, not the examination of the group process, is considered the *raison d'être* for the group.

Serotonin. A monoamine that is believed to be a neurohumoral transmitter. It is found in the serum and, in high concentrations, in the hypothalamus of the brain. Recent pharmacological investigations link depression to disorders in the metabolism of serotonin and other biogenic amines, such as norepinephrine.

Session leader. *See* Facilitator.

Sexual deviation. Mental disorder characterized by sexual interests and behavior other than what is culturally accepted. Sexual deviation includes sexual interest in objects other than a person of the opposite sex, such as homosexuality or bestiality; bizarre sexual practices, such as necrophilia; and other sexual activities that are not accompanied by copulation. *See also* Bestiality, Exhibitionism, Homosexuality, Masochism, Sadism.

Sexual drive. One of the two primal instincts (the other is the aggressive drive) according to Freud's dual-instinct theory of 1920. It is also known as eros and life instinct. Its main goal is to preserve and maintain life. It operates under the influence of the pleasure-unpleasure principle. *See also* Aggressive drive, Libido theory.

Shifting attention. A characteristic of group therapy in which the focus changes from one patient to another so that no one patient remains continuously in the spotlight. It is also known as alternating scrutiny. *See also* Structured interactional group psychotherapy.

Shock treatment. A form of psychiatric treatment with a chemical substance (ingested, inhaled, or injected) or sufficient electric current to produce a convulsive seizure and unconsciousness. It is used in certain types of schizophrenia and mood disorders. Shock treatment's mechanism of action is still unknown.

Sibling rivalry. Competition among children for the attention, affection, and esteem of their parents. The children's jealousy is accompanied by hatred and death wishes toward each other. The rivalry need not be limited to actual siblings; it is a factor in both normal and abnormal competitiveness throughout life.

Slavson, S. R. (1890-　). American theoretician who pioneered in group psychotherapy based on psychoanalytic principles. In his work with children, from which he derived most of his concepts, he introduced and developed activity group therapy. *See also* Collective experience.

Sleep. A temporary physiological state of unconsciousness characterized by a reversible cessation of the person's waking sensorimotor activity. A biological need, sleep recurs periodically to rest the whole body and to regenerate neuromuscular tissue. *See also* Dream.

Social adaptation. Adjustment to the whole complex of interpersonal relationships; the ability to live and express oneself in accordance with society's restrictions and cultural demands. *See also* Adaptational approach.

Social configuration. Arrangement of interpersonal interactions. *See also* Hierarchical vector, Horizontal vector.

Social instinct. *See* Herd instinct.

Socialization. Process of learning interpersonal and interactional skills according to and in conformity with one's society. In a group therapy setting, it includes a member's way of participating both mentally and physically in the group. *See also* Interpersonal skill.

Social network therapy. A type of group therapy in which the therapist assembles all the persons—relatives, friends, social relations, work relations—who have emotional or functional significance in the patient's life. Some or all of the social network may be assembled at any given time. *See also* Extended family therapy, Visitor.

Social psychiatry. Branch of psychiatry interested in ecological, sociological, and cultural variables that engender, intensify, or complicate maladaptive patterns of behavior and their treatment.

Social therapy. A rehabilitative form of therapy with psychiatric patients. The aim is to improve social functioning. Occupational therapy, therapeutic community, recreational therapy, milieu therapy, and attitude therapy are forms of social therapy.

Sociogram. Diagrammatic portrayal of choices, rejections, and indifferences of a number of persons involved in a life situation.

Sociometric distance. The measurable degree of perception one person has for another. It can be hypothesized that the greater the sociometric distance between persons, the more inaccurate will be their social evaluation of their relationship.

Sociometric feedback. Information that people give each other about how much closeness or distance they desire between them. It is a measure of how social one would like to be with another. An example of sociometric feedback would be the answer by a group member to the question, "With what three members of this group would you prefer to spend six months on a desert island?"

Sociometrist. Social investigator engaged in measuring the interpersonal relations and social structures in a community.

Soliloquy. *See* Therapeutic soliloquy.

Somnambulism. Sleepwalking; motor activity during sleep. It is commonly seen in children. In adults, it is observed in persons with schizoid personality disorders and certain types of schizophrenia.

Splitting situation. Condition in a co-therapy group. A patient is often unable to express opposite feelings toward one therapist. The splitting situation allows him to express contrasting feelings—positive-love feeling and negative-hostile feeling—by directing one feeling at one co-therapist and the opposite feeling at the other co-therapist. *See also* Role-divided therapy.

Splitting transference. Breaking of an irrational feeling or attitude into its component parts, which are then assigned to different persons. For example, ambivalence toward a mother may be expressed in a group by reacting to one member as to a good mother and reacting to another member as to a bad mother.

Square interview. Occasional session in marriage therapy in which both spouses and each spouse's therapist are present. The therapists and sometimes the patients are able to observe, experience, and respond to the transactional dynamics among the four of them, thus encouraging a common viewpoint by all four people involved in marital therapy. *See also* Collaborative therapy, Combined therapy, Concurrent therapy, Conjoint therapy, Group marital therapy, Marriage therapy, Quadrangular therapy.

Square situation. *See* Quadrangular therapy, Square interview.

Squeaky wheel. Person who is continually calling attention to himself. Because of his style of interacting, he is likely to get more than his share of a group's effort and energy.

Status value. Worth of a person in terms of such criteria as income, social prestige, intelligence, and education. It is considered an important parameter of one's position in the society.

Steckler anti-Negro scale. A scale designed to measure the attitude of Negroes toward Negroes. It can be of use in ascertaining the degree of prejudice blacks have against their own race and in evaluating the corrective efficacy of group experience. *See also* Ford negative personal contacts with Negroes scale, Ford negative personal contacts with whites scale, Kelley desegregation scale, Rosander anti-Negro behavior scale.

Steckler anti-white scale. A scale designed to measure the attitudes of Negroes toward whites. It can be used to ascertain the amount of prejudice blacks have against whites and to evaluate the influence of a group experience. *See also* Ford negative personal contacts with Negroes scale. Ford negative personal contacts with whites scale, Kelley desegregation scale.

Stegreiftheater. *See* Theatre of Spontaneity.

Stekel, Wilhelm (1868–1940). Viennese psychoanalyst. He suggested the formation of the first Freudian group, the Wednesday Evening Society, which later became the Vienna Psychoanalytic Society. A man given to intuition rather than to systematic research, his insight into dreams proved stimulating and added to the knowledge of symbols. Nevertheless, his superficial wild analysis proved incompatible with the Freudian school. He introduced the word thanatos to signify death wish.

Stereotypy. Continuous repetition of speech or physical activities. It is observed in cases of catatonic schizophrenia.

Stimulant. Drug that affects one or more organ systems to produce an exciting or arousing effect, increase physical activity and vivacity, and promote a sense of well-being. There are, for example, central nervous system stimulants, cardiac stimulants, respiratory stimulants, and psychomotor stimulants.

Stress immunity. Failure to react to emotional stress.

Stroke. In transactional analysis, a unit of human recognition. Early in life, strokes must involve physical contact; later in life, strokes can be symbolic—such as, "Glad to see you!"

Structural analysis. Analysis of the personality into its constituent ego states. The goal of structural analysis is to establish and maintain the predominance of reality-testing ego states, free from contamination. It is considered the first phase of transactional analysis. *See also* Contamination, Ego state, Game analysis, Ogre, Script analysis, Transactional analysis.

Structured interactional group psychotherapy. A type of group psychotherapy, developed by Harold Kaplan and Benjamin Sadock, in which the therapist provides a structural matrix for the group's interactions. The important part of the structure is that a different member of the group is the focus of the interaction in each session. *See also* Forced interaction, Go-around, Up.

Studies on Hysteria. Title of a book by Josef Breuer and Sigmund Freud. Published in 1895, it described the cathartic method of treatment and the beginnings of psychoanalysis. It demonstrated the psychological origins of hysterical symptoms and the possibility of effecting a cure through psychotherapy.

Stupor. Disturbance of consciousness in which the patient is nonreactive to and unaware of his surroundings. Organically, it is synonymous with unconsciousness. In psychiatry, it is referred to as mutism and is commonly found in catatonia and psychotic depression.

Subjectivity. Qualitative appraisal and interpretation of an object or experience as influenced by one's own feelings and thinking.

Subject session. Group technique, used particularly in structured interactional group psychotherapy, in which a topic is introduced by the therapist or a group member and is then explored by the whole group.

Sublimation. An unconscious defense mechanism in which unacceptable instinctual drives are diverted into personally and socially acceptable channels. Unlike other defense mechanisms, sublimation offers some minimal gratification of the instinctual drive or impulse.

Substituting. Providing a nonverbal alternate for something a patient missed in his early life. Crossing the room to sit beside a group member who needs support is an example of substituting.

Substitution. An unconscious defense mechanism in which a person replaces an unacceptable wish, drive, emotion, or goal with one that is more acceptable.

Suggestibility. State of compliant responsiveness to an idea or influence. It is commonly observed among persons with hysterical traits.

Sullivan, Harry Stack (1892–1949). American psychiatrist. He is best known for his interpersonal theory of psychiatry. *See also* Consensual validation.

Summer session. In structured interactional group psychotherapy, regularly scheduled group session during the therapist's vacation.

Superego. One of the three component parts of the psychic apparatus. The other two are the ego and the id. Freud created the theoretical concept of the superego to describe the psychic functions that are expressed in moral attitudes, conscience, and a sense of guilt. The superego results from the internalization of the ethical standards of the society in which the person lives, and it develops by identification with the attitudes of his parents. It is mainly unconscious and is believed to develop as a reaction to the Oedipus complex. It has a protective and rewarding function, referred to as the ego ideal, and a critical and punishing function, which evokes the sense of guilt.

Support. *See* Mutual support.

Suppression. Conscious act of controlling and inhibiting an unacceptable impulse, emotion, or idea. Suppression is differentiated from repression in that the latter is an unconscious process.

Surplus reality. The intangible, invisible dimensions of intrapsychic and extrapsychic life. The term was coined by J. L. Moreno.

Survival. Game used in a professionally homogeneous group. It is designed to create awareness of one another's talents. An imaginary situation is created in which the members are no longer permitted to continue in their particular professions and must, as a group, find some other activity in which to work together meaningfully and profitably. *See also* Game, Hit-and-run game, Million-dollar game.

Symbolization. An unconscious defense mechanism whereby one idea or object comes to stand for another because of some common aspect or quality in both. Symbolization is based on similarity and association. The symbols formed protect the person from the anxiety that may be attached to the original idea or object. *See also* Defense mechanism.

Sympathomimetic drug. Drug that mimics the actions of the sympathetic nervous system. Examples of these drugs are amphetamine and epinephrine.

Sympathy. Sharing of another person's feelings, ideas, and experiences. As opposed to empathy, sympathy is not objective. *See also* Identification, Imitation.

Symptom formation. *See* Symptom substitution.

Symptom substitution. Unconscious psychic process in which a repressed impulse is indirectly released and manifested through a symptom. Such symptoms as obsession, compulsion, phobia, dissociation, anxiety, depression, hallucination, and delusion are examples of symptom substitution. It is also known as symptom formation.

Tachylogia. *See* Logorrhea.

Tactile hallucination. False sense of touch.

Tangentiality. Disturbance in the associative thought processes in which the patient is unable to express his idea. In contrast to circumstantiality, the digression in tangentiality is such that the central idea is not communicated. It is observed in schizophrenia and certain types of or-

ganic brain disorders. Tangentiality is also known as derailment. *See also* Circumstantiality.

Tardive oral dyskinesia. A syndrome characterized by involuntary movements of the lips and jaw and by other bizarre involuntary dystonic movements. It is an extrapyramidal effect occurring late in the course of antipsychotic drug therapy.

Target patient. Group member who is perceptively analyzed by another member. It is a term used in the process of going around in psychoanalytically oriented groups.

Task-oriented group. Group whose main energy is devoted to reaching a goal, finding a solution to a problem, or building a product. Distinguished from this type of group is the experiential group, which is mainly concerned with sharing whatever happens. *See also* Action group.

Tele. In psychodrama, an objective social process that strengthens association and promotes cohesiveness in groups. It is believed to function on the basis of transference and empathy.

Tension. An unpleasurable alteration of affect characterized by a strenuous increase in mental and physical activity.

Termination. Orderly conclusion of a group member's therapy or of the whole group's treatment as contrasted with a drop-out that is not advised by the therapist.

T-group (training group). A type of group that emphasizes training in self-awareness and group dynamics. *See also* Action group, Intervention laboratory, National Training Laboratories, Sensitivity training.

Thanatos. Death wish. *See also* Stekel, Wilhelm.

Theatre of Spontaneity (Stegreiftheater). Theatre in Vienna which improvised group processes and which was developed by J. L. Moreno, M.D.

Theoretical orientation. Alignment with a hypothetical point of view already espoused by a person or group.

Therapeutic agent. Anything—people and/or drugs—that causes healing in a maladaptive person. In group therapy, it refers mainly to people who help others.

Therapeutic alliance. Conscious relationship between therapist and patient in which each implicitly agrees that they need to work together by means of insight and control to help the patient with his conflicts. It involves a therapeutic splitting of the patient's ego into observing and experiencing parts. A good therapeutic alliance is especially necessary during phases of strong negative transference in order to keep the treatment going. It is as important in group as in dyadic psychotherapy. *See also* Working alliance.

Therapeutic atmosphere. All therapeutic, maturational, and growth-supporting agents—cultural, social, and medical.

Therapeutic community. Ward or hospital treatment setting that provides an effective environment for behavioral changes in patients through resocialization and rehabilitation.

Therapeutic crisis. Turning point in the treatment process. An example is acting out, which, depending on how it is dealt with, may or may not lead to a therapeutic change in the patient's behavior. *See also* Therapeutic impasse.

Therapeutic group. Group of patients joined together under the leadership of a therapist for the purpose of working together for psychotherapeutic ends—specifically, for the treatment of each patient's emotional disorders.

Therapeutic group analysis. *See* Group analytic psychotherapy.

Therapeutic impasse. Deadlock in the treatment process. Therapy is in a state of imminent failure when there is no further insight or awareness and sessions are reduced to routine meetings of patient and therapist. Unresolved resistances and transference and countertransference conflicts are among the common causes of this phenomenon. *See also* Therapeutic crisis.

Therapeutic role. Position in which one aims to treat, bring about an improvement, or provide alleviation of a distressing condition or state.

Therapeutic soliloquy. Psychodrama technique that involves a patient's portrayal—by side dialogues and side actions—of his hidden thoughts and feelings that parallel his overt thoughts and actions.

Therapeutic transaction. Interplay between therapist and patient or among group members that is intended to improve the patient.

Therapist surrogate. Group member who—by virtue of experience, intuition, or training—is able to be an effective group leader in the absence of or in concert with the group therapist. He is also known as a nuclear group member. *See also* Leaderless therapeutic group.

There-and-then. Past experience rather than immediate experience. *See also* Here-and-now.

Thinking. *See* Cognition.

Thinking compulsion. *See* Intellectualization.

Thinking through. The mental process that occurs in an attempt to understand one's own behavior and gain insight from it.

Third ear. Ability to make use of intuition, sensitivity, and awareness of subliminal cues to interpret clinical observations of individual and group patients. First introduced by the German philosopher Frederic Nietzsche, it was later used in analytic psychotherapy by Theodor Reik.

Thought deprivation. *See* Blocking.

Thought process disorder. A symptom of schizophrenia that involves the intellectual functions. It is manifested by irrelevance and incoherence of the patient's verbal productions. It ranges from simple blocking and mild circumstantiality to total loosening of associations, as in word salad.

Three-cornered therapy. *See* Co-therapy.

Three Essays on the Theory of Sexuality. Title of a book by Freud. Published in 1905, it applied the libido theory to the successive phases of sex instinct maturation in the infant, child, and adolescent. It made possible the integration of a vast diversity of clinical observations and promoted the direct observation of child development.

Tic. Involuntary, spasmodic, repetitive motor movement of a small segment of the body. Mainly psychogenic, it may be seen in certain cases of chronic encephalitis.

Timidity. Inability to assert oneself for fear of some fancied reprisal, even though there is no objective evidence of potential harm. In a therapy group, the timid person may make others fear the destructiveness of their normal aggression.

Tinnitus. Noises in one or both ears, such as ringing and whistling. It is an occasional side effect of some of the antidepressant drugs.

Tolerance. In group therapy, the willingness to put up with disordered behavior by co-patients in the group.

Too-tired-to-be-polite phenomenon. Phenomenon in a marathon group that stems from fatigue and results in the relaxation of the social facades of politeness. Some proponents of marathon groups have stressed the helpfulness of fatigue in breaking through the social games that participants play in the early stages of the group. *See also* Group marathon.

Totem and Taboo. Title of a book by Freud. Published in 1913, it applied his concepts to the data of anthropology. He was able to afford much insight into the meaning of tribal organizations and customs, especially by invoking the Oedipus complex and the characteristics of magical thought as he had discovered them from studies of the unconscious. *See also* Oedipus complex, Primal father.

Toucher. Someone who enjoys touching another person. When the touching is not of the clinging type, such a person in an encounter group usually helps inhibited people lose their anxiety about physical contact and closeness.

Traditional group therapy. Group therapy of a conventional type in which the role of the therapist is clearly delineated and the other participants are understood to be clients or patients who are attending the group meetings to overcome or resolve some definite emotional problems. *See also* Encounter group, Group psychotherapy, Sensitivity training.

Trainer. Professional leader or facilitator of a sensitivity training or T-group; teacher or supervisor of a person learning the science and practice of group therapy.

Training group. *See* T-group.

Tranquilizer. Psychotropic drug that induces tranquility by calming, soothing, quieting, or pacifying without clouding the conscious. The major tranquilizers are antipsychotic drugs, and the minor tranquilizers are antianxiety drugs.

Transaction. Interaction that arises when two or more persons have an encounter. In transactional analysis, it is considered the unit of social interaction. It involves a stimulus and a response. *See also* Complementarity of interaction, Forced interaction, Group stimulus, Structured interactional group psychotherapy, Therapeutic transaction.

Transactional analysis. A system introduced by Eric Berne that centers on the study of interactions going on in the treatment sessions. The system includes four components: (1) structural analysis of intrapsychic phenomena; (2) transactional analysis proper, the determination of the currently dominant ego state (Parent, Child, or Adult) of each participant; (3) game analysis, identification of the games played in their interactions and of the gratifications provided; and (4) script analysis, uncovering of the causes of the patient's emotional problems.

Transactional group psychotherapy. A system of therapy founded by Eric Berne. It is based on the analysis of interactions and on the understanding of patterns of transactions as they occur during treatment sessions. Social control is the main goal of therapy.

Transference. Unconscious phenomenon in which the feelings, attitudes, and wishes originally linked with important figures in one's early life are projected onto others who have come to represent them in current life. *See also* Countertransference, Lateral transference, Multiple transference, Rapport, Transference neurosis.

Transference neurosis. A phenomenon occurring in psychoanalysis in which the patient develops a strong emotional attachment to the therapist as a symbolized nuclear familial figure. The repetition and depth of this misperception or symbolization characterize it as a transference neurosis. In transference analysis, a major therapeutic technique in both individual and group therapy, the therapist uses transference to help the patient understand and gain insight into his behavior. *See also* Collective family transference neurosis, Dilution of transference.

Trend of thought. Thinking that centers on a particular idea associated with an affective tone.

Triad. Father, mother, and child relationship projectively experienced in group therapy. *See also* Nuclear family.

Trichotillomania. Morbid compulsion to pull out one's hair.

Tricyclic drug. Antidepressant drug believed by some to be more effective than monoamine oxidase inhibitors. The tricyclic drugs (imipramine and amitriptyline) are presently the most popular drugs in the treatment of pathological depression.

Tyramine. A sympathomimetic amine that is believed to influence the release of stored norepinephrine. Its degradation is inhibited by monoamine oxidase. The use of monoamine oxidase inhibitors in the treatment of depression prevents the degradation of tyramine. The ingestion of food containing tyramine, such as cheese, may cause a sympathomimetic effect, such as an increase in blood pressure, that could be fatal.

Unconscious. 1. (Noun) Structural division of the mind in which the psychic material—primitive drives, repressed desires, and memories—is not directly accessible to awareness. 2. (Adjective) In a state of insensibility, with absence of orientation and perception. *See also* Conscious, Preconscious.

Underachievement. Failure to reach a biopsychological, age-adequate level.

Underachiever. Person who manifestly does not function up to his capacity. The term usually refers to a bright child whose school test grades fall below expected levels.

Undeveloped potential. The behavior, feelings, and motivations of a person known neither to himself nor to others. It is the unknown quadrant of the Johari Window, a diagrammatic concept of human behavior. *See also* Blind self, Hidden self, Public self.

Undoing. An unconscious defense mechanism by which a person symbolically acts out in reverse something unacceptable that has already been done. A primitive defense mechanism, undoing is a form of magical expiatory action. Repetitive in nature, it is commonly observed in obsessive-compulsive neurosis.

Unisexual group. *See* Homogeneous group.

Universality. Total effect produced when all group members share specific symptoms or problems.

Up. The member who is the focus of discussion in group therapy, particularly in structured interactional group psychotherapy.

Up-tight. Slang term that describes defensive, rigid behavior on the part of a person whose values are threatened or who is afraid of becoming vulnerable and of experiencing painful emotions. Such a person frequently becomes a target for pressure in a therapy group.

Urine-testing. Thin-layer chromatography-testing for the presence of opiates, quinine, barbiturates, and amphetamines. Addict treatment programs use such testing to verify abstinence from illicit drug use.

Vector. An engineering term used to imply a pointed force being felt by the group. *See also* Hierarchical vector, Horizontal vector.

Verbal-deep approach. Procedure used in small groups in which communication is conducted exclusively through verbal means and is oriented to major goals. It is a technique used in analytical group therapy. *See also* Actional-deep approach, Actional-superficial approach, Verbal-superficial approach.

Verbal-superficial approach. Group therapy procedure in which language is the sole medium of communication and the therapeutic process is structured to attain limited objectives. It is a technique traditionally used in the treatment of large groups. *See also* Actional-deep approach, Actional-superficial approach, Verbal-deep approach.

Verbal technique. Any method of group or individual therapy in which words are used. The major part of most psychotherapy is verbal.

Verbigeration. Meaningless repetition of words or phrases. Also known as cataphasia, it is a morbid symptom seen in schizophrenia.

Verbomania. *See* Logorrhea.

Vertical vector. *See* Hierarchical vector.

Vienna Psychoanalytic Society. An outgrowth of the Wednesday Evening Society, an informal group of Freud's earliest followers. The new name was acquired and a reorganization took place in 1910, when the Society became a component of the newly formed International Psychoanalytical Society. Alfred Adler was president from 1910 to 1911, and Freud was president from 1911 until it was disbanded by the Nazis in 1938.

Visceral insight. *See* Insight.

Visitor. Guest who participates in discussions with patients in group therapy. In family therapy, members outside the nuclear family who are invited to the session are considered visitors. *See also* Extended family therapy, Social network therapy.

Visual hallucination. False visual perception.

Volubility. *See* Logorrhea.

Warming-up session. *See* Premeeting.

Waxy flexibility. *See* Cerea flexibilitas.

Wednesday Evening Society. A small group of Freud's followers who in 1902 started meeting with him informally on Wednesday evenings to receive instruction in psychoanalysis. As the society grew in numbers and importance, it evolved in 1910 into the Vienna Psychoanalytic Society.

West-Coast-style T-group. Sensitivity training or encounter group that is oriented toward the experience of union, intimacy, and personal awareness, with relative disregard for the study of group process. It is a style popular in California. *See also* East-Coast-style T-group.

Wild therapy. Group therapy conducted by a leader whose background may not be professional or whose theoretical formulations include widely deviant procedures when compared with conventional techniques.

Withdrawal. Act of retreating or going away from. Observed in schizophrenia and depression, it is characterized by a pathological retreat from interpersonal contact and social involvement, leading to self-preoccupation. In a group setting, this disorder creates a barrier for therapeutic progress.

Wittels, Fritz (1880–1950). Austrian psychoanalyst. One of Freud's early followers, he wrote a biography of him in 1924, during a period of estrangement, when he was under the influence of Wilhelm Stekel. Later, a reconciliation took place, and Freud conceded that some of Wittels' interpretations were probably correct.

Wolf-pack phenomenon. Group process in which a member or the therapist is the scapegoat.

Word salad. An incoherent mixture of words and phrases. This type of speech results from a disturbance in thinking. It is commonly observed in far-advanced states of schizophrenia.

Working alliance. Collaboration between the group as a whole and each patient who is willing to strive for health, growth, and maturation with the help of the therapist. *See also* Therapeutic alliance.

Working out. Stage in the treatment process in which the personal history and psychodynamics of a patient are discovered.

Working through. Process of obtaining more and more insight and personality changes through repeated and varied examination of a conflict or problem. The interactions between free association, resistance, interpretation, and working through constitute the fundamental facets of the analytic process.

Xenophobia. Fear of strangers.

Zoophobia. Fear of animals.

Contributors

D. Vincent Biase, Ph.D.
Director of Psychological Research for Rehabilitation Addiction Services Agency, New York, New York

John M. Davis, M.D.
Professor of Psychiatry and Associate Professor of Pharmacology, Vanderbilt University School of Medicine, Nashville, Tennessee

Eugene Friedman, Ph.D.
Chairman, Alcoholism and Drug Addiction Committee of the New York Society of Clinical Psychologists, New York; Psychologist in Charge, Department of Psychiatry, Fordham Hospital; Adjunct Assistant Professor, Bronx Community College of the City University of New York, New York, New York

Harold I. Kaplan, M.D.
Professor of Psychiatry and Director of Psychiatric Education and Training, New York Medical College; Attending Psychiatrist, Flower and Fifth Avenue Hospitals; Visiting Psychiatrist, Metropolitan Hospital and Bird S. Coler Memorial Hospital and Home, New York, New York

Nathan S. Kline, M.D.
Associate Clinical Director, Research Center, Rockland State Hospital, Orangeburg, New York; Professor of Psychiatry, College of Physicians and Surgeons, Columbia University, New York, New York

Joyce Lowinson, M.D.
Assistant Professor of Psychiatry, Albert Einstein College of Medicine; Chief of Drub Abuse, Bronx State Hospital, Bronx, New York; Consultant to Methadone Maintenance Treatment Program, Gracie Square Hospital, New York, New York

Mitchell S. Rosenthal, M.D.
Deputy Commissioner for Rehabilitation Programs, New York, New York

Benjamin J. Sadock, M.D.
Associate Professor of Psychiatry and Director, Division of Group Process, New York Medical College; Associate Attending Psychiatrist, Flower and Fifth Avenue Hospitals; Associate Visiting Psychiatrist, Metropolitan Hospital; Assistant Attending Psychiatrist, New York State Psychiatric Institute, New York, New York

Aaron Stein, M.D.
Associate Clinical Professor of Psychiatry, Mount Sinai School of Medicine; Associate Attending Psychiatrist and Chief, Adult Group Psychotherapy Division, The Mount Sinai Hospital of the City University of New York; Visiting Psychiatrist and Director, Department of Group Psychotherapy, Hillside Hospital, Glen Oaks, New York; Attending Psychiatrist, Brookdale Hospital Center, Brooklyn, New York

Israel Zwerling, M.D., Ph.D.
Chairman and Professor of Psychiatry, Albert Einstein College of Medicine; Director, Bronx State Hospital, Bronx, New York